YEATS'S GOLDEN DAWN

YEATS'S GOLDEN DAWN

George Mills Harper

BOOKS
10 East 53d St., New York 10022
(a division of Harper & Row Publishers, Inc.)

© George Mills Harper 1974

First published in the United Kingdom 1974 by
THE MACMILLAN PRESS LTD

Published in the U.S.A. 1974 by
HARPER & ROW PUBLISHERS, INC.
BARNES & NOBLE IMPORT DIVISION

ISBN–06–492718–0

Printed in Great Britain

To

KATHLEEN RAINE

for, in the words of Yeats to Vestigia,
'to whom else could I dedicate this book?'

Contents

Preface

Based primarily on unpublished manuscripts from the library of W. B. Yeats, this book would have been impossible without the hospitality and unfailing generosity of the family of Senator Michael B. Yeats, who now possesses the papers. For other primary materials used in this study, I am indebted to Gerald Yorke, who made his collection of Golden Dawn papers available to Kathleen Raine when she and I planned this book as a collaborative effort in 1969. These papers were also made available to Ellic Howe, who has generously answered my questions about people and events connected with the Golden Dawn. His study of *The Magicians of the Golden Dawn* (1972), which was published after my manuscript was finished, was extremely valuable for my revision. I am grateful also to Anne Yeats, who generously invited me to examine the library of W. B. Yeats, now in her possession. Among the other people to whom I cannot give proper thanks are the many fratres and sorores, often unidentified, who corresponded with Yeats about religious experiences and experiments in the Golden Dawn and related Orders. I am most grateful to the American Council of Learned Societies for a fellowship which enabled me to spend several weeks in England and Ireland examining unpublished materials and talking with informed people.

Although this book is based largely on primary materials, I am indebted to several studies about Yeats – in particular Virginia Moore's *The Unicorn* (1954), Joseph Hone's *W. B. Yeats* (1943), and Richard Ellmann's *Yeats: The Man and the Masks* (1948) – and to many of Yeats's own works.

For the generous permission to quote from the following copyrighted materials of W. B. Yeats acknowledgement is gratefully made to Senator Michael B. Yeats, A. P. Watt & Son,

I am grateful to the Henry E. Huntington Library and Art
Gallery for a reproduction of John Quinn's copy of 'Is the
Order of R.R. & A.C. to remain a Magical Order?' and to the
Kenneth Spencer Research Library, University of Kansas, for a
reproduction of P. S. O'Hegarty's copy of 'A Postcript to Essay
called "Is the Order of R.R. & A.C. to remain a Magical
Order?"'

                                                    G.M.H.

ONE

A Shape for Vague Thoughts

We Easterns are taught to state a principle carefully, but we are not taught to observe and to remember and to describe a fact. Our sense of what truthfulness is is quite different from yours.[1]

'Most of us who are writing books in Ireland to-day', Yeats once observed characteristically, 'have some kind of a spiritual philosophy; and some among us when we look backward upon our lives see that the coming of a young Brahmin into Ireland helped to give our vague thoughts a shape.'[2] Those retrospective words were published on 14 April 1900.[3] At the very hour almost Yeats was engaged in a bitter struggle for the preservation of The Hermetic Order of the Golden Dawn, a secret society to which he had belonged for more than ten years.

Although all serious students of Yeats are aware that he belonged to the Golden Dawn for most of his mature lifetime, no one has made a thorough study of the intellectual climate which nurtured his interest or of the reasons for his commitment to the Golden Dawn rather than some other of the many similar societies flourishing in London and Dublin at the turn of the century. Even more important, no one has made a thorough assessment of the significance of Yeats's involvement upon the art and theory which most certainly would have been greatly different if not impossible without the stimulus of the Golden Dawn.[4] Until quite recent times it has been critically fashionable to follow W. H. Auden's dismissal of Yeats's occult studies in 'all those absurd books' with one contemptuous line: '... but mediums, spells, the Mysterious Orient – *how* embarrassing.'[5] It is, I suggest, unscholarly if not obtuse for those whose epistemology and critical bias run counter to

Yeats's to omit entirely any consideration of the occult tradition. We know now, as a result of recent discoveries in the Yeats papers, that he was a member of the Golden Dawn or its successors for more than thirty years and was corresponding even longer with his 'old fellow students' about occult matters. In July 1892, after receiving a 'reproving post card' from John O'Leary, Yeats defended the study of magic in terms that would have been quite as valid or appropriate at the end of his life and career:

> If I had not made magic my constant study I could not have written a single word of my Blake book, nor would *The Countess Kathleen* have ever come to exist. The mystical life is the centre of all that I do and all that I think and all that I write. It holds to my work the same relation that the philosophy of Godwin held to the work of Shelley and I have always considered myself a voice of what I believe to be a greater renaissance – the revolt of the soul against the intellect – now beginning in the world.[6]

'I sometimes forget,' he added, 'that the word "magic" which sounds so familiar to my ears has a very outlandish sound to other ears.' Yeats went one step further, insisting to O'Leary that 'it is surely absurd to hold me "weak" or otherwise because I chose to persist in a study which I decided deliberately four or five years ago to make, next to my poetry, the most important pursuit of my life'.[7] It is, I submit, quite as absurd for students of Yeats not to appreciate the significance of his 'constant study' of magic.

Surely no one can doubt that the visit of the 'young Brahmin' Mohini Chatterji to Dublin left a profound and lasting impression on Yeats and several of his friends. Nor without evidence to the contrary can we dismiss lightly Yeats's assertion in 1900 that they had been studying occult lore even before that momentous visit: 'When we were schoolboys we used to discuss whatever we could find to read of mystical philosophy and to pass crystals over each others' hands and eyes and to fancy that we could feel a breath flowing from them as people did in a certain German book.' When Yeats and his friends were told by someone who had heard Chatterji in London that he 'knew more of these things than any book' they invited him 'to come and teach us'.[8] Although Yeats does not name the purveyor of the good news about Chatterji, it was probably his friend Charles Johnston. Yeats himself, according to Ernest Boyd, had read A. P. Sinnett's popular books *Esoteric Buddhism* and *The Occult World* and recommended them to Johnston, who went to London apparently to meet Sinnett, Anna Kingsford, Mme Blavatsky, and other occultists, Chatterji among them.[9]

Yeats's interest in Sinnett had already led to the formation of the Hermetic Society, which met for the first time on 16 June 1885, with Yeats presiding.[10] At this meeting were presented two papers (one by Yeats 'upon the objects of the society') and many more in succeeding meetings at which other friends of Yeats were active, notably George Russell, Claude Wright, and Charles Weekes.[11] During the year 1885 Yeats's first published poems and Johnston's article on esoteric Buddhism appeared in the *Dublin University Review*,[12] and Chatterji came to Dublin 'with a little bag in his hand and *Marius the Epicurean* in his pocket'. Talking 'all day long' to the excited young theosophists, 'he unfolded what seemed to be all wisdom'.[13] Although he returned to London at the end of a week, he left an ineradicable imprint on the life and art of two of the most important figures in Ireland's literary Renaissance, George Russell and W. B. Yeats. Fifteen years later Yeats was 'certain that we, seeking as youth will for some unknown deed and thought, all dreamed that but to listen to this man who threw the enchantment of power about silent and gentle things, and at last to think as he did, was the one thing worth doing and thinking; and that all action and all words that lead to action were a little vulgar, a little trivial'.[14] It is clear, I suppose, that the fundamental dilemma expressed in these lines remained with Yeats to the end and is at least partially responsible for the intensity of the art by which he sought to project the ideological tension suggested. 'Ah how many years', he cried in 1900, 'it has taken me to awake out of that dream!'[15] In truth he never fully awakened from that dream, but he was acutely conscious in April 1900 that even poets and prophets are sometimes forced to soil their hands. By that time certainly, Yeats knew that he like Alcibiades must flee from Socrates 'lest he might do nothing but listen to him all life long'.[16] But Yeats was sad that it must be so, for he had hoped that the pathway leading to that crucial battle might have taken him instead to the hermit's cell or a fairer field.

Whatever the reasons for the pathway he chose, Yeats was always the seeker, and he could never have been satisfied with the cell. It was he most likely who organised the Hermetic Society, planned its programmes, and invited Chatterji to Dublin. If so, however, why did he not join the Dublin Lodge of the Theosophical Society founded by Charles Johnston after his visit to London? It is likely, I think, that Yeats preferred the theology of the Hermetic Society founded by Anna Kingsford and Edward Maitland which originated as the Hermetic Lodge of the Theosophical Society but declared its independence on 22 April 1884.[17] Like Yeats, Mrs Kingsford preferred Chatterji to Mme Blavatsky. 'I like Mohini Chatterji', she wrote to Lady Caithness on 12 May 1884. 'I think he knows *more intuitively* than Mme. B. is capable of knowing. I have had two hours' conversation with him, and found him instructed and intelligent.'[18] Two years later, on 10 June, Chatterji, still in London, delivered a lecture on 'Krishna' in the Hermetic series sponsored by Maitland and Mrs Kingsford. Among other illustrious occultists appearing on this series were two men soon to be intimate friends of Yeats: S. L. MacGregor Mathers, who lectured on 'The Kabala' (3 June) and 'The Physical or Lower Alchemy' (8 July), and William Wynn Westcott, who lectured on 'The Kabalistic Book, *Sepher Yetzirah*' (29 July).[19]

There is no easy explanation for Yeats's failure to join the Dublin Lodge organised by his friend Johnston. In May 1887, when he moved with his family to London, Yeats sought out Mme Blavatsky, who had according to Yeats been virtually deserted by her followers as a result of the charges of fraud lodged against her by the Society for Psychical Research.[20] But when he saw her next 'she was surrounded by followers', and he was persuaded to ask for admission to the Society.[21] 'About Xmas 1888', according to the journal he kept, he 'joined the Esoteric Section of TS. The pledges gave me no trouble except two – promise to work for theosophy and promise of obedience to HPB in all theosophical matters'.[22]

It is, of course, significant that Yeats joined the Esoteric Section of the Theosophical Society. According to Ellmann,

Mme Blavatsky formed the Esoteric Section in 1888 'for the sincerest of her "chelas" '. But the division had been suggested in December 1883 by Anna Kingsford in 'A Letter to the Fellows of the London Lodge of the Theosophical Society'. This long pamphlet is a vindication of her position in opposition to that of A. P. Sinnett. She and Maitland, the President and Vice President, recommended that

> two Sections be created in the London Lodge, one of which shall be formed by those Fellows who desire to pursue exclusively the teaching of the Thibetan Mahatmas, and to recognize them as Masters; and that the Presidency of this Section be conferred on Mr Sinnett, the only person now in this country competent to fill such a position. The other Section should be composed by Fellows desirous, like myself, to adopt a broader basis, and to extend research into other directions, more especially with the object of encouraging the study of Esoteric Christianity, and of the Occidental theosophy out of which it arose.[23]

Although Mrs Kingsford and Maitland resigned the following year, they obviously spoke for a significant number of the Society in their desire 'of making known to a desponding and divided Christendom the advent of the "Christ that is to be" '. They were certain that 'sooner or later Esoteric Christianity will be proclaimed as a religious science to the Western half of the world'.[24] The point is that Yeats sympathised with the Esoteric Section of the Society. Like Mrs Kingsford also he had reservations about pledging allegiance to Mme Blavatsky's teachers, the Mahatmas. When the 'London esotericists' passed a resolution of several clauses including a belief in Mme Blavatsky's teachers, Yeats recorded in his journal, 'I had some doubt as to whether I could sign this second clause'.[25] Mrs Kingsford was even more hesitant: 'When I was invited to join the Society, I was emphatically and distinctly told that no allegiance would be required of me to the "Mahatmas," to Mme Blavatsky, or to any other person real or otherwise, but only to Principles and Objects.'[26] It is clear that Yeats and Mrs Kingsford were leaders not disciples. It is also clear, I think, that both of them were seeking a revitalisation of the Western religious tradition, whereas Sinnett and his followers were denying its validity.

Yeats, as always, was sceptical, refusing to decide between alternatives because there were 'too few facts to go on', but he dismissed 'the fraud theory in its most pronounced form ... as it is wholly unable to cover the facts'.[27] Hesitant to commit himself and uneasy about the vagueness of the resolutions, Yeats determined 'to keep a diary of all signings I go through and such like, for my future use; and always to state my reasons for each most carefully and when in doubt as to the legitimacy of my reasons to submit them to some prominent members in whom I have confidence.'[28]

After observing the members of both sections of the Society, however, he came to the conclusion that 'they seem some intellectual, one or two cultured, the rest the usual amorphous material that gathers round all new things.... What effects it [the Esoteric Section] has produced', he concluded, 'are wholly owing to the inherent weight of the philosophy.' 'The one adequate appeal that has been made to cultivated people', in Yeats's judgement, was that of Mohini Chatterji, 'but then he could not write decently'. On 20 December 1889, approximately a year after joining the Esoteric Section, Yeats records that he met with Mrs Annie Besant, Herbert Burroughs, G. R. S. Mead and others to renew the pledge.[29]

Mrs Besant had been introduced to Mme Blavatsky by Burroughs in 1889, and became President of the Theosophical Society after the death of Mme Blavatsky in 1891. A prolific writer and dynamic organiser, she remained one of the most prominent occultists in London for many years, ultimately becoming head of a society called Co-Masonry. Yeats apparently preferred her to other members of the Esoteric Section. A letter to Ernest Rhys, probably written in September 1889, suggests that Yeats may have met Mrs Besant before she was a member of the Theosophical Society : 'Mrs. Besant, you may not have heard, has turned theosophist and is now staying with Madame Blavatsky. She is a very courteous and charming woman'.[30] At any rate, Mrs Besant was already a force to be reckoned with. Some four months later (on 27 February 1890), only a week before his initiation into the Golden Dawn, Yeats wrote to Katharine Tynan about numerous projects in which he was engaged, including plans for an article describing

> experiments lately made by me, Ellis, Mrs Besant, etc. in
> clairvoyance, I being the mesmerist; and experiments in
> which a needle suspended from a silk thread under a glass
> case has moved to and fro and round in answer to my will,
> and the will of one or two others who have tried, no one
> touching the glass, some experiments too of still stranger
> nature.[31]

Unfortunately, Yeats says no more about these 'still stranger'
experiments. Cautious as always, he did not, apparently, complete his article:

> Probably if I decide to publish these things I shall get called
> all sorts of names – imposter, liar and the rest – for in this
> way does official science carry on its trade. But you do not
> care for magic and its fortunes and yet your Church's enemy
> is also materialism. To prove the action of man's will, man's
> soul, outside his body would bring down the whole thing –
> crash – at least for all who believed one; but, then, who
> would believe? Maybe my witnesses, more prudent than I,
> shall bid me remain silent.[32]

Yeats is clearly implying that the experiments conducted by
Mme Blavatsky's circle did not satisfy his restless spirit of
inquiry. As he pointed out in *The Trembling of the Veil*, he was
'irritated by the abstraction of what were called "esoteric
teachings"' and 'began a series of experiments' on his own.[33]
These, I suppose, are the magical experiments of a stranger
nature which he defended in the letter to Katharine Tynan.
Having read 'an essay upon magic by some seventeenth-
century writer', he 'got together a committee' to assist in an
experiment to raise the ghost of a flower from its ashes. Failing
in this, he asked the members of the committee to put portions
of the ashes 'under their pillows at night and record their
dreams'. The primary object of this study was to 'rid the mind
of abstraction'. By this time, probably late 1890, 'it was quite
plain', Yeats recalled, 'that I was not in agreement with their
methods or their philosophy'.[34] He refers here to the Theosophical Society, with which he had become increasingly discontented. And the distrust was mutual: 'Presently a secre-

tary, a friendly, intelligent man, asked me to come and see him, and when I did, complained that I was causing discussion and disturbance'.[35] 'Did they dread heresy', Yeats asked himself some thirty years after the event, 'or had they no purpose but the greatest possible immediate effect?'[36]

If Richard Ellmann is correct, Yeats 'made his last public appearance' in the Theosophical Society in August 1890, when he lectured on 'Theosophy and Modern Culture'. Since Mrs Besant was presiding, this lecture may have been given to the Esoteric Section, of which she and G. R. S. Mead were joint secretaries.[37] By the same logic, Mead might be identified as the secretary whom Mme Blavatsky chose as emissary to deliver her request that Yeats should leave the Society. But it is unlikely that the man Yeats satirised in a journal entry of 20 December 1889 as an 'over-righteous' pedant 'whose intellect is that of a good sized whelk'[38] should be described thirty-two years later as the 'friendly, intelligent' secretary who delivered the notice of expulsion. Mrs Besant, in contrast, was one of the few prominent members of the Theosophical Society for whom Yeats had respect. He surely read her *Autobiography* (1893) and such books as *Esoteric Christianity* (1898) and *The Ancient Wisdom* (1897). After he left the Society in 1890, he no doubt remained in contact with her. When William Q. Judge, an American theosophist, came to England in 1894 and attempted to oust Mrs Besant from the presidency of the Society, Yeats was indignant, writing to his father that he had known the facts about the resulting scandal 'for twelve months or more'.[39] He obviously kept up with the activities of his old friends.

Although Yeats was forced to leave the Society, he was not bitter; and indeed, if he had not been such an inquiring maverick, he might have maintained his membership even though he had already found a more congenial climate for his occult experiments.

On 7 March 1890 he had been initiated into the Hermetic Order of the Golden Dawn.[40] If Yeats remembers correctly, he had belonged for three years to a study group called 'The Hermetic Students', which probably included several prominent members of the Golden Dawn: 'In May or June 1887', Yeats recalled in 1926, 'I was initiated into that society in a

Charlotte Street Studio, and being at a most receptive age, shaped and isolated'.[41] Since only a few years before he had carefully preserved the form which recorded the date of his invitation to join the Golden Dawn, he can hardly have been confusing both month and year. It is more likely that the group of Hermetic Students Yeats joined in 1887 was associated with or an outgrowth of the Hermetic Society founded by Anna Kingsford and Edward Maitland which had withdrawn from the Theosophical Society, becoming an independent organisation on 22 April 1884.[42] Both Mathers and William Wynn Westcott had participated in a series of Hermetic lectures sponsored by Mrs Kingsford and Maitland in 1886.[43] Since the Isis-Urania Temple of the Golden Dawn was 'authorised' on 1 March 1888, eight days after Mrs Kingsford's death, it seems likely that Mathers and Westcott organised the Golden Dawn to carry on her work or at least to fill the vacuum in Hermetic studies left by her death.[44] If this was the society of Hermetic Students Yeats joined in 1887 and if Yeats was still a member in February 1888, we can only wonder why he did not shift allegiance to the Isis-Urania Temple when it was founded. Of course, he might not have been invited, he might have preferred the Theosophical Society, or he might have been displeased at the mystery surrounding the new Order. But he would have been aware of its establishment, and he probably knew Mathers and Westcott, two of the founding Chiefs.

Although the history of the Golden Dawn has been told in recent years,[45] some details of its beginning need to be recounted here. According to a typescript in the Yeats papers entitled 'Investigations into the Foundations of the Order and the Source of Its Teachings (abridged)',[46] the basic written materials for the 'G.D. on the Outer' were contained in 'the Cypher M.S.S.' which 'were discovered by a clergyman the Rev. A. F. A. W[oodford] on an old bookstall in London in 1884'.[47] Excited over the possibilities of his discovery, Woodford took the manuscripts 'to V.O.V. and S.A. both well-known and highly esteemed'.[48] These men, Dr William Robert Woodman and Dr William Wynn Westcott, were officers in the Societas Rosicruciana in Anglia, an occult society of Master Masons.[49] 'Attached to the M.S.S.', according to the account of 'Investigations into the Foundations of the Order', 'was a letter saying that if any one cared to decipher these M.S.S. and would communicate with Sapiens Dominabitur Astris c/o Fraulein Anna Sprengel living in Hanover they would receive interesting information'.[50] After deciphering the manuscripts, Westcott, presumably, wrote to Fräulein Sprengel and asked for further information. She replied that if he and his associates would 'elaborate the notes and . . . [be] diligent they might form an elementary Branch of the Rosicrucian Order in England'. She also authorised Westcott to sign her name to 'any warrant or documents necessary', and she promised 'further rituals' and 'advanced teaching' if the Order flourished. On 1 March 1888 such a warrant was drawn up and signed by Deo Duce Comite Ferro (MacGregor Mathers), Vincit Omnia Veritas (Woodman), and Sapiens Dominabitur Astris (for Fräulein Sprengel by Westcott). It deputed Mathers (as Praemonstrator), Westcott (as Cancellarius), and Woodman (as Imperator) 'to constitute and to rule the Isis-Urania Temple, No. 3, of the Order of the G.D. in the Outer. . . .'[51] They 'received the honorary grade of (7)=[4] from S.D.A. so as to enable them to act as Chiefs in the New Temple'. The Cypher Manuscripts included rough notes and diagrams for the five rituals of the Outer or First Order,[52] some instructions for elementary occult teaching to accompany the degrees, and a rough diagram of the warrant.

The Chiefs of the new Order set to work at once. Mathers, the most creative, accepted the task of composing the rituals as they were needed; and Westcott, who was something of a scholar, began preparing the lectures and study manuals necessary for the attainment of degrees. Among the earliest, possibly the first, of his efforts was 'The Historic Lecture to Neophytes G.D. Written and first delivered by Q.S.N.' (1888).[53] Westcott pointed out that the Golden Dawn was a society devoted to the study of 'Occult science and the magic of Hermes'.[54] He traced its history briefly, naming prominent Adepti of 'public renown' who 'have handed down to us this Doctrine and System of Theosophy and Hermetic Science and the Higher Alchemy from a long series of practical investigators'. Although Westcott mentioned Frater Christian Rosenkreuz, he emphasised the more ancient origins of Rosicrucian doctrine. He outlined the 'scheme of the G.D.', listed names of the Order in several languages, called attention to the 'success of women in occult researches',[55] and praised such recent Hermeticists and Theosophists as Dr Anna Kingsford and Mme Blavatsky. The choice of these two was no chance. They represented a dichotomy in occult study which was to become extremely important in Yeats's thinking – the East versus the West:

> The Eastern School of Theosophy and occultism and our own Hermetic Society of the G D are fraternities of students whose predecessors must have come from the same stock of *Magi* – the Scientific Priests of a remote antiquity –
> The two Societies, differing in mode of teaching and in language, are allied by mutual understanding and respect and their aim is similar.[56]

Westcott assured the neophytes, in conclusion, that the Golden Dawn 'can show you the way to much secret knowledge.... It can, we believe, lead true and patient students who can *Will, Dare, Learn, and be Silent* to the Summum Bonum, True Wisdom and Perfect Happiness'.[57]

Some years after the composition of the 'Historic Lecture for Neophytes' Westcott prepared a lecture or study manual on 'The History of the Rosicrucian Order'[58] for students advancing to $5=6$, the first degree of the Second Order. Insisting that 'the Order of the Rose and Cross hath existed from time immemorial', Westcott observed that there are three important periods in its history: 'the first being the life period of Christian Rosycross' (1378-1484); 'the second, the 120 years of silence and secrecy, being the period from 1484 to 1604'; 'the third the period subsequent ... to the Reformation'.[59] During the third period, as Westcott points out, two books especially important to the Order were published: (1) *Fama Fraternitatis; or a Discovery of the Fraternity of the Most Laudable Order of the Rosy Cross* (1614) and its Supplement under the title *Confessio Fraternitatis R.C. ad Eruditos Europae* (1615); (2) *The Chymical Marriage of Christian Rosencreutz* (1616). Much of the material for Westcott's lecture came from these books, which he certainly knew in the well-known publication of Frater Arthur Waite (Sacramentum Regis), *The Real History of the Rosicrucians*.[60] According to Westcott, 'the *Fama* was an official manifesto ... authorized by the Fratres then empowered', and a 'great stir [was] roused by its publication'.[61] Since Westcott suggests more than he reveals of the contents of these books, he probably assumed that his students would consult Waite's *History*. Westcott concluded by observing that the 'historical element' is 'a minor consideration as compared with the mystic symbolism involved therein'.[62]

The Golden Dawn flourished from the beginning. By the end of its first month there were nine members, including Mina (changed to Moina) Bergson, the sister of the French philosopher Henri Bergson. She was an intimate friend of Yeats and became the wife of MacGregor Mathers in 1890. (I will return to their marriage in another context.) According to a typed document in a Private Collection available to Ellic Howe, 170 people had been initiated by 2 September 1893, and 315 by 1896.[63] Almost half the total in Isis-Urania were women – 84 of 189. By the end of 1890, the year Yeats joined, Isis-Urania had accepted 50 initiates, including two women who are important to this study – Florence Farr Emery and Annie Horniman.

During these early months Westcott was apparently the principal organiser and promoter of Isis-Urania. He claimed 'right and precedence in the origin of the G.D.', and he served as 'Recorder of Minutes, Superintendent of $5° = 6°$ Admissions, Corresponding Secretary and Treasurer'.[64] Although Westcott continued to conduct most of the routine work until 1897, he did not long remain the prime mover. Mathers, a much more imaginative and more aggressive man, soon seized control, insisting after a time that all knowledge for the rituals was transmitted through him from the Secret Chiefs of the Third Order. In 1892, however, 'he was told by his Occult teachers to transfer his centre to Paris',[65] where he founded the Ahathoor Temple Number 7; and his interest in Isis-Urania as well as his control began to slip. After Mathers moved to Paris, Westcott functioned as his London representative until 1897, when he resigned and was replaced by Mrs Florence Farr Emery.[66] Not very disciplined herself and chiefly interested in Egyptology rather than Hermeticism, she did not supervise the records as Westcott had, and she did not insist on the examination system for advancement in grade.

About this time also, according to Mrs Mathers, 'my husband entirely reorganized the school under orders, and further teachings were given him'.[67] This reorganisation may have been a device to inspire awe in a restive and recalcitrant group. At any rate, trouble was brewing in Isis-Urania.

TWO

Ludicrous Proceedings

*How difficult it seems for many of the London Second
Order to comprehend that I am neither to be bought,
bribed, persuaded, tricked, bullied, frightened nor ridiculed into any line of action that I do not see fit to take!*
MATHERS to MARCUS W. BLACKDEN (26 April 1900)

It should have been obvious to Mathers as soon as he moved to
Paris that he could no longer maintain control of his highly
individualistic, often eccentric colleagues in the Isis-Urania
Temple. Autocratic from the beginning, he became increasingly so as he attempted to rule in absentia. In 1896, he sought
to quell an uprising among the senior members in London by
demanding complete submission. As 'Chief Adept and Ambas-
sador of those Secret and Unknown Magi who are the concealed
Rulers of the Wisdom of the True Rosicrucian Magic of Light',
he addressed a Manifesto (dated 29 October 1896) to the Theorici
Adepti Minores of the Second Order. Upon the attainment of
that grade,

> he or she must send a written Statement of voluntary submis-
> sion in all points regarding the Orders of the G.·. D.·. in the
> Outer and the R.·. R.·. et A.·. C.·. to G. H. Frater Deo Duce
> Comite Ferro before being permitted to receive any further
> instruction. Unless he or she is prepared to do this, he or
> she must either Resign from the Order, or elect to remain a
> Zelator Adeptus Minor only. And he or she hereby under-
> takes to refrain from stirring up any strife or schism hereon
> in the First and Second Orders.[1]

Most of the remainder of the Manifesto is devoted to convincing the Adepti that Mathers, with Vestigia Nulla Retrorsum
(Mrs Mathers) as associate 'in a less degree', was the chosen

instrument of the Secret Chiefs for the promulgation of 'the whole of the Second Order Knowledge'. He must obey the commands of the Secret Chiefs 'without question and without argument', and the Adepti in turn must obey him 'by abstaining to the utmost of your power from putting any extra hindrance in my way'.[2] He called attention, without naming the principals, to an internal squabble between Miss Horniman and Dr Edward W. Berridge, who had apparently made sexual overtures to her : 'What I discountenence and will check and punish whenever I find it in the Order is any attempt to criticise and interfere with the *private life of Members of the Order*; neither will I give the Wisdom of the Gods to those who endeavour to use it as a means of justifying intolerance, intermeddling, and malicious self conceit.'[3] Although Miss Horniman returned her 'written Statement of voluntary submission', Mathers was not satisfied with her independent spirit. Even as instructor to the Neophytes of the Outer Order she was 'inclined to treat the instruction rather from the point of view of *scholar* rather than of student'. He also implied that she, like Westcott, had 'deliberately endeavoured to reduce me to the level of a puppet'.[4] Five days later (on 27 November 1896), in a letter appealing for money, Moina Mathers explained and justified her husband's anger to Miss Horniman : '... for in the Order we know that you have not been loyal to him as representing your principal occult teacher (at least in the Outer World)'.[5] When Miss Horniman refused the money and accused him of injustice, Mathers wrote an angry letter on 3 December 1896 :

C et VH Sor F et R[6]

In my letter to you in answer to your reply to my manifesto I insisted upon your complete and absolute submission to my authority as regards the *management as well as the teaching* of both the First and Second orders. You have now had more than sufficient time to send me this. Not only have you not done so, but in your letter to VNR you again tax me with injustice. I do not care one atom what you *think* but I refuse absolutely to permit open criticism of, or any argument concerning my action in either order from you or any other member. The attitude you have chosen to take leaves me no other alternative than (however unwillingly) to remove your name from the roll of the order, for I will not continue to teach one who persistently opposes my authority and endeavours to influence others to do so. Even had you the technical right so to do I could not consider that the person whom I saw shuffling her feet & crying in a hysterical attack at the Musee Guimet because the style of Indian art affected her nerves unpleasantly, (and who on recovering from this attack made VNR & myself solemnly promise not only to warn but to check her in any & every way no matter how, if at any future time we thought she was beginning to show any trace of hereditary mania) such a person I say would be utterly unfit to correct me in the extremely complex administration of the instruction and governance of such an order as the Rosicrucian – This promise of checking you VNR & I have fulfilled. I do not say that I consider you insane, but the intense arrogance, narrowness of judgement & self-conceit you have displayed during the past 12 months (which I saw beginning two years ago, and tried all in my power to check gently then) are, as any physician will tell you, the beginning, believe me, which led to such a result.

As regards your conduct to me & VNR *personally* I consider it *abominable*. It is useless your thinking to raise up fresh dissentions [sic] against me, for I have received thorough and complete submission from SA, LO, SSDD, Resurgam, APS, Vigilate, Non Sine Numine, Sub Spe & Shemeber.[7]

I will therefore take leave of you with much regret, as one whom VNR & myself at one time, both sincerely loved and esteemed and whom also we regarded as a true & faithful friend until recent events had shewn us the contrary.

Deo Duce Comite Fero[8]

Mathers was apparently uneasy about the expulsion of one of the Order's oldest and most dedicated members, and he wrote to several of those who had sworn fealty, though not significantly to Westcott, Acting Chief in London with whom he had been quarrelling. A letter to Frederick Leigh Gardner dated 19 December suggests that Mathers was on the defensive:

Re F.E.R. I have *most unwillingly* been compelled to take the
step of removing her from the roll of the Order; for I will
not permit longer her continued insubordination to me.
She was willing enough, as most of them are, to take all
the knowledge I can teach her; at the same time she does
everything in her power to counteract my authority in the
Order.[9]

In the light of subsequent events Mathers's action proved to be
imprudent. Miss Horniman was a strong and stubborn woman
with more financial resources than any of her fellow members.
Since she had supported Mathers for many years, first through
a job in her father's museum and later by a direct subsidy, her
accusation of injustice was perhaps not without foundation.
Moreover, her termination of the subsidy in 1896[10] was probably the primary cause of her expulsion from the Order,
though Mathers had found another excuse – insubordination.
　　Conspicuously absent from the list of names from whom
Mathers had demanded 'complete submission' in 1896 was that
of an old and dear friend, W. B. Yeats (Demon Est Deus Inversus). Since he was an early member of the Golden Dawn, having
been initiated on 7 March 1890,[11] and had perhaps become
acquainted with Mathers sometime before, the omission of
any reference to Yeats is curious. Although he was a close
friend of both Moina and MacGregor, having been a member
of a 'little group' to whom Mathers's home was a 'romantic
place' while he was curator of the Horniman museum at Forest
Hill,[12] so too had been Annie Horniman and Florence Farr;
hence friendship alone cannot account for the omission of
Yeats's name. Being absent from London frequently, Yeats did
not attend meetings as regularly as the people Mathers named
in the letter to Miss Horniman, and Yeats may have had no
part in the revolt. On the other hand, as subsequent events
suggest, he may have been a leader who refused to submit. In
fact, he preferred the Golden Dawn to the Theosophical Society because submission had not been demanded at the time
he was initiated. When he joined the Esoteric Section of the
Theosophical Society in late 1888, he recorded in his journal
that 'the pledges gave me no trouble except two – promise to
work for theosophy and promise of obedience to HPB [Mme

Blavatsky] in all theosophical matters'. He had apparently hesitated to sign until she assured him that 'this obedience only referred to things concerning occult practice if such should be called for. Since then', he added, 'a clause has been inserted making each member promise obedience subject to the decision of his own conscience.'[13] But if indeed Mathers had asked Yeats for 'complete submission' and had been refused, why did he not remove Yeats's name from the roll as he had Miss Horniman's? Barring the discovery of correspondence from Mathers, that question most likely must remain unanswered. But one thing is certain: if Yeats had been asked to submit, he would have refused. He sympathised with – probably approved – Miss Horniman's refusal, and was responsible, as we shall see, for bringing her back into the Order at the first opportunity.

Nevertheless, Yeats maintained contact and friendship with the Matherses during the more than three years of Miss Horniman's exile from the Order. Yeats sought their advice on both rituals and mythology for a secret Celtic society he and Maud Gonne conceived: 'I go to Paris on the 14th of April', he informed George Russell in March 1898, 'to see the Mathers on Celtic things. I have just heard, curiously enough, that Mrs Mathers has been seeing Conla and without knowing that we have been invoking him constantly.'[14] On 25 April, Yeats wrote to Lady Gregory from Paris, where he had been 'for a couple of days', that he was 'buried in Celtic mythology' and would be 'for a couple of weeks or so'. 'My host', he said in a postscript, 'is a Celtic enthusiast who spends most of his day in highland costume to the wonder of the neighbours.'[15]

It is clear certainly that in April 1898 Yeats not only had affection for Mathers, despite his growing eccentricity, but also respected his learnings.[16] Although we can know very little of what transpired in those two weeks of consultation, we do know, through an unpublished letter from Moina, what kind of help Yeats and Maud Gonne (who was also in Paris) hoped to get from her and MacGregor. Yeats had suggested to John O'Leary as early as July 1892 that they might get assistance on nationalistic questions from Mathers, who 'is a specialist and might have given useful advice to anyone who thinks as you do'.[17] But O'Leary was suspicious of all things occult, and probably had little faith in Mathers's Celticism. His worst fears were no doubt confirmed when Yeats wrote some months later that he was going to Paris for a visit with Mathers, hoping, Yeats said, for 'a quiet dream with the holy Kabala for bible and naught else'.[18]

Although Yeats disagreed with Mathers over the expulsion of Miss Horniman in December 1896 and worked for her recall, he continued to visit the Matherses in Paris, and he sought their assistance in the composition of rituals for his Celtic religious movement. Maud, of course, played an important part in Yeats's Celtic project. Since she too lived in Paris most of the time, Yeats arranged to meet her with the Matherses 'to see visions'. Although she approved of his Celtic Castle of Heroes, Maud did not care for the Golden Dawn or for the Matherses, I suspect.[19] She was initiated into the Golden Dawn on 16 November 1891,[20] but did not remain long or progress beyond the Outer Order. According to her own account, she left when she discovered Mathers making use of 'various emblems' connected with Freemasonry, which she considered a 'British institution'. As a dedicated revolutionary, she was disturbed over receiving 'authentic information' that members of the Golden Dawn 'were holding ceremonies invoking peace'.[21] That was too much for Maud. Her object in establishing the Castle of Heroes was political, Yeats's was religious.

Some time in 1899, as well as I can determine, Yeats cooled towards Mathers. On 31 October 1898 Moina was still writing enthusiastically of her illustrations for Fiona Macleod's *Ulad of the Dreams*, of a translation of Yeats's *Rosa Alchemica*, and of hope of assistance from Bailly, who 'is very much interested in all you & the other Celts write & he wants me so much to go on translating etc & illustrating with him'. 'Am so glad that you are working at the Celtic revival', she continued, then spoke of a new direction or intensified involvement in an old interest for her and MacGregor : 'With some Frenchmen, as I think I told you, we are endeavouring to restore the Mysteries (Egyptian). At last one sees the practicability & possibility of all these things that we have so desired.' Yeats would have disagreed with that. Not only would he have been unhappy with the shift of emphasis away from the Celtic revival, but also he would have disapproved of their fascination with the Egyptian

Mysteries. A year and a half later this interest was to become a point of dissension in the Second Order. Two closing notes were surely an augury of things to come. Moina had not seen Maud since Yeats left (probably in early May), 'but I am writing to her today', she added apologetically. Yeats was no doubt irritated at Moina's failure to keep Maud involved in his project since his pursuit of her was surely a major reason for the Celtic project. And Moina's reference to one of MacGregor's recent projects may have disturbed Yeats even more : 'Is not Abramelin fine? There is any amount of real magic in it. Very dangerous book, however – Mind what you are about (with its material formulas).'[22]

But she closes with an expression of 'Every kind wish from us both', and she was still friendly in a hurried note dated 29 May 1899, but she was 'plunged in "Egypt" ' and apologised for 'leaving Connla for ages', pleading 'many distractions in other directions'. Obviously, her enthusiasm had waned. Yeats's love affair was also going badly, despite the Celtic project; and he went to Paris to see Maud in February 1899. Although, as he wrote to Lady Gregory, 'she made it easy for me to see her', he was depressed. Maud had told him 'the story of her life' and discouraged any further pursuit on his part. Although Yeats does not mention Mathers by name in three letters to Lady Gregory from Paris, he may be referring to him in a brief, perhaps ironic, account of a strange experience. Speaking of a violent cold that kept him in bed 'for a day and then went completely', he said : 'M G is quite convinced that it is the work of a certain rival mystic, or of one of his attendant spirits. She points out that I went to see him without it and came back with it, which is circumstantial evidence at any rate.'[23] By this time (10 February 1899) certainly, if Mathers was the mystic, Yeats's affection for him had waned, in part perhaps because Maud disliked him. The friendship came to an abrupt end in January 1900, when a great quarrel erupted which split the Order badly and from which it never fully recovered. Although I have elsewhere discussed this painful struggle,[24] I must review some details here before considering another internecine quarrel perhaps even more disturbing to the ideological health of the Order and far more significant to the development of Yeats's religious thought.

Although as I have said a revolt was obviously brewing in the Second Order as early as 29 October 1896, the date of Mathers's Manifesto, an uneasy truce existed for three more years. On 13 January 1900 Mathers received a disturbing letter from Florence Farr Emery, whom he had named as his 'Representative in the Second Order in London' after Westcott's resignation in March 1897.[25] Mathers also received a disturbing set of minutes of a meeting held on 12 January. Since neither Mrs Emery's letter nor the minutes is available, I can only guess at the cause of Mathers's unhappiness from a letter to her dated 16 February. He accused her of bringing his 'private affairs' into a discussion at the meeting of 12 January. More particularly, he accused her of 'attempting to make a schism' within the Order to work 'under "Sapere Aude" under the mistaken impression that he received an Epitome of the Second Order work from G. H. Soror, "Sapiens Dominabitur Astris"'. Westcott, he said, had never been in communication with the Secret Chiefs, the supposed correspondence between them and Westcott being '*forged*'. According to Mathers '*every atom* of the knowledge of the Order has come *through me alone* from o = o to $5 = 6$ inclusive', and only he had been in communication with the Secret Chiefs.[26] He warned her of the '*extreme gravity*' of the matter, entreated her 'to keep this secret from the Order', and remarked that Sapiens Dominabitur Astris was in Paris assisting him.[27] Considering the outraged tone of Mathers's letter, I can only wonder why he had postponed answering her letter, which he had received on 13 January, for more than a month. His time, he said, was 'enormously occupied with the arrangements for the Buildings and Decorations of the Egyptian Temple of Isis in Paris'.

He was also slow to reply to a letter of 18 March (which included a copy of one dated 4 March) from P. W. Bullock, who tried to play the role of peace-maker. Speaking as the representative of a Committee (consisting of himself, Mrs Emery, Mr and Mrs E. A. Hunter, M. W. Blackden, G. C. Jones, and Yeats) 'to investigate the questions concerning the circumstances surrounding the foundations of this Order', Bullock remarked that Mathers's charge of forgery was 'likely to shake the confidence of the whole Second Order in some of its fundamental traditions', and he asked Mathers 'to prove the matter completely ... in order to place the Order on its true basis'.

On the same day, 18 March, Mathers wrote to Mrs Emery, refusing to recognise the Committee she had formed to consider information contained in 'my *private* letter to you'. He insisted again on 23 March that his letter was 'personal'. He had not in fact marked the letter 'private', though he had urged her to 'Read this letter carefully before showing any part of it to anyone!' That, she wrote on 25 March, was exactly what she had done: 'I went into the country and spent days of thought on the whole subject. I saw that if I kept silence I should become a party to a fraud, and therefore took the advice of some Members of the Order who have always been friendly to your interests.' One of these must have been W. B. Yeats, who surely had been Mathers's closest friend in the London Temple. Mrs Emery pointed out to Mathers that they had sent him 'repeated messages' which apparently he had ignored; and she closed her letter with a reminder to him that 'our oaths are covered by the written assurance that nothing contrary to our civil, moral or religious welfare is demanded of us'. The quarrel had indeed become serious.

Compromise was no longer possible. In separate letters on 23 March Mathers removed Mrs Emery from her office and charged Bullock 'to abstain from further action in the matter'. Believing that he had been misled by the forgeries, however, Bullock considered it his duty to make a correction. 'Abstention', he said, 'would clearly be the equivalent of compounding a felony.' He called on Westcott to find out whether or not Fräulein Sprengel was in fact 'the author of the letters alleged to be forged by him'. Westcott informed Bullock that he had written to her in Germany and received 'bona fide posted letters' in reply.[28]

After the letter of 23 March removing Mrs Emery from office, Mathers did not write to her again, choosing apparently to ignore her altogether. On 2 April he wrote a strong but courteous letter to Bullock, insisting as usual that the Committee was invalid without his 'authorization and consent': 'I *annul* the Committee', he wrote, 'and I *annul* the Resolutions passed at the meeting of the 24th March, 1900.' Mathers reminded Bullock of the Manifesto issued to the Theorici Adepti on 29 October 1896 demanding and receiving 'a written Declaration of allegiance' from each of them.²⁹ Mathers was particularly incensed at Gardner (De Profundis Ad Lucem), possibly because he had led the effort in the spring of 1897 to get Miss Horniman reinstated and had maintained contact with her during her exile.³⁰ He too had befriended Mathers, having financed the publication of *The Book of the Sacred Magic of Abra-Melin the Mage* in 1898. Mathers insisted again that he owed allegiance only to the Secret Chiefs and the Eternal Gods, he cited the 'turmoil and strife' in the Theosophical Society after the death of Mme Blavatsky as a warning to the investigative Committee, and he threatened to 'formulate my request to Highest Chiefs for the Punitive Current to be prepared, to be directed against those who rebel'. Bullock probably did not answer that letter; if so, he did not enter a copy in the record kept by the Committee, as he had been doing.

All was quiet for some two weeks. On 17 April, according to a statement prepared by E. A. Hunter (Hora Et Semper), he received a telegram urging him to come at once to the Order meeting rooms at 36 Blythe Road. When he arrived he found that Aleister Crowley (Perdurabo) and Miss Elaine Simpson (Donorum Dei Dispensatis Fidelis) had broken into the rooms and seized the property on the authority of Mathers. They remained in possession until Mrs Emery arrived and called a constable.³¹ On the same day all the members of the Second Order received a notice from Crowley cancelling the meeting called for 21 April and demanding an appearance at Headquarters at 11:45 on 20 April.

On 19 April, two days after the seizure, Yeats participated directly in the altercation for the first time. He and Hunter talked with and absolved the landlord at 36 Blythe Road, changed the locks, and prepared to defend the Order properties. 'About 11:30', according to Hunter's account, 'Crowley arrived in Highland dress, a black mask over his face, and a plaid thrown over his head and shoulders, an enormous gold or gilt cross on his breast, and a dagger at his side.' When he was forbidden to enter by Yeats and Hunter, Crowley called for a constable, 'who ... told him to go, which he at once did, saying he should place the matter in the hands of a lawyer.'

On 23 April, still acting as the envoy of Mathers, Crowley sent a message to all members of the Second Order complaining that property of his had been detained and his projected interviews made impossible. He threatened the Order with the courts, denied the 'story of the masked man', and suspended Mrs Emery, Miss Cracknell (Tempus Omnia Revelat), Hunter, Bullock, and Yeats. He also insisted on individual interviews with the remainder of the Order by noon of the next day, threatening 'suspension from both orders' for failure to appear. Before leaving Paris, Crowley and Mathers had formulated a series of questions for this interview. If the refractory members answered 'yes' to all their questions, they were 'to cease these unseemly disputes as to the headship of this Order' and to sign a paper containing a 'solemn reaffirmation' of their obligation as a $5=6$ and a pledge of support for the new regulations. If their answers were 'no', Crowley was to expel them from the Order.[32] Similar tests were planned for the First or Outer Order.

On 26 April M. W. Blackden received a letter from Mathers headed 'This is NOT a private letter!' Declaring that 'there has been much more precipitation than discretion' in Blackden's letters and 'recent action', Mathers condemned 'the liberty of speech' in which Blackden had indulged and declared that 'The only excuse I see in your favour beyond what I have already admitted is that in the midst of a current of absolute mania which appears to be acting in the London Second Order, you would seem to have somewhat of sanity left.' With that limited concession Mathers hoped 'to aid you to arouse yourself to a clearer comprehension of your environment'. The remainder of the letter goes over now familiar issues and complaints with slight variations. The most important of these is an accusation, which Mathers termed a 'Fact', that Yeats had asked Westcott 'to lead them should they succeed in shaking off my authority'. Yeats, who almost certainly prepared the 'List of Documents' against Mathers, noted at the bottom of the page that 'This "fact" is fiction. D.E.D.I.' Mathers defended the 'Mask of Osiris' Crowley had worn as a symbolic device designed 'completely to separate and distinguish between his individuality and the office with which I had invested him'. 'How difficult it seems', he concluded, 'for many of the London Second Order to comprehend that I am neither to be bought, bribed, persuaded, tricked, bullied, frightened nor ridiculed into any line of action that I do not see fit to take!' If the rebels needed further evidence, this outburst was surely proof positive that a change was imperative. As Yeats said, 'his amazing actions showed that a change must be made in our constitution'.

In the meantime important events had transpired. The investigative Committee prepared a resolution to suspend Mathers, Dr Berridge, and Miss Simpson and to withhold any recognition of an uninitiated person – that is, Crowley, who had earlier been denied admission.[33] This resolution was passed on Saturday, 21 April, at a meeting attended by twenty-two members of the Second Order. Following the adoption of the Committee report, Yeats 'gave an address on the history of the Order, and explained the illegalities which had crept in, in recent years'. He spoke of his 'personal sorrow' over Mathers's actions, referred to the 'lamentable, though altogether ludicrous, proceedings' described in the report, outlined 'the legal aspects of the matter', 'explained the pecuniary transactions which had taken place between 1892 and 1896', and introduced 'the resolutions which the Committee proposed for the reconstruction of the Order'.

The gist of the eleven resolutions then passed may be summarised briefly: the past Constitution was declared at an end, the membership was restricted to those present and some few who could not be there or would be invited from the Outer Order, the 'Committee of 7' was asked to administer until a new Executive (of 3 chiefs and 7 members) could be chosen, the Executive was to examine 'the system of teaching and the rituals' to separate the genuine from the fantasy of some member (obviously Mathers), and the change in the Constitution was not to affect 'its connection with the Rosicrucian Order'.

With the adoption of those resolutions a long and painful episode stretching from January to April was concluded. Yeats emerged as the leader of the reorganisation. Although he had avoided a conspicuous role in the first stages of the revolt, he led the way at the end when he was convinced that a change was necessary to avoid chaos. It was probably he who insisted upon the purification of the rituals and the continuation of the Rosicrucian connection, for he had already considered, experimented with, and rejected Freemasonry and Theosophy. He continued to participate in the affairs of the Second Order until

1922 and maintained an active interest and advisory role for many years after that – almost to the end, as I will point out in a later chapter.[34]

THREE

Divisions, Bickerings,
and Scandals

*All went well until September 1900 when I found every-
thing I proposed was objected to, after a few weeks I
discovered that my group which had been working quietly
for 3 years was being violently attacked.*
                    FLORENCE FARR EMERY to J. W. BRODIE INNES
                                        (17 January 1901)[1]

The relief Yeats no doubt experienced at the conclusion of the
momentous meeting on 21 April 1900 was not to last long. Indeed, the next few months were to be especially distressing, and
the affairs of the Second Order were partially, perhaps primarily, responsible for many of his problems. Among the manuscript materials he or Mrs Yeats preserved is a stray sheet of
Coole Park stationery with a most revealing note in Yeats's
hand: '1900 – from April till February 1901 "worst part of
life". Both in regard to ♀ matters & other things.'[2] The
'♀ [Venus] matters' may be a reference to his despondency
over Maud's unwillingness to marry him. Although he was
presumably resigned to the status quo in their affairs after the
mystical marriage of 1899,[3] he continued to hope until her
marriage to John MacBride in February 1903. In *A Servant of
the Queen*, Maud records, with one of the few dates in her
book, that she met MacBride at the end of 1900, having
travelled to Paris with Arthur Griffith to meet him on his
'return from the Transvaal'.[4] She recalls that they had dinner
together and 'sat up all night talking'.[5] 'Impatient with Willie
Yeats, who, like all writers, was terribly introspective and
tried to make me so', Maud had finally found a man of action
who understood why she 'had redoubled work to avoid
thought'.[6] Yeats met Maud in London in the spring of 1901

upon her return from the lecture tour in America. This meeting was the occasion for the composition of 'Adam's Curse'[7] and another (and certainly the most frequently quoted) of Yeats's renewed pleas for marriage.[8] Although Maud gives no date, she recalls that Yeats spoke of William Rooney's death when he took her to Euston Station that evening.[9] The news of Rooney's death (on 6 May 1901) had been cabled to her in America by William Griffith.[10] How soon after this Maud decided that she 'was not really needed' in America I cannot determine. Since, however, she talks of visiting Philadelphia and St Louis after receiving the news about Rooney, she surely did not get to London before late May or early June. Yeats was in Sligo as late as 25 May, being, as he confided to Lady Gregory, 'in rather low spirits about my Irish work lately'.[11] He does not imply or suggest to Lady Gregory that Maud was responsible for his 'depressed state of mind', though 'my Irish work' may be an indirect reference to the Castle of Heroes he and Maud had planned.

Nevertheless, unless Yeats had a more than usual concern over Maud's interest in MacBride – whom she had, after all, 'deserted' in America – there is not, I suppose, any reason to believe that this crisis in his continuing pursuit of her was any greater than any of many others over a period of more than ten years. Since Venus occupies a central position in the symbolism and ritual of the Golden Dawn, Yeats's despair over '♀ matters' is more likely to refer to troubles in the affairs of the Order. As the guardian planet of the Isis-Urania Temple,[12] Venus is the Stella Matutina or morning star which the Order took as a name under Dr Robert W. Felkin (Fenim Respice). An unpublished meditation (dated July 1909) in Yeats's papers sheds some light on what he meant by 'Venus matters': '... this is the morning or evening star – ♀ [Venus] – the star of the side of the vault through which the initiate enters.'[13] The vault is the seven-sided tomb of Christian Rosenkreuz, the mythical founder of the Rosicrucian Society. The evidence suggests, I think, that 'Venus matters' is a reference to the affairs of the Golden Dawn rather than Yeats's love affairs. To be sure, both were in a bad state during the months of April 1900 to February 1901, and they might well have combined to make this the 'worst part of life'. If, however, he had only one set of troubles in mind, it must have been those of the Golden Dawn: the dates cited encompass dramatic quarrels in the Second Order, and Yeats was preoccupied with its problems during the intervening months.

Four days after the disturbing meeting of 21 April 1900, he conveyed his relief and distress to Lady Gregory: 'I have had a bad time of it lately. I told you that I was putting Mac-Gregor out of the Kabbala. Well last week he sent a mad person – whom we had refused to initiate – to take possession of the rooms and papers of the Society.' Yeats then mentioned the suit being brought by Crowley and said that Charles Russell, the lawyer for the Second Order, 'is trying to keep my name out of the business'. Yeats, as usual, had been managing affairs: '... for a week I have been worried to death with meetings, law and watching to prevent a sudden attack on the rooms.... The trouble is that my Kabbalists are hopelessly unbusinesslike and thus minutes and the like are in complete confusion. I have had to take the whole responsibility for everything, to decide on every step.'[14] After some discussion about loss of sleep, Crowley's motives ('vengeance for our refusal to initiate him'), and the Order's reason for refusing admission to Crowley ('we did not think a mystical society was intended to be a reformatory'), Yeats concluded his account of the ordeal with a most revealing paragraph about his respect for Mathers:

I arraigned Mathers on Saturday last before a chapter of the Order. I was carefully polite and I am particularly pleased at the fact that in our correspondence and meetings not one word has been written or said which forgot the past and the honour that one owes even to a fallen idol. Whatever happens the archives of the Society will have nothing unworthy to pass down to posterity. We have barbed our arrows with compliments and regrets and to do him justice he has done little less. The 'envoy' alone has been bitter and violent and absurd. Mathers like all despots must have a favourite and this is the lad.[15]

On Friday, 27 April, with the whole affair very much on his mind, Yeats wrote again to Lady Gregory:

I am expecting every moment a telegram to say how the

case goes at the Courthouse. I have had to go through this worry for the sake of old friends, and perhaps above all for my uncle['s] sake. If I had not the whole system of teaching would have gone to wrack and this would have been a great grief to him and others, whose whole religious life depends on it. I do not think I shall have any more bother for we have got things into shape and got a proper executive now and even if we lose the case it will not cause any confusion though it will give one Crowley, a person of unspeakable life, the means to carry on a mystical society which will give him control of the conscience of many.[16]

After the letter was sealed, he noted on the back of the envelope: 'Just got telegram about law case. We have won. Other side fined £5.'[17] In fact, he was not quite right about the disposition of the case. Some time later in a brief but carefully documented 'Statement of Recent Events which have led to the present Constitution of the Second Order in London',[18] prepared by Yeats most likely, the entire 'Second Order in London (between 50 and 60 members)' was informed that S.S.D.D. (Mrs Emery) had been summoned before a Police Magistrate 'for unlawfully and without just cause detaining certain papers and other articles'. But the case was settled out of court. 'Before it was called on, the Complainant's Solicitor signed the following undertaking – "On behalf of the Complainant I withdraw the summons, and I undertake to pay £5 costs within 7 days." No further proceedings have since been attempted.' Clearly intended as a justification of the Committee's action and headed 'Without Prejudice', this 'Statement' concludes with a list of the ten offices and officers comprising the Executive Council according to the organisation proposed in the eleven resolutions adopted on 21 April. Demon Est Deus Inversus was elected to the post of 'Instructor in Mystical Philosophy'.[19]

An undated letter to George Russell, in a concluding section Yeats marked *private*, contains further information about Crowley's outrageous actions and says again that 'MacGregor apart from certain definite ill doings and absurdities, on which we had to act, has behaved with dignity and even courtesy. A fine nature gone to wrack.' 'At last', Yeats said hopefully, 'we have got a perfectly honest order, with no false mystery and no mystagogues of any kind. Everybody is working, as I have never seen them work, and we have fought out our fight without one discourteous phrase or irrelevant issue.'[20] I suppose Yeats really did believe that he would have no 'more bother' now that 'we have got things into shape and got a proper executive', and he was surely speaking from the heart when he wrote to Lady Gregory on 27 April, 'I hope to be deep in my novel by Monday'.[21] The reference is to his never-finished *The Speckled Bird*, the content and composition of which cast much light on these troubled months, and I will return to it in a later chapter.

If he had hope for peace and quiet after turmoil, he was to be disappointed. 'I wish very much I was at Coole', he wrote to Lady Gregory on 6 June, 'for I am tired of this noisy town, which grows more noisy every day.... Even the fact that MacGregor's masked man Crowley has been making wax images of us all, and putting pins in them, has not made life interesting.'[22]

It is likely that Yeats was uneasy over the effect of the reorganisation and expulsion of Mathers. He was surely aware of the inherent danger of stripping the Order of its mystery by altering the system of teaching and rituals: the search for what is genuine may amount to rewriting the bible. He was aware also that in robbing the Chief of his authority the Committee of 7 had in effect invited every man to become his own priest and had thereby sown the seeds of dissension and dissolution. The problem had, of course, been present from the beginning: it was merely more difficult to resolve or control after the ouster of the autocratic Mathers. New Bye-Laws (dated May 1900) were drawn up, and Yeats was now a member of the Executive Council (see note 19). Also members of the Council were two women who became the mighty opposites in a quarrel soon to develop: Mrs Emery and Miss Horniman. Like Yeats, they had been members of Isis-Urania from an early date. They were strong-minded women, and Yeats, who was a friend of both, was caught in the middle. Although none of the papers available to me make clear the basis for the violence of the differences between Mrs Emery and Miss Horniman, some few facts are suggestive. First, Miss

Horniman, a woman of considerable means, was apparently dominating if not domineering. She had been a friend of Moina Bergson at the Slade School, and her father, at her suggestion no doubt, had employed Mathers in the Horniman Museum at Forest Hill. She financed a 'season of plays at the Avenue Theatre' in 1894 for Mrs Emery,[23] supported the Abbey Theatre from 1904 to 1910, and tried unsuccessfully to get Yeats to write for the Manchester Repertory Theatre (which she founded). Some weeks after her expulsion, as I have said, Fred Leigh Gardner wrote and circulated a petition signed by Mrs Emery, George Pollexfen, and others (but not Yeats according to Ellic Howe)[24] asking for 'a reversal of the Judgement pronounced against her'. Although the petition failed to achieve 'the reconsideration of this decision', Yeats 'invited' her to return and become Scribe in the reorganised Order of April 1900.[25] Because she had leisure time and was willing to help defray many routine expenses, she was particularly useful as Scribe – a role she took most seriously, as we shall see. She admired Yeats greatly, and he defended her staunchly until her interest in Yeats and the Abbey dwindled and died in 1910.[26]

Since there was apparently bad feeling between Mrs Emery and Miss Horniman almost from the date of her return, it is likely that they had disagreed before her expulsion. At any rate, the friction began as soon as she became Scribe. Being a systematic woman, Miss Horniman was appalled at the informality and even laxity which had befallen the Order during her three-year absence corresponding with Mrs Emery's stewardship as Mathers's London representative. Recalling the situation in an open letter of 27 February 1901, Miss Horniman observed, somewhat righteously: 'The long experience of Fortiter et Recte in the business of the Order has taught her that fixed rules and a just enforcement of them would give the members that peace which is necessary for occult study.'[27] If Miss Horniman chose the motto Fortiter et Recte for herself, as she probably did, she may have had a sense of irony not easily found in her work. Mrs Emery and many of her fellow students disapproved of the return to rigidity as well as the tone and attitude of the new Scribe, and she made her position clear in a letter of 17 January 1901 addressed to Sub Spe

(Brodie-Innes), Chief of the Amen Ra Temple in Edinburgh, but obviously intended for others: 'It seems necessary for me to make a semi-official statement to the Theorici regarding my work in the Order during the last 3 years in order to account for the present state of feeling of which naturally you became aware on your visit to London.'[28] Since there is a typed copy of this letter in the Yeats papers, I assume that it was sent to all members of the Second Order, or at least to all the Executive Council. It is clear, at any rate, that Mrs Emery is speaking to the entire organisation as she rationalises an interest which led to a serious rupture: 'You may remember at the end of the year 1895 I came across an Egyptian Adept in the British Museum and freely told other members of the possibilities opened out. On Jan 27th 1896 I received a long letter from DDCF [Mathers] in reply to a letter of mine sending a charged drawing of the Egyptian and asking him if I were not grossly deceived by her claiming to be equal in rank to an $8 = 3$ of our order at the same time giving me numbers which I afterwards calculated to be correct for that grade. I still possess his letter approving altogether of my working with her....'[29] Since this letter was written only a few months after Mrs Emery had worked so hard to eject Mathers, her reliance on him for authority is ironic, to say the least. A few lines further she speaks of developing 'splits in the Order itself' and suggests the 'hopeless state' of the Isis-Urania Temple under Mathers's absentee rule: 'Endless divisions, bickerings, and scandals choked its activity. In the meantime the group I had founded and the groupes [sic] you and others founded continued their work and at last in 1899 the time came. In the early months of 1900 matters were so arranged by the eternal powers that we were freed from the load of dishonesty under which we had been struggling.' The dishonesty she refers to was Mathers's: she suggests that he had deceived the Order about the authenticity of the Cypher MSS upon which the rituals were based and thereby about his own authority as representative of the Secret Chiefs of the Third Order.

But expelling Mathers had not solved the dissension. The uneasy peace lasted from April till September 1900, when Mrs Emery 'discovered that my group which had been working quietly for 3 years was being violently attacked'. Although these attacks concentrated first on the use of the Order Rooms at 36 Blythe Road, the reasons were much deeper. To Miss Horniman, any deviation from tradition and accepted practice was unsound if not evil; to Yeats, the question was philosophical, and he spent much of his time and energy for the next few months trying to resolve the irreconcilable: two fundamentally opposed ideologies represented by two antagonistic women.

The battle lines were drawn when Mrs Emery concluded her open letter to Brodie-Innes by quoting a notice she had 'recently' posted at the Order Rooms: 'SSDD wishes to say that any Member of the Order who feels sympathy either for the study of the Egyptian Book of the Dead or for the symbolism of the Tree of Life projected on a Sphere will be very welcome to join her group on their attainment of the grade of Theoricus. Yours under the wings of the eternal O.'[30] This letter apparently represents a critical point in a debate which had been going on from September to January. An unpublished letter from Yeats to Mrs Emery indicates that he had been engaged in working out a compromise for his quarrelling friends. Although, unfortunately, the letter is not dated, it probably was written in January, after her letter and before an important meeting on 1 February. She had, according to Yeats, agreed on a compromise at two meetings with him. Yeats's chief objection to the group she had sponsored and was proposing to legalise in the Council was that it would admit Zelators, that is members of the Golden Dawn in the Grade of $1 = 10$, the lowest of the ten Degrees, in contrast to the $5 = 6$ which Mrs Emery and Yeats had achieved.[31] Although Yeats had hoped that his compromise would satisfy Miss Horniman, he was motivated primarily by a philosophy of order. But he reminded Mrs Emery that honour was also involved. If after promising to refuse admission to Zelators she could not get her group to agree, Yeats thought she should resign her position in the group. If she did not keep faith, Yeats warned that he could no longer work with her outside the Order on some project which offered great opportunities. The remainder of the letter hinted rather vaguely at Yeats's meaning. A note in Miss Horniman's hand records that it is 'Demon's letter about the compromise to Sapientia'. He had apparently suggested that Mrs Emery should have a prominent part in some theatrical project which he was planning with others whose names he could not reveal. He may have been hinting that she should have the role of Grania in *Diarmuid and Grania*, finished the preceding month if my dating is correct. But Yeats was apparently suggesting that she should also share in some larger enterprise if she were co-operative.[32] If not, he warned, she would make it impossible for him to rely upon her, and he cited an analoguos situation which had led to a break with T. W. Rolleston over the New Irish Library many years before.[33] Although Yeats expressed sorrow at having to write such a letter, he was obviously determined to preserve the traditional structure of the Order.

But threat and bribe were unavailing, and a violent quarrel ensued at a council meeting on 1 February 1901. Reflecting both personal animosities and metaphysical subtleties, the record of this meeting and the subsequent debate leading to another change in the administration of the Order are indispensable to a comprehension of the agony which led Yeats to call these months the 'worst part of life'. The recorded events were influential in his quest for a new style of life and the concomitant literary style of this transitional period of his life.

FOUR

A Record of the Executive Difficulty

Then I dropped details and spoke of the way I had returned from exile, and how painfully suspicions as to the 'group' had grown up in my mind from various irregularities done on their behalf, and then I asked 'Where did these suspicions come from?' Amongst many confused ejaculations and remarks Deo Date's statement 'They came from your own mind Fortiter', was very clear.
From Miss Horniman's record of the Council Meeting
on 1 February 1901

Although the events and the issues at stake are likely to seem trivial and even ludicrous to readers of our time, it is important to remember their influence upon Yeats's thought and possibly the direction of his life thereafter. He did not leave the Golden Dawn for many years – and in fact maintained an interest till the end of his life, but he was disillusioned. Despite his partial defeat, however, he emerged the statesman of the Second Order, and the privately printed essay on magic expressing his religious convictions and addressed to members of the Order is clearly superior to the essay entitled 'Magic', which was written in the same year and published first in *The Monthly Review* and later in *Ideas of Good and Evil*.[1] Indeed, Yeats's dissatisfaction with *Ideas of Good and Evil*, expressed in two letters of May 1903, may be attributable in part to the experiences of these months. 'The close of the last century', he wrote to George Russell, 'was full of a strange desire to get out of form, to get to some kind of disembodied beauty, and now it seems to me the contrary impulse has come.' The following day, in a letter to John Quinn, he related his changed attitude to the weakness of *Ideas of Good and Evil*: 'The book is too lyrical, too full of aspirations after remote things, too full of desires.'[2]

I do not, of course, want to over-simplify a complex mood, but rather to follow some of the events of this depressing period and to suggest their impact on new attitudes which, in Yeats's words, 'have made me look upon the world ... with somewhat more defiant eyes'.[3] Fortunately, we have a fairly complete record of Yeats's participation in the crisis. Although there are no available minutes of the critical meetings, Yeats preserved two copies (one typed, one hand-written) of 'The Scribe's Account of the Executive Difficulty'. Written by Miss Horniman five days after the event, this careful recording of the tempestuous Council Meeting on 1 February 1901 outlines all the issues but presents only one side of the debate. The typed copy has numerous annotations by Yeats which clearly reveal the stance he had taken.

The opening paragraph suggests that Miss Horniman was well aware of smouldering discontent in the Order:

> For the Council Meeting on Feb. 1st, 1901, I had drawn up a long and important agenda paper which contained a careful scheme for the coming election besides much Order business. On Jan. 25th I received a letter from Ma Wahanu Thesi proposing four motions, one of which he called 'a slight amendment' for my election scheme. This I placed on the Agenda with the election affairs and the others, of which more anon, at the end; as likely to cause contention. My Agenda was accepted by the Moderator.[4]

Yeats apparently agreed with Miss Horniman. In the left margin he noted: 'misleading description of motions'. But he changed her heading, substituting 'Council Meeting, Feb. 1' for 'Executive Difficulty'. His change suggests that a still further revised copy may have been sent to the entire Council. If so, it is surprising that Yeats made so few revisions in the body of the Account.

The anticipated contention was not slow to come: 'After the Minutes had been read the Moderator said that we would take Ma Wahanu Thesi's resolutions first. I asked her to let the Bruce Pledge Form take precedence as it had been long in hand.

But she over-ruled me and said we would begin with my election scheme.'[5] To which Yeats observed in the margin: 'preconcerted actions. Inconceivable that she did not know of his resolutions nature.' *She* refers to the Moderator, Mrs Emery. Yeats obviously felt that she had failed to keep faith.

But worse was to come, as Miss Horniman records the action, at any rate:

> I read it out with some small interruptions, asking them to hear it through first and then to discuss it step by step. The first portion was violently contested until I explained that my proposal that the Twelve Seniors should nominate such Adepti as they thought fit and then send their motions direct to me would save time.... The extremely simple proposal that I should send out a list of candidates to each member and to tell him to put a cross after the mottoes of the ten he thought most suitable brought forth an extraordinary proposal from Ma Wahanu Thesi. He at first said it was to save future scribes from embarrassment, but when he launched forth and his words were neither hushed down nor disapproved of, I saw that it was an organised attack. He proposed that *two more Scribes should be appointed and that there should be a triple election to avoid errors!*

Yeats drew lines under all or parts of the words I have italicised, apparently intending to call attention to the entire sentence rather than particular words, and penned a note in the margin: 'Unheard of proposal described in manifesto of majority of council as "more usual lines" & according to custom'. This annotation is a direct reference to a passage in Robert Palmer Thomas's 'Statement Issued to the Adepti by the Majority of the Council' (see Appendix I). By repeating such words and phrases as 'unheard', 'majority of Council', 'more usual lines', and according to 'custom', Yeats is drawing attention to the difference between Miss Horniman's Account and Thomas's Statement. Since the Statement was written on 25 February, the day before the momentous Council Meeting, Yeats may have been reminding himself of discrepancies as he annotated Thomas's Statement (see Chapter 5) in preparation for the Meeting. If so, he perhaps annotated Miss Horniman's Account the same day. At any rate, Miss Horniman and

Thomas disagreed violently about 'methods adopted at elections', and Yeats agreed with her.

She then 'spoke of the extra liability to errors', but reminded the readers for whom her Account was intended that she 'took no notice of his idea that three postage stamps should be enclosed, one with each voting-paper, for the use of electors!' Yeats scratched an asterisk above *enclosed* and noted at the bottom of the page: 'Fortiter pays all the expenses of the scribes work. DEDI.' Miss Horniman was upset, but she controlled herself for the good of the whole: 'My first impulse was to shut my Minute Book and leave the room, but then I remembered that my duty is to the Order, not to the Council; so I sat quietly and reasoned with him until the proposal to confuse the electors was dropped.'

At this point in her Account the real issue is suggested: the question of whether or not splinter groups could legally exist within the Order. According to the record, the group members sided with Blackden in opposition to Miss Horniman's election scheme. Yeats was disturbed at their encouragement. After Miss Horniman had gained her way, 'the Demon [i.e., Yeats] got very excited' and 'burst out with something like this, – "You let that proposal drop when you found that Fortiter could not burn the ballot-papers she objected to".' Although Yeats did not apparently object to Miss Horniman's phraseology when he read the manuscript, it should be said, I think, that the emotional outburst she describes is not typical of Yeats, if we can believe published accounts of his participation in other meetings. At any rate, his observation 'made a great scene of excitement, the "group" all calling for "order" as soon as a voice was raised in defence of the Scribe'. After some 'fuss' over the 'examination of the voting-papers', Robert Palmer Thomas (Lucem Spero) 'began to cross-examine' Miss Horniman. Yeats continued to object, but the group shouted him down with 'let Fortiter speak'. The group, according to the harassed victim, seemed to enjoy 'the following scene': 'Sapientia [Mrs Emery] lent [sic] back and I sat forward. Lucem Spero asked me *where* I intended to open the ballot papers; I was confused and puzzled, the various rooms in my flat came into my mind. He then said, raising his finger in front of my face, "Now mind – think – where did you intend to open the *papers?"* ' Yeats underlined this question and commented in the margin: 'Lucem Spero tries to get her to admit that she intended to violate [?] the secrecy of the ballot'. Miss Horniman answered that the ballots would be opened in her own house 'by the Scruteneers'. According to her, she 'was not in the least angry at his impertinence', having made up her mind 'not to take charge of the elections under the circumstances', and being 'determined to see how far he would go'. When she asked for other suggestions, 'someone said "36"' [i.e., the Order Rooms]. Miss Horniman construed that as an attempt to put an unqualified member of the group into her position: '... but I could not refer to her with decency, as though present at the Council meetings, she does not sit nor speak on it'. Unfortunately, I cannot identify this interloper, who obviously represents the kind of irregularity Yeats and Miss Horniman objected to. Such interruptions of the narrative make it difficult to determine what audience Miss Horniman had in mind if indeed she was trying to influence other members of the Order with her Account.

By this time apparently the whole proceeding had become a great debate with her. She argued that the Order Rooms were 'comparatively unguarded', and she 'firmly refused to allow the voting-papers ... to be sent to any house but mine'. Thomas dropped that point and asked her for the origin of her scheme. She replied that she 'got the idea from the voting of the Fabian Society a year ago', and 'the Demon' compared her plan to 'that of the Irish Literary Society'. Yeats's blood-pressure must have risen when Thomas was 'most scornful' of both procedures, and Miss Horniman was disturbed that 'he was not checked at all by the Moderator', who showed no 'displeasure at his behaviour'. When he suggested that all elections ought 'to be personal', Miss Horniman objected that this would keep many country members ('not "group" as it happens') from voting. 'The Demon' also objected on the basis that such a rule would be 'fining them heavily' and noted in the margin: 'proposal to disfranchise country members'. Among others, George Pollexfen, his favourite uncle, must have been in his mind. Being far from London, Pollexfen borrowed the instructional manuals and copied them carefully. Since many of these copies are now in the Yeats papers, I assume that they were left to him upon Pollexfen's death in September 1910.[6]

The issue was compromised at last through an agreement to write the following on the back of the card of directions: 'To be brought to the Ballot Meeting if possible. If you cannot possibly attend send this by post before the—'. Miss Horniman was instructed by the group to 'bring the envelopes complete to Blythe Road and put them in the box and that *all* members present would remain to watch the counting'. 'I let that go', she added, 'as too bad to be worth making any objection to on my part'. Yeats drew a line across the page at the end of this paragraph and made two notes: 'group to be scruteneers'; 'end of election discussion'.

According to Miss Horniman, 'the "group" all seemed quite pleased at the way they had insulted the whole Order in my person'. At this stage 'Sapientia took Ma Wahanu Thesi's famous three motions' which he had served notice of in his letter of 25 January. Since the real issue was the legalising of groups within the Order, Miss Horniman was perhaps justifiably confused in her attempt 'to fit them [the motions] into what went on at the Council', but she tried: 'As far as I can write out such a scene, this is what happened.' According to a notation by Yeats, the motions were now read, but the Scribe did not get a copy 'as I believe is the usual custom'.

First Blackden wanted the omissions from one clause of the Obligation replaced. When Miss Horniman explained that the Twelve Seniors were considering alterations in the $5 = 6$ Ceremony,[7] this motion was dropped, and Yeats noted it in the margin. Blackden 'made no fuss', the Scribe observed wryly, 'as he had plenty more to bring forward'.[8] He then read a letter from Miss Horniman agreeing 'with the compromise between Sapientia and the Demon' and declaring that 'although I disapprove of "a group" I would show my fraternal feeling by helping to hush up the scandal'. Yeats wrote in the margin: 'cross examination of Scribe on her statements about group'. Miss Horniman declared at this point that she had written 'this phrase seriously and with good intention' because she believed the 'doings' of the group would be 'harmful to the Order and certain to bring suspicion and curiosity of an unpleasant kind and every sort of ill-feeling amongst us', but her opponents

were neither charitable nor tolerant. 'Instead of showing gratitude for my forbearance', she observed, the group 'indulged in
further insults towards the Scribe'. Thomas continued his cross
examination, and Mrs Emery called for ' "order" whenever
the Demon showed signs of his non-group mental attitude'. In
defending herself, Miss Horniman cited such services to the
Order as fighting 'the mutilation of the $5=6$ Ceremony diagram' and correcting 'a proposed irregular initiation'[9] – suggesting, of course, the kind of righteous rigidity of character
the group had obviously found unpleasant in her conduct of
the office. The next few lines are especially revealing: 'Then
I dropped details and spoke of the way I had returned from
exile, and how painfully suspicions as to the "group" had
grown up in my mind from various irregularities done on
their behalf,[10] and then I asked "Where did these suspicions
come from?" Amongst many confused ejaculations and remarks Deo Date's[11] statement "They came from your own
mind Fortiter", was very clear.' But But the group 'took no
notice' of her protestations, and the 'cross-examination continued', as Yeats noted in the margin. The many changes in
the manuscript at this point indicate how careful Miss Horniman was to set the record straight. Also, apparently, she was
quite as careful in the meeting itself, as one attached insertion
will illustrate: 'I spoke slowly as my words were written down
or notes taken of what I said. I drew their attention to this,
but again my politeness was not appreciated.'[12]

At this point in the Account, Miss Horniman reveals, with
some pride obviously, what a gadfly she was and why most of
the Second Order both feared and disliked her. When Thomas
charged her with having 'accused them of *evil*', she

> ... stretched out my hands and said words like these 'I
> solemnly declare on my word of Honour that I have never
> accused you of Evil, that I have never thought that you
> were working for Evil, and I have never been tempted to
> think that your work was evil but I cannot judge of your
> working except by its fruits such as I know them, they are
> Ignorance, Selfishness and Discourtesy.' I might have added
> 'an absence of a sense of humour', for as soon as I stopped
> they all began to ask me for evidence! I then noticed that

my out-stretched left hand had been pointing to the Cross of the Obligation, my right at Lucem Spero. I explained how more than three years ago when many of the 'group' were still beginners in the Order, that I had been shown their first Diagram by one of themselves, a Soror of the highest honour, who had never thought that she, a Zelator, was not free to show to a Theoricus, a G. D. paper which she did not understand; how I had found one trivial error and one most serious omission, – that their sphere left a larger portion open to the Lower forces below them than to the Higher above. A few days later, Sapientia had written to me that the matter was to be a secret, that I was to be silent on the subject and if I thought about it at all, that I was to consider myself in the centre. I wrote back to her that as I did *not* like it at all I should try to forget it. Much later when in the British Museum I had by chance felt a force which was not harmonius to my nature coming from a small statue which I found to be that of their Adept. At that time it gave me a sense of ruthless destruction and a sweeping away of obstacles and a disregard of the weak and helpless.[13]

It is not surprising that 'Things now grew very confused'. In the estimation of Miss Horniman the only other person who 'spoke for the general good of the Order' was Yeats: 'The Demon made a speech which by its beauty enforced silence but it fell on the ears of an audience who were on a different plane of thought.' So the prosecution continued. Thomas called Yeats's speech ' "a pretty sermon but not to the point" or words to that effect', and Mrs Emery 'made her only speech': 'She energetically enquired from the Demon "who and what are *you* in the Order" or words to that effect.' To this the outraged Miss Horniman commented: 'Motives of delicacy to the "group" might have urged her to be silent as to Order progress as he is one of those who are next to the Seniors in the Order.'[14]

The cross examination had stopped by now, and Miss Horniman had the floor. She pointed out the 'horrible dangers for us all' in legalising the groups. We 'would be helpless', she said, 'to even object to the most pernicious practices in our Tomb.'[15] When Blackden 'pointed to the Cross and talked of the Obligation', she reminded him that Aleister Crowley, who had been denied membership the year before, had taken the oath of Obligation in Paris.[16] She reminded them also of Dr Edward W. Berridge (Resurgam), who had been ejected with Mathers in April 1900.[17]

By this time, apparently, the meeting had been going on for hours. Two key members (Vigilate, Mrs Helen Rand, and Dum Spiro Spero, Henrietta Paget) were gone, and all were tired no doubt. But the speeches went on. 'Silentio [Reena Fullham-Hughes][18] made a little speech telling us how *she* had not been offended when she heard of the beauties of the "group" studies.' During the confusion Blackden revealed that there were more groups than one, and Miss Hughes admitted membership in one of them. By this time, obviously, the excitement was high. Miss Horniman interrupted the narrative to observe ironically that 'At some time during the turmoil the Demon proposed arbitration; but he was told that there was nothing to arbitrate and the idea was scouted.' Thomas then spoke, telling Miss Horniman how sorry he was for her and how he hoped that her ignorance would protect her 'from the terrible consequences of resistance against or objection to their workings'. Another insertion in the manuscript at this point refers to the expulsion of Mathers: 'He [Thomas] told us how he had aided the rebellion against one tyranny, and would never allow another tyrant to arise. This must have meant the Demon as several weeks earlier I had arranged to leave the Twelve Seniors and not to stand for office again.' It is fairly clear that the reference was in fact to Miss Horniman, not Yeats.

'The motion as now put', according to the Account;[19] ' "groups" were to be legalised, no one of any seniority or grade is to be allowed to make any enquiries or to see after the working of members in any way.' By the time the vote was taken, only nine members were present. Six voted 'aye' and two voted 'nay' ('the Demon and I'). William Peck (Per Aspera Ad Astra)[20] did not vote, but he helped the losing cause by insisting upon the removal of 'and prying' from the motion. 'We were beaten', Miss Horniman wrote, 'and the "group" triumphed on the Council'. Despite the lateness of the hour she asked the Council to transact some 'ordinary business' but proposed that consideration of the Bruce Pledge Form should wait until a later meeting 'as naturally we were all tired'. She appealed also for a General Meeting in the near future. It was set up for 'today',[21] and Thomas was invited to take the chair. Why he rather than Mrs Emery I can only guess. It may be that Yeats, as Imperator, had been conducting the general meetings and had now asked to be relieved.

When the meeting was over and Miss Horniman could speak 'as Fortiter', she apparently expressed very strong opinions about 'their treatment of such an old member'.[22] She was, of course, most harsh with Blackden, pointing out gleefully to him how easy it would be for her with 'a little hot water and neatness of hand' to open the country envelopes and mark the ballots any way she liked. When he assured her that 'he had meant no insult', she accepted his apology but observed that his denial did not 'fit' in with his actions or the Moderator's. As first written, apparently, the Account was ended at this point, but it was amended in revision to conclude with the following frustrated observation: 'it would indeed require a high Adept of piercing intellect and great knowledge of human nature as well as the skill of an able lawyer to gather together the "group" information I have received into a coherent whole. As it is, maybe the common sense of the Adepti will show them what they may expect if they legalise "groups"'. Yeats's marginal observation was simply: 'on groups'. At this date he must have been weary of the whole affair. He certainly did not expect common sense of his misguided colleagues.

FIVE

The Case for the Minority

I ask you to examine this Resolution carefully, and to ask yourselves whether it has come from the Powers who represent the Personality of this Order, its Constitution, its Tradition and its future, or whether it has come from powers that could see, with indifference, the dissolution of this Order, its Constitution, its Tradition and its future. All that we do with intensity has an origin in the hidden world, and is the symbol, the expression of its powers, and even the smallest detail, in a professedly magical dispute may have significance.

Yeats, 'A Final Letter to the Adepti of R.R. et A.C. on the Present Crisis' (21 February 1901)

Most readers will be disappointed not to know more about Yeats's feelings, which were, if we can believe Miss Horniman's Account, quite as strong as hers. Fortunately, for the record, we have preserved among his papers the typescripts of four open letters or essays which reveal the intensity of his emotions. The first, 'To the Twelve Seniors', is dated 2 February 1901, the day after the tempestuous Council Meeting. Since the salutation to 'Care et V H Fratres & Sorores' is in a hand other than Yeats's, I imagine that it was distributed by someone else[1] and that it may have gone to the entire membership of the Second Order. At any rate, he probably wanted all the members to be aware of his stance. 'I do not know', he begins, 'whether it would be your wish to nominate me as a member of the Executive Council. But I think that it may save you trouble if I asked you not to do so, you will have no difficulty in understanding my decision when I have brought to your attention a very remarkable scene which took place yesterday at a meeting of the Executive Council.'[2] The scene Yeats described is the wrangle over the election schemes. In the light of later letters and the essay on magic which in effect concluded the episode (see Appendix K), it is surprising that Yeats made no mention of his opposition to legalising the groups. From the injured tone of the letter 'To the Twelve Seniors' it is clear that he was more concerned with the undignified treatment (or lack of deference) he and Miss Horniman had received than with the doctrinal dispute over group study. 'It is my duty', he continued,

> to add that only one of the Adepti and he not the most guilty has apologized. I feel that it would ill become my dignity to continue longer than my duty towards the Order requires, an elected member of a Council where party feeling has run to such extravagance. I am ready to teach anything I may know of magical philosophy to any fratres and sorores who may desire; but I shall take no other part in the business of the Second Order until its moral health has been restored.

It should be noted that, in spite of his obvious unhappiness with the course of events, Yeats did not resign (as Miss Horniman had) and that he was inviting retention in an instructional capacity, but not on the Executive Council. In the reorganisation following the expulsion of Mathers, he had been elected as one of 'the seven Adepti Litterati' to instruct in Mystical Philosophy.[3] It is obvious that he was deeply committed to the Order and enjoyed his role as the unquestioned authority in a complex area of study. The hieratic prose of the remainder of the letter projects Yeats's reflections on the position he so obviously enjoyed:

> I have sat on many committees in my own country and elsewhere, but I am proud to say that I have never met among the mechanics, farmers and shop-assistants with whom I have worked in Ireland, a stress of feeling so ignoble or resolutions so astonishing as those I had to listen to yesterday. I desire to keep my reverence for the august symbols of our Order, but I could not do so if I had to sit through more scenes of the kind before the very door of the Tomb of Christian Rosenkreuz in the very presence of the Cross of the Obligation.

In the last sentence of the typescript two intentional blanks are filled in by hand – 'Tomb of Christian Rosenkreuz' and 'Cross of the Obligation', suggesting obviously that this is knowledge forbidden to the typist. This writing is not in Yeats's hand, but the 'D E D I' is.

The letter ends with an elaborate complimentary close, some variations of which were used for the three letters to the Adepti which were to follow :

> Vale Sub Umbram Alarum Tuarum.
>
> יהוה
> *DEDI*
> 18, Woburn Buildings
> Euston Road.

After these letters Yeats did not again, to the best of my knowledge, sign any of his correspondence or work with the four Hebrew letters of the Tetragrammaton for Jehovah (I H V H or Y H V H) or the Latin valediction. The purpose of Yeats's valediction in these letters was to remind his colleagues of an instructional manual they all knew well – Flying Roll No. XVI, 'The History of the Rosicrucian Order' by G. H. Frater N. O. M. (that is, William Wynn Westcott). In 'Suplementary Notes' Westcott suggested that 'it is especially desirable' for 'our brethren' to use the ancient forms of salutation and valediction:

> ... they should salute each other in the following manner 'Ave Frater'.... Members are moreover further requested to endeavour upon all occasions when taking leave of each other to use the old formula Vale, adding 'Sub umbra alarum tuarum, Jehovah !'[4]
>
> The effect of the foregoing observance is to directly maintain the psychic link which has ever served to bind the Members of this Ancient and Honourable Order one to the other; – in this light it is something more than a mere form.

Thinking perhaps that further explanation was needed for beginning students of the Golden Dawn, Westcott added a note after 'Jehovah' relating the valediction to the holy Mountain of Abiegnos and the Cabbalistic Tree of Life :

> A Wand to guide you and protect you in the ascent of the

Mountain is the Staff of Hermes, about which the twin Serpents of Egypt twine: above the wings of Binah and Chokmah – shrouding the sacred Diamond lying on the Crown of Kether – the Supernal. *Sub umbra alarum tuarum*; beneath the rays of spiritual *Understanding* emanating from Divine *Wisdom*, you may indeed be safe, trusting to the protection and aid of the High and Holy Powers summed up in the great Name J H V H.[5]

These two brief passages are most important to our under-standing of Yeats's argument against the establishment of groups within the Second Order. He expected his reference to 'the old formula Vale' to emphasise the importance of unity and the danger of fragmentation to the 'moral health' of the Order. That, as we shall see in Chapter 6, was the thesis of his eloquent plea, 'Is the Order of R.R. & A.C. to remain a Magical Order?' which closes with an allusion to the Mountain of Abiegnos.

Yeats had been beaten in the first round, but he did not concede. In preparation for the General Meeting set for 26 February, he composed three open letters which were typed and circulated to the entire membership of the Second Order. The first, without a date unfortunately, is headed 'A First Letter to the Adepti of R.R. et A.C. upon the Present Crisis'[6] and addressed 'Care et V. H. Fratres & Sorores' in the same hand as the letter 'To the Twelve Seniors'. All four letters were com-posed during the period of 2-22 February, and the 'First Letter to the Adepti' was probably written on 2 February, or at least soon after the 'Executive Difficulty' on 1 February. It begins with a reference to Mathers and the cleavage of the year before. Yeats hints at his own role in the expulsion and suggests how optimistic he had been that the grave problems of that crisis had been solved by the reorganisation: 'I was among those who invited you some months ago to throw off an unendur-able burden and to make this order worthy of its high purpose. The complicated reorganization made necessary by this change came about swiftly and quietly, and there is now more ardour of study and of labour among us, than at any time I can remember.' These lines are reminiscent of a letter to George Russell in May 1900, only a few days after the victory over

Crowley: 'At last we have got a perfectly honest order, with no false mystery and no mystagogues of any kind. Everybody is working, as I have never seen them work, and we have fought out our fight without one discourteous phrase or irrelevant issue.'[7]

Yeats had obviously been too optimistic. If we can trust his letter of 25 April 1900, to Lady Gregory, he had been forced 'to take the whole responsibility for everything, to decide on every step' because 'my Kabbalists are hopelessly unbusinesslike'.[8] Three days later another letter to Lady Gregory corroborates Yeats's faith in his ability to solve their problems and also casts additional light on his motivation: 'I have had to go through this worry for the sake of old friends, and perhaps above all for my uncle['s] sake. If I had not the whole system of teaching would have gone to wrack and this would have been a great grief to him and others, whose whole religious life depends on it.'[9]

If, as Yeats suggests, his own religious life was not wholly dependent upon the Golden Dawn, one can only marvel at his patience and tenacity. He had, of course, been wrong in his confident assertion of ten months before: 'I do not think I shall have any more bother for we have got things into shape and got a proper executive now....'[10] He knew by February 1901 that the Order did not have a 'proper executive' – at least from his viewpoint, and he probably realised that their problems were more complex than his 'First Letter to the Adepti' suggests:

> One anomaly was however forgotten, and it is now causing the only trouble that has arisen among us. We have cast out the tyrannical rule of Frater S.R.M.D., and we must see to it that a 'group' which originated from that tyranny does not bring the Order into a new subjection, which would be none the less evil because purely instinctive and unconscious, and because the mutual distrust and suspicion it would spread among us would have their foundation in good intentions.[11]

Yeats had been aware of the existence of 'private groups' bound together by secret promises. As early as 1897, when 'the Order had lost much of its central fire' 'through distrust of

S.R.M.D.', Mrs Emery in London and Brodie-Innes in Edinburgh had formed groups.[12] With the expulsion of Mathers, Brodie-Innes's group 'abandoned its secrecy', but Mrs Emery's group did not. Yeats insists that he would have 'urged their immediate dissolution' if he had not 'forgotten their existence'. But Miss Horniman did not forget. Almost as soon as she rejoined the Order, apparently, she began to find 'various irregularities' which she traced to the secret groups, and she set out to correct the irregularities. But she soon discovered, in Yeats's words, that 'if she complained of one member, all the members were indignant, that everything she said had as many echoes, and often very distorting echoes as there were members in the group'. The meeting of 1 February certainly proved that. She also discovered that seven of the eleven Council members belonged to Mrs Emery's group, that one other belonged to another group, and that one of the three remaining was married to a member of Mrs Emery's group.[13] Only Yeats and Miss Horniman were outside.

Deciding that she was powerless, Miss Horniman chose not to seek re-election, and Yeats thought he had arranged a compromise with Mrs Emery. If no more Zelators were admitted, he reasoned, 'the "group" would gradually be asorbed by the Theorici degree, where it would be a strength and not a weakness to the Order'. But the group was not pleased with the compromise and insisted upon the meeting which Yeats had described 'to the Twelve Seniors in the first heat of my indignation'. At this point he inserted the whole of his letter to the Seniors.

He then identified 'the Frater who so insulted your Scribe' as Lucem Spero (Thomas), 'who has never past an examination in the Second Order, who has not even consecrated his implements'. Because he has flouted 'our traditions of courtesy' and denied proper respect 'to the Heads of our Order', Yeats continued, 'I have requested him to resign his position as Sub-Imperator of Isis-Urania till he has apologized to your Scribe, but no apology can make amends for such a scene'.

Yeats argued that the existence of a secret society within the Order had reduced its 'well bred and friendly people'[14] to 'a wonderful state of suspicion'. At this point he inserted a footnote which reveals his own ironic awareness of Miss Horniman's flaw as the source of trouble: 'Their suspicion was an outburst that they doubtless remember with astonishment. It was perhaps irritation masquerading as suspicion. They all knew in their hearts that our Scribe's sense of law is almost too great. Party feeling is a wonderful thing.'

Yeats professes not to understand the object ('if indeed it had any ... which I doubt') of this great scene, and he comes to the point of his letter, the resolution declaring all groups 'legal and admirable' which the entire membership of the Second Order are to vote upon at a General Meeting on 26 February. Apologising for being unable to quote the resolution because 'no copy was given to the Scribe, an irregularity she is accustomed to', Yeats says that he has 'given its sense with accuracy', then comments ironically that 'Its oratory, which was all about freedom, if I remember rightly, I cannot give'. That, I suppose, reveals more of Yeats's personal social and political philosophy than it does of the debate at the meeting. By this time he may have been regretting the loss of a strong central authority with the expulsion of Mathers. Always the advocate of order, peace, and unity, Yeats now offers a compromise amendment: 'That this Order, while anxious to encourage among its members, friendly associations which are informal and without artificial mystery, cannot encourage associations or "Groups" that have a formal constitution, a formal obligation, a distinct magical personality which are not the Constitution, the Obligation, or the Personality of this Order.' After some comment upon signatures, which appear to amount to pledges, from the group, Yeats makes one further request: 'I shall ask you also, and this is the most important point of all, to call upon Soror S.S.D.D. to admit no more Zelators into any formal Group.' Finally, he concludes his letter with the sardonic observation that he would be happy if the Order would call upon Mrs Emery to 'dissolve her "Groups"', then adds that such a request may be asking 'too much of human nature'. The letter closes, in a hand other than Yeats's or Miss Horniman's, with 'Vale sub Umbram Alarum Tuarum', followed by Yeats's motto and title, both typed: 'Demon est Deus Inversus, – Imperator of Isis-Urania Temple'.

Disappointed in the response to his long and carefully reasoned letter, Yeats decided several days later to write 'A Second

Letter to the Adepti of R.R. et A.C. on the Present Crisis'.[15] Typed like the first, it is addressed in Miss Horniman's hand to 'Care et V.H. Fratres & Sorores'. After chiding his colleagues gently for confining their responses to 'private letters' which he could not answer because only 'faint rumours of their contents have come to me',[16] Yeats writes that he must 'go into certain details' over the 'business capacity of the organizer' – that is, Mrs Emery. Declaring that he had rather pass over these details in silence, Yeats insists that he would have nothing but praise for her if he were speaking of her 'in any other capacity than that of an official of this Order'. Since he remained her friend and correspondent until her death in India many years later,[17] there is no reason to doubt Yeats's sincerity. But their continued friendship is a little surprising in the light of his harshness. Recalling the proceedings that led to the 'expulsion of Frater S.R.M.D.', he declares that her inexperience was so great that she could not guide the Order until the new Constitution could 'become a habit'. He accuses her also of not following established practices in arriving at and reporting decisions of committees.

The point of this argument is that the Second Order would have broken up for lack of attention to 'the little wearisome details on which its stability depended' if Miss Horniman had not been ready to return in April 1900. Yeats himself had 'invited Soror Fortiter et Recte to return to the Order and to become its Scribe'. Though he was aware that it would appear 'bad taste' to invite her back 'almost in the very hour of S.R.M.D.'s own expulsion', Yeats thought it was for the good of the Order, and he did get 'the unanimous consent of all the working members'. As he summed it up, 'We had all perfect confidence in her business capacity'. With better hindsight than foresight, I suspect, Yeats remembers saying 'something like this' to Miss Horniman as he prepared to get away to Ireland: 'You will have a hard task, you will have to see that laws and precedents are observed, that everything is recorded'. He also remembered warning her in effect 'that in every society or movement that succeeds there is some person that is built into it, as in old times a sacrificial victim was built alive into the foundations of a bridge'. Even then, of course, he knew how zealous she would be. For him, as for most others, the

Order was merely 'one of several things we cared for', but for her 'it would be the chief thing in life', in part no doubt because she had leisure and no other compelling interest. By the time Yeats returned to 'this noisy town', he 'found that she no longer considered it possible to carry out her duties successfully'. She discovered that 'laws and precedents' were being evaded; she 'noticed great irregularities in the list of members and in the book of Admissions and Examinations, the most important record that we possess'; and she complained that 'the Moderator tried continually ... to act without consulting the Council'. That failure Yeats attributed to 'unusual inexperience, and a constitutional carelessness in all such matters' rather than 'any deliberate desire' on the part of Mrs Emery.

Despite his long friendship with her, Yeats felt compelled to summarise these irregularities for the entire membership with a promise to place full details 'in the hands of the Chairman of the General Meeting'. As a strict constructionist, Yeats was primarily concerned with Mrs Emery's attempts to make changes in rituals and study manuals. Chief among these irregularities were an addition to the Corpus Christi Ceremony, an alteration of the diagram of the Minutum Mundum ('the central diagram of our system'), and a modification of the Portal Ceremony. Most serious of all, however, was her 'perfectly serious and decided proposal to admit a candidate "privately" with "a modified $0 = 0$" ceremony without the consent of the Council'. If allowed to continue, such irregularities would, Yeats said, establish 'an autocracy like that we have thrown off with so much difficulty'. Because they disturbed the bonds 'formed in the super-conscious life' and raised a 'general irritation', these careless irregularities threatened the very constitution of the Order. Yeats confesses that he had thought upon his return from Ireland that anyone who had caused as much irritation as Miss Horniman 'could hardly be in the right'. But he had discovered by going 'through all her papers carefully' that her position was right, and he concluded that she must be supported. Otherwise, Mrs Emery and her group 'would have modified beyond recognition the Constitution, that we formed with so much difficulty'. I rather imagine that Yeats was in fact the chief author of the 'Second Order Bye-Laws' (May 1900).[18]

One member, possibly Mrs Emery, had written to Yeats that

'Our group is bound by no oaths nor ruled by any Constitution'. Although Yeats had 'never said' that they were bound by oaths, he did insist that they had made a 'formal constitution', which would in time destroy the Order. This point is the heart of his argument:

> The members of the chief 'group' have certainly formed themselves into a *magical* personality made by a very formal meditation and a very formal numerical system. Unless *magic* is an illusion, this *magical* personality could not help, the moment it came into contact with the larger personality of the Order, from creating precisely the situation it has created. It was a formal evocation of disruption, a formal evocation of a barrier between its own members and the other members of the Order, a formal intrusion of an alien being into the conscious and what is of greater importance into the super-conscious being of our Order, an obsession of the magical sphere that has descended to us, as most of us believe, from the *Frater Christian Rosencreuz* by a sphere created at a time of weariness and disappointment. Such a personality, such a sphere, such an evocation, such an obsession even if it had not supported the real disorders I have described, would have created, so perfectly do the barriers of the conscious life copy the barriers of the super-conscious, illusionary suspicion, illusionary distrust more irremediable than if they had real cause. We who are seeking to sustain this great Order must never forget that whatever we build in the imagination will accomplish itself in the circumstance of our lives.[19]

I have quoted at length because this passage reveals so much of Yeats's personal philosophy and aesthetic. To him, membership in the Order represented a symbolic search for membership in the ideal order of the universe. Magic, as he uses the term, is a means of breaking down the barriers between the phenomenal or conscious world and the spiritual or super-conscious world. Therefore, magic must never be used to evoke distrust or erect barriers between members. These impassioned lines make clear that Yeats's faith in the 'magical sphere that has descended to us, as most of us believe, from the *Frater Christian Rosencreuz*' was no passing fancy, was in fact central to his thinking for a significant portion of and period in his life. He was, without doubt, working as hard as possible 'to sustain this great Order', which had become the religious instrumentality for closing the doors of his imagination against a pushing world. Magic was no illusion. The Golden Dawn was the ideal brotherhood for its practice, and any proposal which threatened to fragment the Order was clearly evil. Therefore, Yeats appeals, 'I have a right to believe that you will not pass a law giving your sanction and the sanction of this Order to this "group" or to any "group" of the kind'.

This 'Second Letter' then closes with a repetition of Yeats's proposed amendment and a postscript explaining that he had suspended Thomas for 'his principal share in the scene of February 1st'. It is signed, 'Vale, s.u.a.t. יהוה D.E.D.I.'

Yeats apparently intended this as his last appeal before the meeting planned for 26 February, but he was prompted to write 'A Final Letter to the Adepti of the R.R. et A.C. on the Present Crisis'[20] when he received from Percy W. Bullock, the Chairman for the General Meeting, a copy of the Resolution prepared by Mrs Emery's group for consideration by the Second Order. Yeats's letter, drafted 21 February, is so openly satiric that I rather imagine he already thought the battle lost. 'It is long', he said, 'the longest Resolution I have ever seen made out of such light material, and yet it contains but a single sentence'. Because 'this sentence winds hither and thither with so much luxuriance', Yeats proposes to give it 'a closer study than you could give it at the General Meeting'. He begins by quoting the Resolution in full:

If the liberty and progress of individual members – and of this Order as a whole – is to be maintained – for progress without liberty is impossible – it is absolutely necessary that all members of the 2nd Order shall have the undisputed right to study and work at their mystical progress in whatsoever manner seems to them right according to their individual needs and conscience – and further it is absolutely necessary that they shall be at perfect liberty to combine, like minded with like minded, in groups or circles formed for the purpose of that study and progress, in such manner as seems to them right and fitting and according to their consciences, and that – without the risk of suffering from interference by any member of any grade whatever, or of any seniority whatever, – and furthermore that this is in perfect accord with the spirit and tradition of our Order which is always to allow the largest liberty for the expansion of the individual, and has always discountenanced the interference of any and every member with private affairs, whether mystical or otherwise of any other member.

'Amid all this luxuriance' Yeats discovers four 'distinct ideas: (1) that all fraters and sorores shall be free to do anything they like so long as it is something mystical, (2) that they shall be free to form any kind of groups they like so long as they are mystical, (3) that to do so is true not only to the spirit but to the letter of the *Father Christian Rosencreuz*, (4) that nobody, no not the highest or the oldest of our Adepti, shall "interfere" with them in any way.'[21] At this point Yeats was a bit discouraged if not disgusted with his colleagues. In particular, he was unhappy that the Order could not, under this Resolution, interfere with members 'who flagrantly misuse their *magical* knowledge' even in the 'Rooms of the Order itself'. He was fearful that this misuse might take the form of black magic: to '*evoke the genius* of another', to 'cast about that *genius* an enchantment of sensual passion', to '*evoke the spirits* of disease to destroy some enemy',[22] or to 'hold any kind of Witches Sabbath they like before the door of the Tomb'. Moreover, in the disregard 'of any grade whatever, or of any seniority whatever', this Resolution would, Yeats perceived, destroy the whole structural hierarchy and in time the Order itself. And he was, of course, quite right.

Reminding his colleagues once more that they had only 'recently expelled certain fratres whose "consciences" and whose expression of what "seems to them right" were not to your minds', he points out that the same logic applies now, and suggests that another great schism is in the making. He insists also that they are responsible not only to the 'Laws of this Land' but also to 'far subtler Laws' for what happens in the Order Rooms. Despite veiled threats of 'the worst of evil *magic*', he argues, you are being asked to trust everybody and 'to believe no longer in the ancient *magical* tradition that bids even the highest look lest he fall' and 'to trust to your clair-voyants and introducers so profoundly that you are to believe no unfit person shall ever again enter this Order'. As strangely ironic as these lines are, they nevertheless reveal Yeats's basic scepticism. He wanted to believe implicitly, but he continued to probe and question, to measure his fellow members, to sift the ideal questers from those who merely sought diversion. If you adopt this Resolution, he warns, 'The medium, the mes-merist, the harmless blunderer or the man who seeks a forbid-den pleasure by symbols that are now better known than they were, may form his secret "group" from the moment he has passed the ceremony of $5 = 6$, and gather his secret "group" about him in the rooms of your Order.' He suggests, moreover, that this Resolution does not come from powers representing the true 'Personality of this Order' (he is certainly thinking of himself) but rather from 'powers that could see, with indiffer-ence, the dissolution of this Order, its Constitution, its Tradi-tion and its future'. These powers, in Yeats's opinion, 'seek ends that are not the ends of this Order, and that say to their followers as the Evil Powers once said to theirs "Your eyes shall be opened and ye shall be as Gods knowing Good and Evil"'. Such biblical references remind us of the distinction Yeats was seeking to establish between the truly religious and the black magicians. To him, at least, the Order represented a means of effecting the 'reconciliation of Paganism and Christ-ianity', and he therefore warned the dabblers: 'All that we do with intensity has an origin in the hidden world, and is the symbol, the expression of its powers, and even the smallest detail in a professedly *magical* dispute may have significance.'

Yeats closed his 'Final Letter ... on the Present Crisis' with a fine metaphorical passage suggestive of the spheres, gyres, and cones of *A Vision*, for which in fact he was already forming the convictions and storing the philosophic materials:

Sometimes the sphere of an individual man is broken, and a form comes into the broken place and offers him know-ledge and power if he will but give it of his life. If he give it out of his life it will form a swirl there and draw other forms about it, and his sphere will be broken more and more, and his will subdued by alien wills. It seems to me that

such a swirl has been formed in the sphere of this Order,
by powers, that though not evil in themselves are evil in
relation to this Order.

The letter is dated 21 February, and signed, like the others,
'Vale s.u.a.t. יהוה D.E.D.I.'[23]

The following day Yeats added a postscript. In answer to a
letter received that morning, he replied to the argument that
only a group could decide whether or not it should have a
'formal constitution' and that therefore no group should be
condemned. 'This', Yeats says, 'is an example of the confusion
of mind that hangs over this dispute'. Although Yeats opposes
'legislation against groups', he insists that the Order must not
surrender supervisory powers over 'collective or individual
practice of a distinctly mystical kind' or over the meeting
rooms themselves. He considers any such surrender 'a dangerous breach of our obligation'.

Three days later, on 25 February, all the appropriate members received what amounted to a rebuttal of Yeats's open
letters. Signed by Lucem Spero (Thomas) and headed simply
'Statement Issued to Adepti by the Majority of the Council',[24]
it is directed specifically against Yeats and Miss Horniman.
The copy of the Statement in Yeats's papers has notes by both
of them, suggesting, I think, that they analysed it and plotted
strategy together for the General Meeting called for the following day. Yeats made his brief notes in the margin, but Miss
Horniman made numbers at various points and wrote more
extended answers on separate sheets, which fortunately are
attached to the Statement.

Ostensibly, Thomas's purpose is simply to convey 'further
information with regard to the subject for the consideration
of which the General Meeting on the 26th Feb has been called
– i.e. the advisability of working in private groups'. He begins
his argument by citing the Minute Book of 1 April 1897 to the
effect that on the very appointment of Soror SSDD as head of
the London branch 'the formation of secret groups was advised
and legalized on the same occasion with the consent of DDCF'.
Yeats underlined 'secret groups' and wrote in the margin: 'if
not a formal obligation there is a formal understanding or how
can they be secret'. He also drew a line beside the first dozen

or so lines and wrote 'secresy', and Miss Horniman made her first number at the same point. Her first observation adds little to the debate, though she does end with a suggestive note we might wish she had finished: '... and the Grail Cup symbol in their sphere etc'.[25]

One argument for the secret groups is especially strange: the writers reason that members ought to 'be encouraged to investigate freely and to use the knowledge already received as much as possible as a basis for further development' because 'there is no prospect of further official Knowledge'. This, I suppose, is a clear indication that Moina and MacGregor Mathers had indeed been transmitting all 'official Knowledge', which was no longer available now that they were out of the London Temple.[26] If Mathers had seen this admission, he would have been exultant: it corroborates his warning that disruption and dissension are certain to come without his strong leadership and (he would have added) his ties with the Secret Chiefs of the Order.

The following sentence, insisting that 'the Oath of fraternity should protect members from the suspicion and criticism of those with whom they do not happen to be working at the time', is circled and marked A, but there is no record of the special comment which the labelling suggests. Yeats wrote 'criticism' in the margin and underlined, without comment, two phrases in the succeeding sentence: 'formal obligation' and 'Formulae opposed to the Order'. By this time, apparently, he did not think it necessary to answer the denial of the group that had taken the one and were working on the other.

Having dispensed with preliminary matters, the letter gets to its real business, the indictment of Miss Horniman and Yeats. 'The case of Very Hon. Sor. F. E. R. (hereafter called Fortiter)' is first. The chief objections to her are stated in two paragraphs:

This Soror was out of the Order from 1896 to 1900 when we were all very glad to welcome her back from what we considered an unjust exile. She had left us when many members were her juniors to whom 3 years of hard work had naturally made considerable difference. They gladly yielded to her her old seniority as a matter of courtesy. Unfortunately she considered her position gave her the right to find fault with their methods and override their teaching. This no doubt caused great friction, as different occultists have widely different views as to the relative importance of different details in teaching.

One of Fortiter's first actions was to try and reestablish the supreme right to honour and authority in the Order of those who had passed examinations. D.D.C.F., our late chief, neglected examinations because he came to see the practical imperfections of the system in dividing the fit from the unfit. Sapientia agreeing with him did not enforce examinations during her term of office, 1897 to 1900, though members were free to go through this curriculum if they found it helpful.

Miss Horniman made three numbers in this passage and offered the following rebuttal in her notes: (2) 'The phrase "gladly yielded to her, her old seniority" is a contradiction in terms'; (3) 'If I found fault with some of the new methods it was because of my long experience. I do not know what "override their teaching" means'; (4) 'I certainly advocate the examination system, which D.D.C.F. neglected from idleness, as I saw in Paris in 1895'. Yeats wrote 'seniority' in the left margin, then repeated Miss Horniman's indictment of Mathers's dereliction of duty in a note at the bottom of the page: 'neglected from idleness – (consider also lack caused from money matters)'.[27] Neither Yeats nor Miss Horniman commented on Thomas's insistence that 'due recognition should be given to those whose interest is centred in one branch of occultism....' But Yeats drew a line opposite and wrote 'exams'.

The letter next turns to Miss Horniman's opposition to groups, especially to their use of the meeting rooms, and Thomas accuses her of asking 'various members to make formal complaints'. Yeats wrote 'use of rooms' in the margin, and Miss Horniman made note 5: 'When about Nov. 15th the "group" had drawn attention to itself I asked Igitur alone if she had ever been turned away from the Library. The complaint made to me by Servio[28] on Nov. 13th or 14th I requested her to put in writing as I felt that I must lay the matter before the Council.'

The first sentence of the next paragraph is circled and marked B, apparently for some special attention which is not clear: 'Since last November Fortiter has literally persecuted persons she suspected of belonging to the Sphere Group by word of mouth and in written letters and lectures, endeavouring to prove that it is a disintegrating force.' Yeats noted 'criticism again', then added (in words difficult to decipher) something about 'persecution'. Thomas calls her accusation 'absurd', pointing out that the group included members who had been active in the service of the Order both 'before and since the Revolution'. 'Nearly all of you have the lecture on the star maps', he continues, 'and know the desirability of turning the Kether of the earth to the true Kether.[29] That is the object of the Sphere group work. There is no secresy or heresy about its formulae.' Miss Horniman noted (no. 6) that ' "Turning the Kether of the earth to the True Kether" is referred to in the Tarot Lecture', then added that 'in regard to the working of the "group" these words are a confirmation of the faint murmur which has reached me'. To Thomas, her suspicions are baseless and the present scandal entirely her fault.

At this point, he passes to particular issues: first, Miss Horniman's criticism of Blackden's not having passed his D examination. The justification certainly would not have pleased her: he had been translating a part of the Egyptian 'Book of the Dead for the Lecture on the Pillars'. But most of her malice, according to Thomas, had been directed at Mrs Emery: that she had 'conducted examinations unfairly', that she had 'altered the Minutum Mundum diagram' to suit the more esoteric teaching of the group, that she had withheld dates and information. To Thomas, most of these difficulties could be traced to Miss Horniman's upset nerves: she took jokes seriously and exaggerated the most casual remarks of the group, considering many of them serious offences 'against rectitude'. (The play on the word is surely intentional.) Throughout the autumn and winter she had been apparently compiling a list of black marks against the group.

Miss Horniman had an answer for all Thomas's charges. In

the space of some twenty-five lines she made five numbered
notes :

(7) My 'suspicion & distrust' have been proved to be founded
on experience.

(8) I never accused Sapientia of conducting examinations
unfairly : I remarked that as I could not take those of Adepti
who had worked with me privately, that it would not do for
her to superintend those of her 'group'.

(9) In regard to the Minutum Mundum Diagram – is the $5 = 6$
ceremony for the Order or for the 'group'?[30]

(10) I was never informed by Sapientia that she had a complete copy of the Examination book. The Council agreed
that the examiner was to inform the Scribe. Her postcard
on Dec. 19th about Sub Hoc[31] on July 16th answers this
assertion.

I was grateful for her courtesy in sending me the missing
mottoes, names, & dates.

(11) I do not know what happened on Jan. 12th, no meeting
is recorded on that date in the Minute Book. What I have
placed in the archives as 'an example of a serious offence
against rectitude' I cannot identify.

Although these responses to Thomas's accusations may represent a fundamental difference in viewpoint, they also suggest
a kind of head-on collision of two egoistic and determined
women, and Yeats was in a difficult position. But he had sided
with Miss Horniman, so he too must be called to account. 'The
Case of V. H. Fra D.E.D.I.'[32] opens on a conciliatory and flattering tone which illustrates ironically the kind of mingled
dislike and respect he commanded :

This frater did you all great service during the Revolution
as you know from your printed documents. Since then he
has attended the council meetings at intervals and we all
bear him witness that he has talked at greater length than
all the other members put together. His position among us
is due to his long connection with the Order, the originality
of his views on Occult subjects and the ability with which
he expresses them rather than the thoroughness of his knowledge of Order work and methods which is somewhat scant.
He is however a shining example of the help we may get

from Members who have no special talent for passing Examinations.

The statement that Yeats had done 'great service during the Revolution as you know from your printed documents' makes it clear, I think, not only that he prepared the printed 'List of Documents' (Appendix A) and 'Statement' but also that he was the leader in the revolt. Miss Horniman's note 12, made in the middle of the paragraph above, observes that 'D.E.D.I. has been at only ten out of the seventeen Council Meetings, owing to absence from London. In examinations he stands next to the Twelve Seniors'.[33]

At this point the gloves came off, and the battle was on. 'Unfortunately', Thomas continues, 'he has put himself forever beyond our sympathy by a recent flagrant piece of audacity before which the little tyrannies of our late Parisian Chief pale. As Emperor he has, without attempting to consult the Prae-monstratrix or Cancellaria, demanded the retirement of a Vice Chief of Isis Urania Temple because they had had a difference of opinion on Council.' Miss Horniman's note 13 defends Yeats on legalistic principles: 'This action in regard to the Sub-Imperator is supported by Bye-law 6 of the Inner'. She refers apparently to the statement in the Bye-Laws of May 1900 (see Appendix N) that each Chief is to have two subordinates 'who shall be responsible to him for the performance of their duties, with the right of appeal to the Executive Council'. According to Thomas's version of the dispute over election procedures, 'D.e.d.i. lost his temper completely' over Blackden's proposal, 'pretending that our desire to act in accordance with custom was a personal attack on the integrity of the Scribe'. Miss Horniman's note 14 observes that she was not 'a person interested in the result': 'I had already announced my intention of neither nominating, voting nor standing for election'.

As the seconder of Blackden's motion, Thomas was incensed at Yeats's opposition. Pointing out that he is 'a freemason[34] and a member of many occult bodies', Thomas insists that 'the motion was impersonal and was simply an effort to secure a ballot to which less exception could be taken'. 'This however was of no avail', he continues, 'V.H. D.e.d.i. insisting on the idea of suspicion which was introduced on the Council by him

& by him alone'. Miss Horniman's note 15 comments on this section:[35] 'I alone was responsible for the scheme. Before D.E.D.I. shewed anger I had had the impulse to resign on the spot; this impulse was only conquered by my sense of duty towards the Order'.

After noting proudly that he and Blackden had been willing to compromise by allowing the country members 'to ballot in the ordinary way' at 'the general meeting in March', Thomas summarised the allegations 'made by V. H. D.e.d.i. regarding myself':

> A That I was solely responsible for Mawahanu's ballot proposal. This is incorrect.[36] [Yeats wrote 'I did not' at this point.]
> B That my action caused V.H.F.e.n. to decide on resignation. This is also incorrect as I understand the Soror in question expressed this determination previously.[37] [Again Yeats wrote 'I did not.']
> C That I have not consecrated my implements. It is somewhat difficult to see what this has to do with the case, or how the information was obtained. It is equally incorrect.[38]
> D That I relied for courage on some Hierarchy.

Thomas professes that he is 'really at a loss to understand what is meant by this', that he had not, in fact, 'relied on anything but the common sense of the majority of the council'. According to Miss Horniman's note to *D*, she too is 'ignorant as to the meaning of Lucem Spero's reference to "Hierarchy"'.

Thomas might have ended here, but he had a personal issue to raise. Angry at Yeats's 'illegal attempt' to suspend him from his position of Vice-Imperator, and thinking ironically of their suspension of Mathers, Thomas insists that Yeats's action is 'a specimen of the kind of Tyranny that we are endeavouring to render impossible in our Order'. He concludes with a denial of personal ambition for office or influence but admits to 'a great pleasure' in the confidence that his colleagues have reposed in him. The letter proper ends with a typed identification: 'signed, Lucem Spero'.[39]

Although he may have written the letter himself, it appears to represent a 'group' effort. At any rate, the rebels decided to add a postscript to which all of them would subscribe. Both a summary and a warning, it needs to be quoted in full:

To sum up.

We wish to state that we do not allow that the Theoricus rank warrants those who hold it in taking upon themselves the responsibility of acting as the conscience of other members of the $5=6$ grade. The whole spirit of the Revolution was to exalt the expert at the expense of the seniors, if a senior happens to be an expert so much the better, but we refuse to be controlled in any way by seniors simply because they have passed examinations. We believe that in countenancing a system of carefully organised groups we are advocating a policy which will give the order the status it abandoned when it abandoned the authority of D.D.C.F. And we do not believe that any occult work can be benefitted by the criticism or supervision of those not actually engaged in it. We have now to state that if the General meeting decide to take away the right we at present enjoy to form groups in which we are at liberty to work with any members who have special knowledge or qualities whether they have passed examinations or not, the following members will withdraw, taking no further active part in an order in which such stultifying regulations are approved. Sapientia. Vigilate. Deo date. Silentio. Dum Spiro Spero. Hora et Semper. Ma Wahanu Thesi. Lucem Spero.[40]

Miss Horniman made three comments about the postcript. First, she observed, 'any "rank" entails "responsibility", in our Order as in daily life'. Second, she asked, 'Who is to organise "groups"?' Third, 'Are only those Theorici who are attracted by Egyptian symbolism responsible for the welfare of the Order?' Then, characteristically, she signed her notes and dated them carefully: 'Fortiter et Recte, T.A.M. Feb. 25th, 1901'. Yeats, as usual, was more succinct, and more devastating. In the left margin he wrote a single word: 'chaos'.[41]

Although Yeats did not receive or preserve a copy of the minutes of the momentous General Meeting on 26 February, we know something of what transpired from an open letter dated 27 February and signed by Miss Horniman, Yeats, and J. W. Brodie-Innes,[42] all of whom resigned their positions. The letter begins by quoting in full an amendment by Brodie-Innes to Blackden's Resolution at the meeting of the night before:

That before any other matter can be considered it is necessary that the Constitution and Rules of the Order shall be revised and formally adopted and that a small Committee be forthwith appointed to draft and submit to the Order a scheme for this purpose. And that in the meantime there shall be no interference with any group which does not transgress the laws of the Order, and that no group shall interfere with or alter the working of the Order.

Speaking to his amendment, Brodie-Innes described the 'state of things ... in the language of Mediaeval politics as a "Truce of God"'. His amendment was 'negatived apparently by a mechanical majority, who failed to comprehend its effect, for the same proposals were afterwards affirmed by the same majority'.

After the failure of Brodie-Innes's amendment, Yeats then proposed an 'amendment in the following modified form':

That this Order while anxious to encourage among its members associations which are informal and without artificial mystery neither desires to encourage nor condemn associations, or 'groups' that have a formal constitution, a formal obligation, a distinct magical personality which are not the Constitution, the Obligation or the Personality of this Order. That the resolution proposed by Frater Ma Wahanu Thesi and this amendment be submitted in writing to all the Adepti of the Second Order and that this Meeting adjourn until the votes have been received, those who cannot attend personally to be permitted to vote through the post.

This too, as Yeats no doubt expected, was 'negatived'.

When Blackden, explaining his 'vague resolution' to the assembly, declared that 'he did not ask for a vote of confidence in any "group" or for any positive action being taken', Brodie-Innes voted for the motion, but Yeats and Miss Horniman voted against it. Brodie-Innes rationalised his vote by affirming that the Meeting could not express confidence in groups because it had no authority to give them legal status: 'Nothing that has happened has any force either to reduce the primary authority of the Obligation nor the right and responsibility of the Order which it derives from the Obligation itself to enforce it.'

There was apparently unanimous agreement that the rules must be revised immediately since the Order was now operating without any binding rules except the Obligation. Because 'the power heretofore possessed by D.D.C.F. resides in them as a whole', the 'body of Adepti' must vote unanimously to authorise a committee to 'draft a constitution and revise rules'. 'The necessity for such rules was abundantly proved and acknowledged at the Meeting' in the opinion of the three signers, who added, with obvious self satisfaction, that 'the long experience of Fortiter et Recte in the business of the Order has taught her that fixed rules and a just enforcement of them would give the members that peace which is necessary for occult study'.

But they were less happy over the next action of the assembly : the reinstatement of Thomas by a 'large majority', who made it known emphatically that they considered Yeats's action both 'illegal and unjust'. According to the three authors, however, Yeats 'has resigned his position as Imperator of Isis-Urania Temple', not because of the vote but because the tribunal lacks authority and because 'he does not wish to be a cause of dissension in the Order'. The letter closes with an expression of Yeats's hope that the Order 'will return to its normal state' when the new rules are approved. The expected 'Vale s.u.a.t.' is followed by the Order Mottoes of the three : 'Fortiter et Recte T.A.M. Late Scribe', 'Sub Spe T.A.M. Late Imperator of Amen Raa', and 'Demon est Deus Inversus Late Imperator of Isis-Urania'.[43] Two postscripts follow. In the first Miss Horniman 'categorically' denies 'various accusations ... made against me'. In the second Yeats writes :

> I do not think the letter of 'the majority of the Council' calls for any comment from me. Nobody untroubled by party feeling will believe that I removed Frater *Lucem Spero* from his office because of a difference of opinion at a meeting of the Council, and the other statements in so far as they concern myself are unimportant. D.E.D.I.

It is clear that Yeats's emotional response to the letter of the majority was strong. Both he and Miss Horniman were greatly disturbed, as subsequent events were to prove.

SIX

Defending the Magic of Power

If we preserve the unity of the Order, if we make that unity efficient among us, the Order will become a single very powerful talisman, creating in us, and in the world about us, such moods and circumstances as may best serve the magical life, and best awaken the magical wisdom. Its personality will be powerful, active, visible afar, in that all powerful world that casts downward for its shadows, dreams, and visions.

Yeats, 'Is the Order of R.R. & A.C. to remain a Magical Order?'

At the time, surely, Yeats must have felt there was nothing more to say or do; but he was a determined man, and the issue had, for whatever complex of reasons, assumed tremendous proportions. As a proud man of strong principles, he was infuriated by Thomas's attack upon his personal integrity. Far more important, however, was the ruin he foresaw for an Order which embodied in its teachings and rituals his profoundest religious and philosophical convictions about man's place in the universe. So, as usual, he sought an artistic means for the ordering of his thought and for the reunification of a religious organisation he thought could not exist in fragments. He must have begun almost at once to write the striking and thoughtful essay entitled 'Is the Order of R.R. & A.C. to remain a Magical Order?' The title page of the privately printed pamphlet records that it was 'Written in March, 1901, and given to the Adepti of the Order of R.R. & A.C. in April, 1901'.[1]

The essay is divided into five numbered parts. The first, very brief, section is little more than a transition linking the essay to recent events and Thomas's Statement in particular. 'I regret', Yeats wrote, 'that differences have arisen among us, but none the less I must submit to you a system which is not, so far as I can judge from a recent open letter, the system of "the majority of the Council".' Although the meaning of 'system' in this context is ambiguous, Yeats apparently sought to imply that his religious philosophy as well as his conception of the organisation and government of the Second Order differed fundamentally from the beliefs of the majority. Referring to the 'legal constitution' about to be made as a result of 'the vote of all the Adepti', Yeats insists strongly that 'we must ... go to first principles, and decide what we mean to do with the Order'. In one sense the remainder of the essay is his attempt to formulate and explain these 'first principles'. As a traditionalist, he preferred keeping the Order 'as it has come down to us' rather than changing it 'into some new shape'. Although it is difficult to imagine that Yeats had any real faith that he could stem the rising tide of disunity, he must have thought that contrary viewpoints needed the kind of logical analysis which had been impossible in the heated debates of the weeks just past. Disregarding emotional differences, he stated the issue with admirable clarity : 'We have even to decide whether we intend it to remain a Magical Order at all, in the true sense of the word'. Before we swear allegiance to a new set of laws, he is saying in effect, we must determine if possible what the true sense of the word 'magic' is and by extension what metaphysical basis there is for faith in a magical cosmic order. Because it is Yeats's only extended analysis of a fundamental cosmological question basic to an understanding of his art and life, 'Is the Order of R.R. & A.C. to remain a Magical Order ?' deserves a significant place in his canon. Coming as it does at the end of the 'worst part of life', it represents his most thoughtful philosophic observation about the nature of the universe and of man's relationship to everything outside himself.

In another sense, of course, the essay is a defence of 'the Magic of power', the quest for knowledge, of man's desire to ascend the 'ladder into heaven'. Part II is devoted primarily to Yeats's argument for restoring 'the Order to that state of discipline' necessary to the acquisition of this divine wisdom. The first step must be a return to the practices of eight or nine years ago – that is, to the date of Yeats's initiation into the Second or Inner Order in 1893.[2] 'This can be done', Yeats thinks,

(1) By insisting on a strict obedience to the laws and by-laws.

(2) By making the giving out of the knowledge lectures dependent on the passing of examinations.

(3) By giving the highest Degree (or Grade) weight in the government of the Order, and by retaining the old respect for the Degrees and seniority.

(4) By restoring the oath taken upon the Cross on Corpus Christi Day, until recent years, by one of the seniors as a representative of the Third Order.[3]

All these except the last are directly related to issues in the quarrel of the preceding weeks. Number four is important, I think, in emphasising that the Golden Dawn was conceived as a Christian organisation. Since Mathers, Westcott, and Woodman had been members of the Societas Rosicruciana in Anglia,[4] an organisation comprised entirely of Master Masons, it was inevitable that the Golden Dawn should be indebted to and compared to Freemasonry. A major difference, apparently, was the emphasis placed upon Christian doctrine in the Golden Dawn, especially in the beginning. The distinction in the minds of the members of the Order is suggested in the answer to a lost letter which Yeats must have written during the very weeks of the ideological quarrel with the groups. On 22 January 1901 an acquaintance (who signs only with initials I cannot decipher) responded to some question about 'the subject of confession in relation to the Society you wot of'. He had taken Yeats's question to 'a very high church (Anglican) parson' who had in turn asked a priest for the Roman Catholic view. The answer was that 'if the Society has for its aim good it need not be mentioned in confessions'. More to my point, however, was an observation that the Catholic Church 'denounced' such continental societies as 'Freemasons who ... do not hold a belief even in a god'.[5] Yeats made a similar comparison between the regular or true members of the Golden Dawn and those who organised themselves into groups for the study of Egyptology. I am not, of course, trying to make Yeats into an orthodox Christian but rather to point out that he continued to insist upon the Christian foundation of the Golden Dawn. Like Anna Kingsford, I suspect, he believed that 'the initiate has no quarrel with the true Christian religion or with its symbolism, but only with the current orthodox interpretation'.[6]

He had looked upon the Order as microcosmic in its original organisation. Always a believer in strong central authority, he approved in principle of one supreme head such as Mathers, whose authority in the Order had been unquestioned because all spiritual knowledge came through him to other members of the Order. He was in effect God's vicegerent. And in creating an Order with three Chiefs, Mathers no doubt had in mind the analogy with the trinity, he being the head. Yeats was aware when Mathers was being ejected in 1900 that his going would destroy this symbolic analogy and that fragmentation might result. A year later, in the shattering divisiveness of a new quarrel, he admitted to himself that his worst fears were being realised, though he still insisted that unity was possible without strong central authority:

> The passing from among us of Frater S.R.M.D. has thrown the whole burden of the unity and continuity of the Order upon the Order itself. They have no longer the artificial support of his vigorous and imaginative personality, and must be supported alone by the laws and by-laws and symbols, by the symbolic personality of the Order, a personality which has, we believe, an extreme antiquity, though it would still be alive and active, had it arisen out of the evocations of these last years.

To this Mrs Emery commented ironically in the margin: 'That is they must become a learned Society without any farcical pretences'.

Yeats himself is subtly ironic. Why, for example, has he chosen to refer to Mathers as S.R.M.D., an early motto with links to the Societas Rosicruciana in Anglia? During the quarrel and expulsion of the year before, Mathers signed his letters and was addressed in return as D.D.C.F. This may be simply Yeats's sly way of suggesting that Mathers had been something of a fraud, at least in the claims he made for himelf. Yeats was no doubt remembering that during the quarrel of 1900 Mathers had consistently denied the authority of the Second Order to elect a committee or arrest the work of the Order 'save and only by my direct commands'. He had, in fact, insisted on his supreme authority: 'I have always acknowledged and shall always maintain the authority of the Secret Chiefs of the Order, to whom and the Eternal Gods I bow, but to *none* beside!' In the same letter (dated 2 April 1900), addressed ostensibly to P. W. Bullock (Levavi Oculos) but intended for Yeats and Mrs Emery, Mathers drew an analogy between his expulsion and the death of Mme Blavatsky and predicted 'turmoil and strife' 'were it *possible* to remove me from my place as the Visible Head of our Order (the which *cannot* be without my own consent, because of certain magical links)'.[7] Whatever Yeats may have thought of these claims in March 1890, when he joined the Order, by March 1901 he was disillusioned: Mathers's '*artificial* support' (my italics) must be replaced by something more enduring, that is, 'laws and by-laws and symbols'. Yeats argues now for a 'symbolic personality of the Order', and he suggests, I think, that he had always looked upon Mathers as a unifying figurehead rather than a divine agent. He suggests also that he is sceptical (as usual) about the claims for the 'extreme antiquity' of the Order, possibly the authenticity of the Cypher Manuscripts themselves.

In one sense the remainder of the essay is Yeats's carefully reasoned attempt to convince his colleagues of the spiritual validity of 'a discipline that is essentially symbolic and evocative'. Unity of purpose and of being can be maintained, he argues, only under a 'system of Degrees that is a chief element in this magical personality'. He is obviously referring to the laxity of discipline under the stewardship of Mrs Emery, but more importantly he is arguing for the metaphysical validity of a hierarchic order of existence. He obviously does not believe in election to salvation, in divine bestowal of grace. As might be expected, his religious convictions are essentially Catholic rather than Protestant, high Church rather than low. The 'magical examinations' are not simply a 'test of efficiency' or an 'Ordeal, which selects those who are most devoted to the Order', both valid in themselves, but rather a ritualistic and symbolic means of attaining union with (or in) divinity:

The passing by their means from one Degree to another is an evocation of the Supreme Life, a treading of a symbolic path, a passage through a symbolic gate, a climbing towards the light which it is the essence of our system to believe,

flows continually from the lowest of the invisible Degrees
to the highest of the Degrees that are known to us.

These lines clearly reveal the basic reason for Yeats's devotion
to the Golden Dawn. To Yeats, the search for meaning in the
multiplicity and profusion and seeming chaos of nature
required a framework, a system. The discipline of the magical
examinations represented a search for truth, a striving for
union with the ideal in the invisible world. In the broadest
sense all Yeats's creative energies were devoted to this religious
quest. In the context of this quest his poetry was but one means
of invoking the magical powers of the invisible. It was a concrete device for the ordering of his thought and therefore of
existence itself; it was in effect a search for meaning; it 'Prepared a rest for the people of God', to quote his words from
'Under Ben Bulben'.

He was concerned primarily with the discipline, the system,
the ordering of his thought, the symbolic evocation rather than
the authenticity of manuscripts, the historic facts surrounding
the Order, or even the name and nature of the Secret Chiefs: 'It
matters nothing whether the Degrees above us are in the body
or out of the body, for none the less must we tread this path
and open this gate, and seek this light, and none the less must
we believe the light flows downward continually.'

In his faith in order, authority, and degree Yeats was closer
to the Renaissance than to his own time; in his faith in the
invisible world he was closer to the Romantics. He was, I
suspect, far more idealistic – and more religious – than most,
perhaps any, of his fellow members in the Second Order. And
he was aware that his aims and faith were not always theirs.
He was, moreover, the admitted authority on mysticism, the
true magic. In the reorganisation of the Second Order after the
expulsion of Mathers, Yeats had been nominated 'by the twelve
most advanced adepts and elected by the members' to the post
of Instructor in Mystical Philosophy.[8] Always the teacher,
Yeats was, as he assured the Twelve Seniors, 'ready to teach
anything I may know of magical philosophy to any fratres and
sorores who may desire'.[9] Although such prophetic self-
assurance must have irritated many of his colleagues, they did
recognise, however grudgingly, his superior insight. Like his

master Blake, Yeats was offering to the unilluminated 'the end of a golden string' which 'will lead you in at Heaven's gate'. Because 'the Degree of Theoricus is our link with the invisible Degrees', it demands 'respect and attention':

> If the Degree has too little knowledge or too little authority, we must give it knowledge from our intuitions and our intellect and authority from the laws and by-laws of the Order. If we despise it or forget it, we despise and forget the link which unites the Degree of Zelatores, and through that the Degree of the Portal and the four Degrees of the G. D. in the Outer, to the Third Order, to the Supreme Life.

Mrs Emery's note reveals the irritation many of them felt over the mantle Yeats assumed: 'Who are "we" to give anything to our seniors?'

Yeats did not achieve the Degree of Theoricus Adeptus Minor until 10 July 1912,[10] more than eleven years after the composition of this essay; and he believed that its attainment must represent the acquisition of some form of knowledge beyond mere 'erudition' or 'traditional knowledge', valuable though they were. Seeking always for some mystical apprehension, Yeats insisted upon a more meaningful discipline: 'some simple form of meditation to be used at stated periods, some symbolic vigil in the mystic tomb of which ours is but the image....' Here as usual Yeats is careful to remind his readers that the invisible world is the real, ours but a symbolic image. Through the intuitive apprehension of reality Yeats hopes 'to bind them [the Adepti] together in a strong indissoluble bond' and ultimately to achieve 'some new descent of the Supreme Life' into the entire Order. Although Yeats is not certain whether this 'new descent' will be 'in the body or out of the body', he appears to be thinking of the second coming 'of some great Adept, some great teacher'; and Christ is obviously in the back of his mind. Mrs Emery's note is caustic: 'They have not any desire to be bound together for many of them distrust each other'. That distrust Yeats had certainly discovered in the weeks just past.

At this point Yeats used two prominent symbols of the Order to illustrate the cosmic vision: the Adepts' link to the Supreme Life is double, ascent being symbolised by 'the climbing of the

Serpent through the Tree of Life' and descent of divine benevolence being 'symbolised by the Lightning Flash among the
sacred leaves'. Since the climbing of the Serpent was related to
the attainment of Degrees, Yeats was obviously referring
again to the laxity of Mathers and Mrs Emery in advancing
candidates without examinations, a weakness both Yeats and
Miss Horniman considered fatal to the Order.

Both the Tree of Life and the Serpent of Eternity are, of
course, well-known symbols to all students of the occult. Less
well-known perhaps is the Lightning Flash, usually pictured as
the Flaming Sword. Like the Serpent, it is always superimposed
on the Tree of Life. Yeats knew that the reference to the Lightning Flash would raise the pictorial image in the minds of his
readers, for all of them had studied the symbolic properties
and applications of the Tree in a lecture on 'The Alchemic
Sephiroth' which was a part of the preparation for advancement from $2 = 9$ to $3 = 8$. Divided into twenty-two brief
sections (reflecting the numerological value attached to the
letters of the Hebrew alphabet and the major cards in the Tarot
deck), this lecture is devoted almost entirely to the Tree and
related matters such as the planets and the Zodiac. Number
twenty-one is described as 'The Flaming Sword, the Natural
order of the Sephiroth when placed in the Tree of Life. It
resembles the course of a flash of Forked Lightning'.[11] This
heading is followed by a diagram tracing the path of the flash
from Kether at the zenith to Malkuth at the nadir. In Yeats's
library also is a copy of the ritual for advancement from $0 = 0$
to $1 = 10$ Degree of Zelator 'Corrected to the Revised Version,
Jan 1901' by F.E.R. (Miss Horniman). One full page near the
end is a carefully drawn picture of 'The Flaming Sword' with
the hilt at Kether and the point at Malkuth. On the left is the
head of a woman and on the right that of a man, both with
horns. All the ten points and the heads bear Hebrew inscrip-
tions.[12] Though the religious quest was a stern discipline, truth
came at last, Yeats insisted, like 'the Lightning Flash among the
sacred leaves'. To Mrs Emery, on the other hand, 'the result of
this is usually disastrous'.

Yeats's object was subtle. He wanted to warn his colleagues
against the danger of fragmentation: the 'new descent of the
Supreme Life' 'should be symbolised, if the Order had not

abandoned an essential part of its ritual, by the obligation[13] spoken on the day of Corpus Christi by some senior in the name of the Third Order, which thereby takes upon itself the sins of all the Fratres and Sorores, as wisdom takes upon itself the sins of the world.' As an Egyptologist, Mrs Emery was no doubt disturbed at the Christian overtones of this suggestion. When Yeats insisted that the Obligation is necessary to awaken 'the stream of the lightning' in the Order and bring 'the Adepti of the Third Order and of the Higher Degrees of the Second Order ... to our help', she declared that 'Mathers found the consequences of taking it so unpleasant he tried to foist it onto S A [Sapere Aude, Westcott] who did it for 1 year & said he never would again'. Also, she added, 'Peck has taken it with no very marvellous result in Edinburgh'.[14]

In Yeats's debate with Mrs Emery, he consistently contended that the group she advocated would become simply 'a society for experiment and research', whereas a Magical Order 'is an Actual Being, an organic life holding within itself the highest life of its members now and in past times'. There is not any doubt of Yeats's sincerity in arguing thus, though the bickerings and turmoil of the past few months must have made him wonder whether in fact the idealistic unity he envisaged was possible. But he was a debater, and he argued strongly on the basis of the microcosmic theory, which was an important part of Golden Dawn doctrine: '... to weaken its Degrees is to loosen the structure, to dislimn, to disembody, to dematerialize an Actual Being; and to sever the link between one Degree and another, above all between the Degrees that are in the heart, in the Tiphereth, in the $5=6$, is to cut this being in two, and to confine the magical life of its visible Adepti to the lower substances of this being.'

The reference to the Tiphereth was designed to set strong symbolic resonances in motion. As the central and only internal Sephira on the tree of life, it was in effect a mid-point between Malkuth and Kether, matter and spirit; and Yeats was reminding his readers of the Second Order that they were at a kind of mid-point on the 'ladder into heaven', having passed through the degrees associated with Malkuth, Yesod, Hod, and Netzach, in that order. His readers would be aware that the symbolic metal of Tiphereth is gold and its planet the sun. They would be reminded also that the 'Deity name' associated with Tiphereth is Tetragrammaton or יהוה, a signature Yeats had intentionally associated with himself by using it at the end of the open letters to the Twelve Seniors and the Adepti of R.R. et A.C. (and nowhere else in all his writing, to my knowledge). As the heart or mid-point of the Tree of Life, Tiphereth linked the invisible world to the visible. To confine the magical life of the Adepti to the visible, as the groups proposed to do in Yeats's estimate, was 'to create an evil symbol, to make the most evil of all symbols, to awaken the energy of an evil sorcery'. He was perhaps reminding his colleagues that all the planets had both 'ill dignified' and 'well dignified' qualities.[15] Whatever the allusions or overtones, Yeats's purpose was clear to his readers: the creation of groups as 'centres of astral activity' which disregard 'the Degrees of this Order ... is to create centres of life, which are centres of death, to this greater life'. Division leads to disorder and dissolution.

The substitution of groups for 'the old discipline, the old tradition' will produce not only this 'magical evil, and the complex and obscure practical evils' which are its 'shadows' but also 'certain practical evils' which are obvious to the well informed. In Part III Yeats proposes to point out these obvious evils and anomalies. The great danger will come from the assumption of authority by 'irresponsible and semi-official' members who will subject students to 'undesirable secret teaching.' To that, Mrs Emery's response is vague: 'What about the member who you wish to take Obligation'. Moreover, Yeats suggests, 'the magical teaching of this Order' may pass into a number of hands who will hide their 'ill-balanced ideas' from each other and the Order as a whole. This kind of secrecy will result in an absence of mutual criticism which, in Yeats's mind, is 'the essence of all collective life, and of nearly all sane life'. The satiric note in the margin suggests the fundamental difference between the thinking of Yeats and his opponents: 'but not of the sane life of Mysticism'. Mrs Emery obviously considers Yeats a mystic, a derogatory term to her. In hiding their doctrines as well as their membership from each other, the groups will promote 'distrust and misunderstanding' or at best 'the indifference that must arise among people who live in separate rooms with perpetually locked doors'. Mrs Emery remarks ironically that such mutual understanding 'never existed & never can exist when the Order is as large as it is at present'. Yeats was, of course, right in suggesting that the groups 'can hardly avoid passing from the quiescence of a clique to the activity of a caucus'. He must have had tongue in cheek with an observation, more history than prophecy, that 'the Council will become a place of battle between people who vote upon a prearranged plan'. He predicted, sadly, that the groups would bring the Order 'to an ignominious end'.

That judgement rests on Yeats's absolute faith in discipline manifested in the Degrees of the Order. He feared, correctly no doubt, that every one of the groups would have a 'separate numerical arrangement on which it will meditate at stated times, every member representing one of the sephiroth; and will have in its midst what professes to be an Egyptian or other spirit seeking to come into relation with our life'. Taking this as a personal reference, Mrs Emery noted that she had 'no desire to come into relation with your life'. To Yeats, it is clear, any 'numerical arrangement' not based on traditional order is certain to be destructive of unity and to grow at the expense of the one life represented by the Order. His expression of this basic faith deserves special attention : 'Incarnate life, just in so far as it is incarnate, is an open or veiled struggle of life against life, of number against number, and of all numbers against unity'.[16] In using the numerical arrangement of the Order without regard for traditional Degree, the groups were guilty of calculated deception if not evil. The branches of the Tree of Life must be ascended in proper order if human beings are to avoid 'warring upon one another and upon the great life they come from'. 'It is', Yeats insists, 'but a necessary foundation for their separated lives, for were they not established in the sephiroth they could not exist for a moment'. That is, without the sustaining strength of degree, chaos would come again. Art (or philosophy or religion) was itself a means of establishing the order which would keep man from falling into non-entity, to use a Blakean term which Yeats liked to depict the absolute formlessness of spiritual death. The members of the groups are instruments of 'the Powers of Disruption' who may have discovered, Yeats suggests, that the Order could overcome the attacks of single individuals but would have difficulty with

massed attacks of groups. Because they invoke the White Light
in their meditations, they emphasise their personal lives, which
'diverge from the general life'. The White Light, Yeats explains,
is 'an undifferentiated energy' which 'receives its differentiated
impulse from the symbol that collects it'. Mrs Emery's note is
sardonic: 'Really! I thought it was the supreme Mystery'.

Yeats too is ironic in suggesting that any change in the
system of Degrees should be complete rather than piecemeal.
Borrowing an image from Blake, he contrasts the system of
Degrees, 'like wheels turning upon a single pivot', to the
groups, 'like toothed wheels working one against the other'.[17]
This he foresees as the 'surrender of ancient unity to anarchic
diversity'. The alternative was to reshape the Order entirely,
'destroying that symbolic Organization which ... must evoke a
Being to a continuous strife with these alien bodies within its
spiritual substance'. Even if everyone at last became a member
of some group and no one stood for the Order, 'this Being'
would always be present 'in that deeper life that is beyond
even dreams and visions, seeking to answer the but half-
forgotten evocation of the Degrees and symbols, and throwing
all into disorder and disquiet'.[18]

Obviously, Yeats was satiric, though he no doubt still hoped
to win supporters for his viewpoint. Tired of compromise and
piecemeal destruction, he posed the issue as a choice of
extremes 'to remain a Magical Order ... or to become wholly a
mere society for experiment and research'. If indeed they were
forced to choose, Mrs Emery was still positive: 'Certainly', she
noted, 'do you suppose 100 people can have any magical
significance unless they are carefully organized in groups'.
Although she chose one extreme, she did not have Yeats's
strong spiritual convictions. With her, I think, the struggle was
more political than religious. With Yeats, in contrast, the whole
business was 'folly' unless 'the doctrine of talismans and symbols is true'. Compromise was unthinkable because truth was
absolute. Therefore, 'there is no position between these
extremes that is not dangerous to our spiritual and material
welfare.' Yeats, as usual, linked the two worlds: they were
necessarily complementary. It was the function of magic to
link the soul and body, or rather to enable man to comprehend
their oneness:

The central principle of all the Magic of power is that everything we formulate in the imagination, if we formulate it strongly enough, realises itself in the circumstances of life, acting either through our own souls, or through the spirits of nature.

In Part IV Yeats returned directly to the debate, attacking strongly one of the most objectionable features of the groups, their secrecy. It was 'unintelligible' to Yeats that keeping both doctrines and membership secret was 'necessary for magical progress'. 'Does the circulation of the "Microcosm Ritual" among us make its formulae powerless', he asked, 'or has our Magic been struck by palsy because the Fratres and Sorores of the Outer know our names?' The answer in the margin is 'No but only because it is so complex very few understand it'.

Yeats denied also the necessity of these 'alien personalities' (that is, groups) to Adeptship, calling the argument 'sheer dillettanteism, mere trifling!' Mrs Emery replied that she had 'never heard of this before'. To illustrate his point, Yeats asked rhetorically if Plotinus had been a member of 'a "group" organized on "the globular sephiroth" when he was thrice united with God while still in the body?' Neither the choice of Plotinus nor the faith in mystical union with God would have been convincing to the groups, whose concept of magic did not include the kind of mystical apprehension Yeats believed in. Men do not come to Adeptship 'by the multiplication of petty formulae' but rather 'by sorrow and labour, by love of all living things, and by a heart that humbles itself before the Ancestral Light, and by a mind its power and beauty and quiet flow through without end'. Mrs Emery's note suggests that such a conception of the fountain of all knowledge and goodness is beyond her comprehension: she underlined 'multiplication of petty formulae' and asked, 'Exactly what is the Order except this'.

In the heat of his one-sided debate Yeats clearly imputed motives (and even practices) to the groups which may never have occurred to them. It is not likely, for example, that they ever conceived their formula (if it had been clearly worked out) 'to be a ladder into heaven'. To Yeats, in contrast, the system of Degrees in the Order surely did represent such a ladder. Although he apparently conceived the ladder pictorially as the Cabbalistic tree, he was probably aware of Christian imagery depicting the cross as the ladder into heaven. When he tried to explain that the 'simple meditation' used by the group would result in its becoming 'segments of a circle that has no very great or rich life to give them in payment', Mrs Emery responded that 'it does nothing of the kind'. And when he imagined 'another effect' to be 'the awakening of a sympathy, which is limited to those who use this meditation at the same hour and as part of the same sphere', she called it a 'Loathsome idea'. But she may have been responding to Yeats's analogy of 'a partly similar meditation ... used by lovers or friends' to make their love more intense. He cited 'one rather terrible case' in which the resulting union had become 'so close that those who use it share not only emotions, but sicknesses and follies', and he doubted 'very much if these meditations should ever be used without certain ceremonial precautions of a rather elaborate kind'. He is, I suppose, thinking of the kind of black magic, including the emphasis on sexual abnormality, which Aleister Crowley and his followers had practised in Paris, in the Sahara Desert, and later in Sicily.[19]

Whatever Yeats implies, it is clear that he considers their magic spurious, concerned with 'experiment and research' in this world rather than union with divinity. But Yeats was no pantheist, and he never suggests that the ideal can be achieved through loss of individuality in some abstract state of oneness. In theory at least he was much closer to traditional Christianity than to theosophy. Although he does not mention Christ by name in 'Is the Order of R.R. & A.C. to remain a Magical Order?' Yeats frequently thinks along Christian lines. For example, in the insistence upon the necessity 'in an Order like ours', of 'the ceremonial sacrifice of one through whom the Third Order takes upon itself and gathers up into its strength ... the frailties of all',[20] he was surely conscious of Christ's sacrifice, though he no doubt thought of it in terms of mythopoeic truth rather than historic event. In a group, Yeats argues, 'frailty must bear the burdens of frailty ... without the joy of a conscious sacrifice, and with none to lighten the burden but some wandering spirit'. The difference between his concept of magic (or religious truth) and the group's theory and practice reveals clearly that he relates his thinking to the Christian tradition, interpreted perhaps through the doctrines of the Cabbala : 'Surely Adeptship must come more easily in an order that "reaches up to the throne of God himself, and has among its members angels and archangels," than in a "group" governed by an Egyptian spirit found, it may be, by accident in a statue'.[21] Here, as elsewhere occasionally, Yeats seems to be referring to Mrs Emery's 'semi-official statement to the Theorici' in her letter to Brodie-Innes of 17 January 1901 (see Appendix B).

In the attempt to distinguish between the eclectic Christian doctrine of the entire Order and the Egyptology of the groups, Yeats rose to eloquent heights, indicating how deeply moved he was by the issue and how firmly rooted his faith was :

> If any were to become great among us, he would do so, not by shutting himself up from us in any 'group', but by bringing himself so near to that continual sacrifice, that continual miracle, whose symbol is the obligation taken by the Senior, that he would share alike in its joy and in its sorrow. We receive power from those who are above us by permitting the Lightning of the Supreme to descend through our souls and our bodies. The power is forever seeking the world, and it comes to a soul and consumes its mortality because the soul has arisen into the path of the Lightning, among the sacred leaves. The soul that separates itself from others, that says 'I will seek power and know-ledge for my own sake, and not for the world's sake', separates itself from that path and becomes dark and empty.

It was, he thought, the duty of 'the great Adept' (which he no doubt considered himself) to seek 'ways of giving the purest substance of his soul to fill the emptiness of other souls'. Even though his own soul should be weakened and 'kept wandering on the earth', he must seek to help other souls, for 'he has been sent among them to break down the walls that divide them from one another and from the fountain of their life, and not to build new walls'. Again Yeats illustrates his faith with an image of supreme self-sacrifice, 'the Pelican feeding its young with its own blood'. Here, as in the following sentence, Christ's sacrifice is uppermost in his mind : '. . . and when, his sacrifice over, he goes his way to supreme Adeptship, he will go absolutely alone, for men attain to the supreme wisdom in a

loneliness that is like the loneliness of death'. He is also recalling, of course, a favourite image from Plotinus: 'a flight of
the alone to the alone'.[22] Yeats warned his readers, as he summarised the negative, that 'No "group", no, not even a "group"
"very carefully organized", has ever broken through that
ancient gate'.[23]

But Yeats was not content to close his argument on a negative note. In the fifth and final section of his essay he imagined
what might happen 'if we preserve the unity of the Order':

> ... the Order will become a single very powerful talisman,
> creating in us, and in the world about us, such moods and
> circumstances as may best serve the magical life, and best
> awaken the magical wisdom.

The 'personality' of the Order will be 'powerful, active, visible
afar', for it is in fact a microcosmic reflection of the 'all powerful world that casts downward for its shadows, dreams, and
visions'. Moreover, he said, 'if we make that unity efficient
among us ... the right pupils will be drawn to us from the
corners of the world by dreams and visions and by strange
accidents'. As a crusader, in particular an Irish crusader, Yeats
could not be satisfied in parochial isolation. Like his master
Blake, he was a prophet and seer with an indefatigable missionary zeal. For this reason, even if there had been no other,
he would have been opposed to the separatism represented by
the groups. He liked to remember that Irish monks had been
the teachers of medieval Europe, and he was convinced that
the Fratres and Sorores of the Golden Dawn 'will send out
Adepts and teachers, as well as hidden influences that may
shape the life of these islands nearer to the magical life'. These
words reveal not only the metaphysical foundation for his faith
but also the strength of his religious convictions. His hope for
himself and for the world rested in the unity of culture which
he thought was possible of achievement through the Order
– or at least through the ancient doctrines upon which it was
founded – and in no other way.

To Yeats, also, the organisation as well as the occult
doctrines of the Order provided a structural framework for his
social and political faith. Like Blake, in fact, he believed
'religion and politics the same thing'. A strong believer in order

and discipline, in art as well as life, he was most unhappy with 'those who would break this unity ... in the name of freedom'. He was acutely aware of the irony and hypocrisy in the argument of those to whom freedom meant unrestraint and intolerance. 'I too might talk of freedom', he said, 'for I do not recognise as its supporters those who claim the right to do and teach in secret whatever pleases them, but deny me the right to oppose them with the only means I have used or desired to use, criticism'. Equally timeless and quite devastating was his observation that 'in our day every idler, every trifler, every bungler, cries out for his freedom'. Meditating upon the course of Irish political events, especially Maud Gonne's commitment to extremism, Yeats had become increasingly certain that the only meaningful freedom men could achieve was the 'right to choose the bonds that have made them faithful servants of law'. As a great Romantic artist, Yeats believed with Coleridge and Shelley and Blake that art itself was an instrument of divinity for imposing order on the chaos of existence. Although Yeats was ostensibly writing his essay for a very small circle of the discontented, he was no doubt addressing an entire generation in his oracular illustration: 'It was the surrender of freedom that taught Dante Alighieri to say "Thy will is our peace"'. Indeed, he asked ironically, 'has not every man who ever stooped to lift a stone out of the way, or raised his hand to gather a fruit from the branch, given up his freedom to do something else?' The subtle allusion to two of the world's great myths (one Irish, one Greek) is significant: Oisin, who had lifted the stone to help the peasants, had chosen the flames of hell in 'godless and passionate age' rather than renounce his friends; Tantalus, who raised his hand to gather fruit which always receded, likewise was doomed to suffer in Hades for a deliberate choice. In their reckless audacity which Yeats so admired neither had stopped to count the cost. By linking these two with Dante in his discussion of freedom within the law, Yeats was suggesting the comprehensiveness of his own religious commitment to 'the reconciliation of Paganism and Christianity'. Assuming this posture, he could insist that 'Greek and Roman antiquity were as sacred as that of Judea, and like it "a vestibule of Christianity"'.[24]

With that Yeats's argument was complete. He concluded his

impassioned plea for magic with an optimistic prediction for the future of the world if his counsel were heeded and a veiled warning if it were not: 'We have set before us a certain work that may be of incalculable importance in the change of thought that is coming upon the world. Let us see that we do not leave it undone because the creed of the triflers is being cried into our ears.'

The essay is signed 'D.E.D.I. *In the Mountain of Abiegnos*'. By omitting his name, Yeats signified that the essay was intended only for the members of the Second Order. The reason for including 'In the Mountain of Abiegnos' is not clear, as he had not done so before and never did again, to the best of my knowledge. But we can be certain that Yeats intended to convey something of significance by its inclusion in this context. As the sacred mountain of initiation, Abiegnos is located symbolically at the centre of the universe. For the purpose of the initiatory ceremony of admission to the Second Order, it is said to conceal the body of Christian Rosenkreuz, which was to remain in the tomb until his second coming. The ceremony for advancement from the Grade of $4=7$ to $5=6$ concludes with a reference to both tomb and mountain: 'Thus have I closed the Tomb of the Adepti in the Mystic Mountain of Abiegnus'.[25] A. E. Waite's *The Real History of the Rosicrucians*, a book Yeats no doubt knew well, contains an extended discussion of the Tomb in the famous *Fama Fraternitatis*,[26] which does not mention the Mountain of Abiegnos. In the 'Appendix of Additional Documents', however, Waite included a two-page description of the holy 'mountain situated in the midst of the *earth* or *centre* of the *world*, which is both *small* and *great*'. Invisible, encompassed by cruel beasts and ravenous birds, and containing 'ample treasures', it can be reached 'only by the worthy man's self-labour and investigation'.

A more obvious source of information about the holy mountain was Flying Roll No. XV ('Man and God') by Westcott. Designed for the instruction of 'Members of the Adeptus Grade of the Order R.R. et A.C.', this Roll was well-known to all Yeats's audience. A part of one paragraph will illustrate the eclecticism of the doctrines of the Second Order and suggest the seriousness of the message he was conveying from 'the Mountain of Abiegnos':

Now Moses had gone up into the holy mountain to seek divine help: this Sinai was the Mountain of God – the Mountain of the Caverns, the Mountain of Abiegnus, the mystic Mountain of Initiation – that is of divine instruction. Even so do we seek inspiration in the mystic Mountain, passing through the wilderness of Horeb, that period life which is *at first* a desert to us, as we cast aside worldly joys, and seek to pass through the Caverns – our Vault, to union with the spiritual powers above us, which send a ray of light to illumine our minds and to fire our hearts, the spiritual centre, with an enthusiasm for the higher life of greater self sacrifice, more self-control – by which means alone can man reach up to the Divine and become one with the All self – the great One-All.[27]

If Yeats meant to imply that he, like Moses, had 'gone up into the holy mountain' seeking divine guidance, he was surely suggesting also that he was the prophet who could lead the erring fratres and sorores 'through the wilderness of Horeb'. Since the Vault itself was the symbolic centre of the mountain, Yeats may have been implying that his essay was in fact written, or at least completed and signed, 'in the Mountain of Abiegnos' – that is, in the Vault. At any rate, it was a part of his ironic purpose to remind his rebel colleagues of these symbolic narratives. He may also have been urging himself to be armed 'with a resolute, heroic courage, lest you fear those things that will happen, and fall back'.[28] He obviously intended to remind his readers of Christian parallels – to the tomb, to the Garden of Gethsemane, and perhaps even between Christ and himself or everyman.

Some weeks later the myth of the holy mountain of Abiegnos was still in his mind as he planned *Where There Is Nothing*,[29] which became in revision *The Unicorn from the Stars*. The heroes of both versions are clearly autobiographical, and the substance of both is deeply indebted to Rosicrucianism. When Martin Hearne, the Christ figure of *The Unicorn*, dies he ascends the holy mountain in a vision:

Martin [*looking at his hand, on which there is blood*]. Ah, that is blood! I fell among the rocks. It is a hard climb. It is a long climb to the vineyards of Eden. Help me up.

I must go on. The Mountain of Abiegnos is very high – but the vineyards – the vineyards![30]

In March 1908, recalling the creation of Paul Ruttledge (predecessor to Martin Hearne), Yeats wrote of him in terms that suggest how much of himself he had put into Paul: 'Whether he understand or know, it may be that the voices of Angels and Archangels have spoken in the cloud and whatever wildness come upon his life, feet of theirs may well have trod the clusters'.[31] In composing 'Is the Order of R.R. & A.C. to remain a Magical Order?', perhaps the most careful analysis he was ever to make of his fundamental religious convictions, Yeats surely believed that 'the voices of Angels and Archangels have spoken in the cloud'. He was quite as sure as Blake (to whom he referred in the same note) that 'the Authors are in Eternity'.[32]

Written in March 1901 and published as soon as possible, Yeats's essay carried a warning on the cover that 'This essay must not be given to any but Adepti of the Order of R.R. & A.C.'[33] It was issued in April, and Mrs Emery apparently took exception almost at once in a letter I have not been able to locate. Yeats responded with 'A Postscript to Essay called "Is the Order of R.R. & A.C. to remain a Magical Order?"' Issued in the same brown paper covers as the essay, the 'Postscript' carries the same warning and notes that it was 'Written on May 4th, 1901'.[34]

Yeats begins by observing that 'Soror S.S.D.D., the founder of the "groups," has written asking me to tell all to whom I have given my essay, that "she strongly disapproves of the kind of magic alluded to on page 24" of my essay, "and has never suggested and still less encouraged any practice of the kind"'. She was referring to a kind of 'meditation' for 'welding those who use it' which Yeats had compared to 'an egotism of two' 'sometimes used by lovers or friends to make their union the closer'. As she noted in her copy of the essay, this was a 'Loathsome idea'. Yeats understood her 'to mean that she never intended to create any kind of astral union among the members of the "groups"'. Although he denied saying that she did, he knew her 'over-watchful individualism' so well that he was certain 'it did not blind her to the obvious effect of a formula, which must seek continually to perfect a spiritual and astral union that I am not alone in believing already to exist'. Yeats here developed a strong argument which I quote at length because it explains a fundamental premise of his theory of symbolism frequently overlooked or not understood by critics and interpreters:

> It is a first principle of our illumination that symbols and formulae are powers, which act in their own right and with little consideration for our intentions, however excellent. Most of us have seen some ceremony produce an altogether unintended result because of the accidental use of some wrong formula or symbol. I can see nothing to limit the intensity of the union evoked by the meditation of the Globular Sepheroth, except the degree of power of those that use it and the lack or plentifulness of other occupation. Such a formula is seldom able to produce the full effect I have spoken of, but I know from the experience[s] of a number of people – experiences which I have carefully recorded – that it soon produces a nearly perfect communion of mood and a somewhat less, though very marked, communion of thought and purpose. This communion, which pre-supposes the creation of a powerful collective personality, is not an evil in itself, for individuality is not as important as our age has imagined. It becomes an evil when it conflicts with some larger communion, some more powerful or more wise personality, or when its relation to the supernatural life is imperfect, or when its constituents have been unwisely chosen.

At this point art and religion are one.

Several assumptions are worthy of special attention: first, that symbols are powers which act in their own right – that is, they are not simply mental constructs for the convenience of the creative imagination but part of the *anima mundi*; second, that the intensity of the union evoked by the meditation is related to the power of those who use it – that is, the power cannot be invoked at will by any ordinary person but must be developed through discipline; third, that Yeats had been carefully studying and recording experiences, his own no doubt as well as others; fourth, that individuality is not as important as his age has imagined it – that is, individuality is an evil when it conflicts with the collective personality or relates imperfectly to the supernatural life or consists of unwisely chosen constituents. The denial of the importance of individuality is sure to seem strange to most readers of Yeats. He is, of course, thinking of man's place in the universe, of his relationship to the world soul, of his function in the larger *communion* rather than *community*. He is making the point – over subtly, I suspect – that the formation of groups represents an emphasis on individuality which destroys the larger communion in part because 'its constituents have been unwisely chosen'.

One other important issue of the essay had been misunderstood by Mrs Emery – 'the oath that should be spoken by a senior upon Corpus Christi Day'. Yeats wants to correct the impression that the senior who repeats the Obligation actually 'takes upon himself the sins of the Order' in the way that 'the legendary Sin Eater takes a dead man's sins upon himself'. Although Yeats had been careful to talk about a 'ceremonial sacrifice', he had not made his meaning clear. Now there must be no doubt: 'The senior who speaks the oath is the Chief Adept, whose office is now so purely ceremonial, that it can be taken, if necessary, by any senior who happens to be present'. As 'the symbolical representative of the Third Order', the Chief Adept lays the sins of the Second Order, including his own, 'in the hands of the Third Order'. In so doing, he 'lightens his own burden and the burden of others'.

With that the great debate was ended. All the logic and most of the work had been Yeats's, but he had been outvoted, though a complete break-up of the Second Order was avoided and valuable time gained through a motion by Brodie-Innes to resolve the issue through another revision of the Constitution and Bye-Laws. As the mover of the motion, Brodie-Innes was made the chairman of the committee, and he wrote a pamphlet 'Concerning the Revisal of the Constitution and Rules of the Order R.R. & A.C.'.[35] Reminding his colleagues briefly of what had happened to their organisation over the past few months, he asked them in effect to help decide what form of government they desired. Once the question of the new constitution was settled, he said, they must then turn their attention to new rules and bye-laws. In conclusion, he recognised the division in the Order and maintained that any institution with health and vitality has two similar parties – 'the one desiring to preserve all our old customs and rules, even where notoriously faulty, the other desiring to make a clean sweep of all that we have, and make an entirely fresh start'. Although he refused to say which he thought better, suggesting that neither was 'absolutely right', he was clearly on the side of change. He asked for 'a free and unfettered expression of opinion', but pointed out that as 'an occult and magical Order' they should put their faith in 'the guidance and supervision of higher powers' (presumably the Third Order) who 'will take care that all that is worth preserving in the Order as we know it will be preserved'. Thinking apparently of the discord in the ranks, Brodie-Innes implies that 'our particular Branch' of the Order may not be worth preserving, not unless they are willing to work together in defeat as well as victory for the common good. 'If we do this faithfully', he concluded, 'I believe the Order will flourish and go on from strength to strength and from knowledge to knowledge and that the Masters of Wisdom will guide our counsels. But if we fail herein, and supinely allow the affairs of the Order to drift, and say to ourselves that "others will manage them", I believe that our Branch will perish as no longer worth preserving.' It is clear that the 'Former Imperator of Amen Ra', as he identified himself, is sceptical about their future and doubtful of the willingness of some members to accept the decision of the group.

Although he might have been thinking of Yeats and Miss Horniman, it is more likely that he was referring to the eight members who had threatened on 25 February to withdraw if 'such stultifying regulations are approved'.[36] In fact, the last two paragraphs of Brodie-Innes's proposal sound very much like the first paragraph of the fifth part of 'Is the Order of R.R. & A.C. to remain a Magical Order?' Yeats may well have written the entire pamphlet 'Concerning the Revisal of the Constitution....' Since he and Miss Horniman had joined forces with Brodie-Innes in the letter of 27 February (Appendix J), it is unlikely that Yeats would have been content not to share in the composition of the proposal for reorganisation. Moreover, since Yeats had been the leader of the opposition throughout the altercation, I rather imagine that the motion to revise was his idea rather than Brodie-Innes's.

SEVEN

Unity of Will?

*Unity of will is the occult condition precedent to a realiza-
tion of our aspirations, unswerving fidelity on your part
both to the ideals of the Higher Life & to the Chiefs of the
Order will constitute the most practical evidence you can
give of your desire to assist your brethren. To know, to
do and to be silent is the triad of Occult Obligation.*
'Manifesto from the Three Chiefs', 26 June 1902

Whether or not Yeats wrote the pamphlet on revision, he certainly shared the fear that 'our Branch will perish' if its affairs
continued to drift, and he was right, as subsequent events were
to prove. Sick of the discord and political manoeuvring no
doubt, Yeats must have left town before the furore died down.
'Is the Order of R.R. & A.C. to remain a Magical Order?' was
distributed sometime in April, possibly after he had already
gone. On 25 April he wrote to Lady Gregory from Stratford
as though he had been there for several days, 'working very
hard, reading all the chief criticisms of the plays and I think
my essay will be one of the best things I have done'. He had
apparently already attended several plays, had seen 'a good
deal of the Company', and was working steadily (from ten to
six) 'in the library of the Shakespeare institute'.[1] Stern of
discipline though he was, Yeats surely must have been, in the
words of a sonnet he quoted in the essay he was engaged upon,

> Tired with all these, from these would I be gone,
> Save that, to die, I leave my love alone.[2]

After the 'noisy time' of the past few weeks in London, Yeats
looked upon Stratford as a 'retreat' 'shut away from the world'
where 'one does not hear or see an incongruous or noisy
thing'.[3] He finished the essay 'At Stratford-on-Avon' (published

in *The Speaker* on 11 and 18 May)[4] in a burst of energy – or relief. But the interlude was brief. Mrs Emery's letter of irritation over the essay to the Adepti either followed him to Stratford or was waiting on his return to London, for his answering 'Postscript' was written on 4 May.[5] Again he fled from the strife and bickering, this time to Sligo, where he arrived no later than 20 May, having stopped in Dublin on the way. 'In rather a depressed state of mind', Yeats had as usual sought for peace with George Pollexfen in Sligo : 'I am in an ebb tide', he wrote from Thornhill, 'and must wait the flow'.[6] As a 'country' member of the Golden Dawn, Uncle George no doubt appreciated the news from London, though he must have been concerned over the break-up of the Second Order.

Yeats was in Ireland all summer, going from Sligo to Coole Park, where he remained for most of the time until the performances of the Irish Literary Theatre which began on 21 October.[7] Sometime in early November he wrote that he had been 'shifting from Dublin to London and very busy about various things'.[8] In January 1902 he confided to Lady Gregory that he had 'emerged into fairly good spirits' 'after a rather gloomy time'.[9]

Among the 'various things' he was busy with during this 'gloomy time' were surely the affairs of the Second Order. During his absence from London the committee headed by Brodie-Innes had been preparing a revised Constitution and Bye-Laws, which was printed and distributed in June 1902, having been approved some time earlier.[10] Under the revised Constitution three new Chiefs of the Second Order were appointed : Dr Robert W. Felkin, 'Finem Respice' (the Imperator, who rules); P. W. Bullock, 'Levavi Oculos' (the Praemonstrator, who instructs); J. W. Brodie-Innes, 'Sub Spe' (the Cancellarius, who records). Their appointment in itself appears to be an attempt at compromise : Bullock had leaned towards the groups, Brodie-Innes towards Yeats and Miss Horniman, and Felkin towards neither apparently. At any rate, the record does not suggest that he had taken part in the quarrel. Although he remained prominent in the Order from this time until the break-up in 1922, he had played no significant role until this reorganisation. According to Ellic Howe, Felkin was the one member of the Second Order who remained 'on the fence' when the petition to reinstate Miss Horniman was being circulated.[11]

Although Yeats's name does not appear in the materials I have seen concerned with the adoption of the new Bye-Laws and the appointment of the new Chiefs, he was still active and was probably influential behind the scenes in subsequent events. By November 1901, if not before, the rift with Mrs Emery was smoothed over. Upon returning to London, he renewed discussions with her and Arnold Dolmetsch about speaking poetry to the accompaniment of the psaltery. When he discovered that 'she had arranged to give Dolmetsch £4 for psaltery' on which he had spent £10, Yeats decided to 'do an article ... and then give the lecture' to get her 'out of the difficulty'. She, not surprisingly, had 'paid part of the money by performances of a very amateurish Egyptian play'.[12] In a letter to Lady Gregory on 13 January 1902, Yeats spoke of his ' "chanting" essay' as 'a necessity that I may launch Mrs. Emery'.[13]

The final brief paragraph of this letter to Lady Gregory suggests that Yeats was deeply involved in the changes in the Second Order and that he probably had an important part in the revision of the Bye-Laws:

> I have done a great deal of work at my Magical Rites, sketched them all out in their entirety. I have gone through some black spots too but have emerged at last into a cheerful mood, which really seems as if it were going to last for a while.[14]

The reference to a melancholy period, linked here to his work on Magical Rites, suggests that the troubles in the Second Order are directly responsible for the 'gloomy time' he has passed through.

It may be also that the revision of the Bye-Laws was completed by this time. Moreover, the language of the revision as well as the subsequent action of the group demonstrates that Yeats had snatched a limited victory from the jaws of defeat. Hence the 'cheerful mood' of 13 January. A brief look at the revised Bye-Laws will illustrate.

The new administrative structure is similar to that provided for in the Bye-Laws of May 1900. The Executive Council (consisting of Moderator, Warden, Scribe and seven Adepti Litterati) is to be replaced by Three Chiefs chosen by the Second Order and Subordinate Chiefs appointed by the Three. The Three Chiefs are to hear and decide all matters referred to them, but their decisions may be appealed. Most importantly, 'the Three Chiefs and Subordinate Chiefs must see that the Bye-Laws are strictly enforced'. That surely was a victory for the strict constructionists (especially Yeats and Miss Horniman), and must have been resented by Mrs Emery and her followers. It was also a blow to the groups to have strong emphasis placed upon 'passing an examination in the requisite knowledge' for advancement in grade. Mrs Emery and Mathers had been lax. The new Bye-Laws are strict about time between examinations, how they are supervised, and how authenticated, none of which are mentioned in the Bye-Laws of 1900.

Finally, under 'Conduct', an entirely new section of the Bye-Laws, members are enjoined to 'preserve inviolable secrecy concerning the Order, its name, the names of its members, and the proceedings which take place at its assemblies'. Moreover, 'members are forbidden to permit themselves to be mes- merized, hypnotized, or to lose the control of their thoughts, words or actions'. Much of this section appears to be aimed at the laxity of the groups.

But the new Chiefs were conscious that the mighty opposite, Miss Horniman, would still pose a problem. Almost their first order of business, therefore, was a kind of open letter to her which is both a plea and a threat.[15] Writing on 21 May 1902, 'as the *recently appointed* chiefs of the Second Order',[16] (my italics) they addressed Fortitre et Recte 'personally and for- mally' and reminded her that 'our commission comprises a return to the original constitution as far as practicable'. They affirmed, moreover, that they had assumed 'the active govern- ment of the Order and incidentally of every matter pertaining thereto including all questions of symbols used and of the form which teaching should take'. The emphasis on the 'original constitution' and a strong central authority appears to be directed at the groups as well as (or rather than) Miss Horni- man; and the sentiments expressed if not the language sound very much like Yeats. Whether or not he shared in the compo- sition, he certainly was sympathetic, as he was with the insis- tence upon unity and co-operation : 'Having this responsibility, it is essential that we assert and uphold our absolute authority and require the loyal cooperation of all members of the Order in securing and preserving the fraternal and benevolent relationship required by our obligation'. Thinking of 'the recent "group" disturbances and other differences which have caused disharmony', the Chiefs request all members 'not to enter into any controversy' but to bring all complaints directly to them. Although they profess to believe that Miss Horniman's object is 'identical' with their 'commission to restore the original constitution and strict adherence to the Obligation', they are obviously uncertain of her loyalty and restraint. In return for her co-operation they promise to deal expeditiously with any 'serious breach of the obligation or improper conduct by any member of the Order'. They close with a request for an acknowledgement of the letter and a promise of compliance 'because it is necessary for us to satisfy ourselves, prior to the ceremony of C.C. [Corpus Christi] that true harmony prevails'. It is signed in ink with three sets of initials: L.O., F.R., S.S., in that order. Miss Horniman must have thought that the shade of Mathers was stalking the Order rooms.

It was clear, of course, that 'true harmony' did not prevail. Sometime during the spring of 1902, the Chiefs informed the Members of the Outer Order of a change in name and enclosed a full list of members, the new Bye-Laws, and labels containing the new name of the Order for use in instructional manuals.[17] One category of members indentifying those who 'have died or resigned during the past 18 months' includes five of the eight who had signed the accusatory statement against Yeats and Miss Horniman on 25 February 1901: Mrs Emery, Mr and Mrs E. A. Hunter, Henrietta Paget and Robert Palmer Thomas.[18] They had, as they threatened, withdrawn, 'taking no further active part in an order in which such stultifying regulations are approved'. The other three signatories (Mrs Helen Rand, Mrs Reena Fullham-Hughes, and M. W. Blackden) remained in the Order.

In explaining the reason for the name change to members of the Outer Order, the Chiefs hint at troubles in the Golden Dawn which may have had something to do with the 'gloomy time' Yeats mentioned on 13 January:

We have, with some reluctance, decided to change the Name of the Outer, and in future it will be known as – The Hermetic Society of The M.R. These letters convey the same meaning as the letters G.D., indicating as they do the German word Morgenröthe. We have taken this step owing to matters which happened at the end of last year and which rendered the retention of the letters G.D. inadvisable.

The remainder of the 'Manifesto' reminded the members of their 'pledge of secresy', commented that 'a certain slackness has obtained recently', urged them to attend the ceremonies and work for advancement, asked for regular payment of dues, and warned them 'to maintain a benevolent and fraternal attitude towards each other'. The last was especially important in what must have been a trying time: 'the Chiefs will not tolerate disregard of this most essential condition'.

Six days later, on 26 June, the Chiefs issued another 'Manifesto',[19] repeating in even sterner language many of the injunctions in the first 'Manifesto' but without reference to advancement and therefore probably intended only for the Second Order. Desiring, in their words, 'to consolidate & establish the fraternal link binding every member to each other & the Order', they ask for 'earnest cooperation in the resolution to permit no discord to mar our harmony'. Pleading and threatening in the same breath, the Chiefs declare that they will not 'tolerate disregard' for the 'essential conditions' of benevolence towards each other and 'strict silence towards all the outer world'. In the emphasis upon the need for secrecy the Rosicrucians were diametrically opposed to the Theosophists, who welcomed all interested parties and made allowance for considerable diversity of thought and practice. The Rosicrucians, in contrast, insist that 'unity of will is the occult condition precedent to a realisation of our aspirations'. 'To know, to do and to be silent', the Chiefs insist, 'is the triad of Occult Obligation.' This stern warning is surely not greatly different from the 'direct commands' of Mathers, and Yeats must have been aware of the ironic implications in the new authoritarianism.

Like the other, this 'Manifesto' includes a list of members with an admonition 'to avoid any mistake in speaking to anyone who has resigned'. It also announces the name change and urges the 'vital importance' of keeping it 'absolutely secret from everyone not on the enclosed list'. Under no circumstances 'must persons who have resigned be told of it'. Since Mrs Emery and four of her strongest supporters had resigned by this time, this reference may be to them. If so, they could be at least partially responsible for the name change explained in the note: '... there are some persons in London who have *no* connection with us whatever who have taken the name G.D. & you must be careful not to identify yourself with them'. Also, if indeed the reference is to the defecting group, it is easier to understand why Mrs Emery had no qualms over selling to John Quinn her copy of 'Is the Order of R.R. & A.C. to remain a Magical Order?' By the same token, however, it is somewhat surprising to find that Yeats and Mrs Emery managed to maintain a good if not close relationship throughout these troubles and in fact to the end of her life.[20]

It is more likely that the warning about the persons with 'no connection ... whatever' was a reference to a pair of imposters, Theo and Mme Horos, whose notorious escapades had been linked with the Golden Dawn and had, as I shall suggest in a subsequent chapter, caused Yeats and his friends considerable embarrassment during the summer and autumn of 1901.

Yeats himself was not in London for all the fire-works. In March he was again in Stratford for the Shakespeare Cycle; in early April he was in Dublin for the production of his own *Kathleen ni Houlihan* and AE's *Deidre*; by 10 April he was back in London hard at work on *The Speckled Bird*; on 13 June he informed Lady Gregory that he was leaving for Ireland on the nineteenth. On 27 June he mailed several of the essays for *Ideas of Good and Evil* to Bullen from Coole Park.[21] Since both *The Speckled Bird* and *Ideas of Good and Evil* reflect directly Yeats's thinking and activities of this period of unrest in the Golden Dawn, especially the months from January 1900 until June 1902, some consideration of them and related compositions is important to an understanding of this 'worst part of life'.

EIGHT

The Antagonism between the Poet and Magician

The difference of opinion about proper kind of symbolism between Michael and Maclagen must be accentuated. Maclagen had better be quite definitely a disciple of the Rosy Cross as that is embodied in the Fama. Michael should as definitely insist on the introduction of such a symbolism as will continue and make more precise the implicit symbolism in modern art and poetry. The antagonism must be made the antagonism between the poet and magician.[1]

Poetry is magic, Yeats would have said, but the poet is not a magician in the tradition of Mathers and Crowley. Conscious that many members of the Second Order had not thought carefully about the distinction or did not agree with him, Yeats concluded that some explanation was desirable. Having explored the nature and function of magic for his colleagues in the Second Order, he continued writing and thinking about the subject in works intended for the public at large. Especially important in the context of Yeats's debate with his colleagues is his essay entitled 'Magic'. It received wide distribution in *Ideas of Good and Evil* (1903), but had appeared earlier in *The Monthly Review* for September 1901. If we allow some interval between composition and publication, we may conjecture that it was written about the same time as 'Is the Order of R.R. & A.C. to remain a Magical Order?' At any rate, they are companion pieces, one written for the Second Order alone, the other for the public. Somewhat frustrated, I suspect, that only a limited number (and those as members of the Order already partially convinced) would see his impassioned argument for union of spirit and faith in the invisible world, Yeats probably composed 'Magic' soon after its companion; and it is important for my purpose to see what it adds and how it differs.

'Magic' is clearly intended as a kind of credo of the Romantic artist. Although Yeats's thoughtful development of a theory of magic would not have shocked well-informed readers of 1901, his opening sentence may have startled a few, as he surely hoped it would: 'I believe in the practice and philosophy of what we have agreed to call magic, in what I must call the evocation of spirits, though I do not know what they are, in the power of creating magical illusions, in the visions of truth in the depths of the mind when the eyes are closed.'[2] Like any good debater, Yeats begins with 'we have agreed', though in fact he was very much aware of the general disagreement, even in the Second Order, over one of the most controversial subjects of the day among the intelligentsia to whom it was directed. Among the occultists of London, many professed greater certainty about the nature of the spirits, but very few of them were pursuing 'visions of truth' as he conceived it. He continues with the well-known summary of the three doctrines which have 'been the foundations of nearly all magical practices':

(1) That the borders of our mind are ever shifting, and that many minds can flow into one another, as it were, and create or reveal a single mind, a single energy.

(2) That the borders of our memories are as shifting, and that our memories are a part of one great memory, the memory of Nature herself.

(3) That this great mind and great memory can be evoked by symbols.

Yeats's function as artist is to arrest 'the slow perishing ... of a quality of mind that made this belief and its evidences common over the world'.[3]

The remainder of the essay is concerned chiefly with examples (that is, 'evidences') from Yeats's experience, and is, therefore, an extension of or complement to its companion essay.[4] Since 'Magic' is readily available, I will call attention only to what is pertinent to Yeats's debate with his colleagues. The first of the evidences recounts a kind of Frankensteinian seance which is chiefly interesting because it was conducted by MacGregor and Moina Mathers, who were living at Forest Hill near London at the time of the experience. Mathers was curator of the Horniman Museum, a position he had no doubt received through the good offices of Miss Horniman, who had also been a schoolgirl friend of Moina Bergson.[5] If Yeats is correct in dating the experience 'some ten or twelve years ago', it most likely occurred soon after the marriage of Moina and MacGregor (performed by the Rev. W. A. Ayton) in June 1890, and the initiation of Yeats in March. If so, eleven years is the outside limit.

When the first experiment of that memorable afternoon was completed, Yeats 'asked to have some past life of mine revealed, and a new evocation was made before the tablet full of little squares'.[6] Yeats thought this vision 'strange and beautiful', though he 'alone seemed to see its beauty'; but he was, as always, sceptical and felt it incumbent to explain : 'In coming years I was to see and hear of many such visions, and though I was not to be convinced, though half convinced once or twice, that they were old lives, in an ordinary sense of the word life, I was to learn that they have almost always some quite definite relation to dominant moods and moulding events in this life'. 'They are, perhaps', he decided, 'symbolical histories of these moods and events, or rather symbolical shadows of the impulses that have made them, messages as it were out of the ancestral being of the questioner'. At the time, Yeats recalled, the visions were little more 'than a proof of the supremacy of imagination, of the power of many minds to become one, overpowering one another by spoken words and by unspoken thought till they have become a single, intense, unhesitating energy'. He recognised one mind as the master but concluded that all minds gave a little, 'creating or revealing' what he called 'a supernatural artist'. In the words of Blake, whom he cited, 'the author was in eternity'.[7] These are acute observations about the working of the creative imagination, but would not have been, I suspect, very convincing to fellow members of the Second Order.

From an account of this unusual day, Yeats passes on to experiences of 'some years afterwards' when he was visiting friends in Paris. Again he is surely referring to Moina and Mac-

Gregor Mathers, with whom he stayed frequently after they moved to Paris in 1892. After narrating brief accounts of two instances of thought transference, Yeats insists that he could 'tell of stranger images, of stranger enchantments, of stranger imaginations ... were it not that the greater energies of the mind seldom break forth but when the deeps are loosened'. Because 'they break forth amid events too private or too sacred for public speech, or ... belong to hidden things', they must not be revealed: 'I have written of these breakings forth, these loosenings of the deep, with some care and some detail, but I shall keep my record shut'. 'After all', he continued, 'one can but bear witness less to convince him who won't believe than to protect him who does, as Blake puts it, enduring unbelief and misbelief and ridicule as best one may'. To avoid these, Yeats must 'be content to show that past times have believed' as he does, and he turns to the account of the scholar-gypsy by Joseph Glanvil, who is dead and will not mind.[8]

Although I have no way of knowing what specific records Yeats has in mind, I think he is probably referring to such experiences as seances, the Celtic visionary explorations of 1897-8, and the 'spiritual marriage' with Maud Gonne in 1898 or 1899 – all of which he recorded, dated carefully, and preserved in his papers. 'If all who have described events like this have not dreamed', Yeats said of Glanvil's story, 'we should rewrite our histories'.[9] In our time 'history speaks of opinions and discoveries', but in ancient times it 'spoke of commandments and revelations'. Or, as he was to suggest in *Where There Is Nothing*, which he may have composed soon after 'Magic', 'not reformation but revelation' is the function of artists, priests, and all thinking men. Education and urban life have deadened the sensitivities of modern man. In more primitive times men 'looked as carefully and as patiently towards Sinai and its thunders as we look towards parliaments and laboratories'.[10] The primary object of this portion of the argument is to prove that the spiritual life of primitive peoples – and Yeats is thinking of Irish peasants in particular – is far richer than that of 'the separated, self-moving mind'. The 'evidences' to illustrate the conviction that primitive people 'were always praising the one mind' Yeats discovers among the people of west Ireland. In one district of Galway he could find 'but one man who had not seen what I can but call spirits, and he was in his dotage'. 'There is no man mowing a meadow', he was told, 'but sees them at one time or another'.[11] The remarkable thing, Yeats discovered, was that many of the peasants under-went profound trances in which the visions they related con-tained traditional archetypal symbols he had found recorded in such repositories as Mathers's *The Book of Concealed Mystery*. He cited two, one of Eden on a high mountain and the other of The Tree of Knowledge of Good and Evil.[12] Both symbols are important in the rituals of the Golden Dawn. In his diary for 27 December 1897 Yeats had recorded a seer's vision of 'Brigid, the goddess, holding out "a glittering and wriggling serpent"', which is also an important symbol of the Golden Dawn. All these he cites as 'proof that there is a memory of Nature that reveals events and symbols of distant centuries',[13] and he quotes Paracelsus and Blake as support.

After citing additional evidences recorded in his 'diary of magical events', Yeats comments upon the magical power of symbols in terms which perhaps had little meaning for Mathers and his followers in the Order: 'I cannot now think symbols less than the greatest of all powers whether they are used con-sciously by the masters of magic, or half unconsciously by their successors, the poet, the musician and the artist'.[14] The emphasis, at any rate, is surely different, and Yeats was acutely aware that he was, like the hero of his novel in progress, a speckled bird. He closed the essay in a memorable section which is more a metaphysical explanation of his theory of symbolism than a justification of magic as it is commonly con-ceived: 'I have now described that belief in magic which has set me all but unwilling among those lean and fierce minds who are at war with their time, who cannot accept the days as they pass, simply and gladly'. Fearing that he may have revealed 'more of the ancient secret than many among my fellow students think it right to tell', Yeats says that he has torn up more than one paragraph about 'some incident or some sym-bol' which belonged to 'hidden things'. 'Yet I must write', he explains, 'or be of no account to any cause, good or evil'.[15]

At this point precisely, I think, Yeats found himself strongly at odds with his fellow Rosicrucians. As the only important artist in the Isis-Urania Temple – or any of the sister temples so far as I am aware – Yeats felt the urge of the poet-prophet, not to reveal hidden secrets but to commit 'what merchandise of wisdom' he has to 'written speech' whether in this essay or in rhyme. Yeats did not enjoy secrecy for the sake of secrecy. Rather he sought and found in Rosicrucianism a system of thought which explained his profoundest convictions concerning the relationship of man to the universe, his place in the total scheme of things. Like the more traditional magicians in the Order such as Crowley and Mathers, however, Yeats was convinced of the awful force of the human mind, not to raise powerful spirits, as many of his fellows believed, but to remake the world nearer to the heart's desire:

> And surely, at whatever risk, we must cry out that imagination is always seeking to remake the world according to the impulses and the patterns in that Great Mind, and that great Memory? Can there be anything so important as to cry out that what we call romance, poetry, intellectual beauty, is the only signal that the supreme Enchanter, or some one in His councils, is speaking of what has been, and shall be again, in the consummation of time?[16]

By means of magic, as Yeats conceived it, man can understand, not control nature. Once he understands nature as a sentient unity, a Great Mind or Memory, he may discover the secrets of the universe, of the past as well as the present, of the invisible as well as the visible. These truths are revealed or transmitted in abstract or metaphysical language; and it is the function of the chosen spirit, the seer, to project his visions in the concrete imagery and symbolism of art. For this aesthetic doctrine Yeats's most consistent model was Blake: it is no accident that he is cited several times in 'Magic'. Yeats does not denigrate Mathers and those of his persuasion, but he is certain that the artist has a higher function than the 'magician'.[17] The artist, in effect, goes one step further. The differences in understanding and function are made clear in the final version of *The Speckled Bird*, an autobiographical novel which Yeats struggled with for several years.

Since he began composing it as early as 1896 and was still engrossed in it as late as April 1902, *The Speckled Bird* is obviously important to an understanding of Yeats's thoughts and possibly his plans during the period I have been exploring. *The Speckled Bird*, as it is preserved, consists of several hundred manuscript pages in Yeats's hand and 179 typed pages (plus three pages of an Abstract of Book IV), much of which apparently was dictated in the spring of 1902. Since only two brief articles,[18] including passages from the typed version, had been published until the recent Cuala Press edition of the typescript, little has been known about the novel. Unfortunately, considerable mystery will remain until the publication of the manuscript, which differs significantly from the typescript. The setting, the names of the characters, and the plot (outlined in fourteen chapters) of the first version in manuscript were changed in the typed version, and the change is important. The first version was to be a fairly conventional story of Michael De Burgh's love for his cousin Margaret De Burgh with some minor and rather vague references to occult materials and two people who may be Moina and MacGregor Mathers. The characters of the typescript are more clearly recognisable. In the early pages the heroine, named Olive Henderson, may be a portrait of Olivia Shakespear, but she soon becomes and remains Margaret, who is clearly patterned on Maud Gonne. Through Book III apparently Yeats still intended to place the emphasis on the love story,[19] but in Book IV he made a shift which would surely have been disastrous to the novel and may account in part for his decision to abandon it. According to the 'Abstract of Book IV', the remainder of the novel was to be devoted to an extended meeting with Maclagen (Mathers) and his circle in Paris, after which Michael was to journey 'to the East where he hopes to learn about astral union'.[20]

Bradford is, of course, wrong in the conjecture that Yeats 'abandoned his manuscript' late in 1901 when Bullen offered to accept a book of essays (*Ideas of Good and Evil*) in lieu of *The Speckled Bird*, for which £50 had been advanced.[21] A letter to Lady Gregory on 10 April 1902 makes clear that Yeats had returned to the novel, probably with some inspiration for its completion: 'I am working at my novel – dictating to a typewriter. I dictated 2000 words in an hour and ten minutes yesterday – and go on again tomorrow. This dictation is really a discovery'.[22] But Bradford is correct, I believe, in his assumption that the first seventy pages of the typescript were made by a typist who had difficulty reading Yeats's hand. At that point apparently he began dictating, probably not from his own manuscript, as Bradford conjectures,[23] but in further composition. For the manuscript version which is transcribed in the typescript breaks off at this point (unnumbered page following manuscript page 118, page 71 of typescript). Since the break does not come at a logical or expected point such as the end of a chapter or book, I assume that he had not put the novel aside for a time at this point but rather merely shifted from one method of recording to another. If so, however, he must have dictated some 110 pages (including the 'Abstract of Book IV') after his 'discovery' described on 10 April. If he did, he obviously had not abandoned the novel he had promised Bullen. By 27 June, however, Yeats sent 'a lot more of the book of essays' to Bullen and spoke as though he were engaged in writing two other essays 'not yet finished'.[24]

My own guess is that the switch with Bullen was not prompted by an unwillingness or inability to finish the novel (Yeats has a remarkable record of finishing his projects) but rather by a change in the theme of the novel. At some time during this unhappy period Yeats decided that the novel should focus, in conclusion at least, on the affairs of the Golden Dawn, in particular his relationship to Moina and MacGregor Mathers. If he conveyed this decision to Bullen, as he surely would have, Bullen just as surely would have been unhappy with it. Some months before, at a chance meeting in Dublin, Bullen told Yeats that 'he was amazed to find the hostility to me of the booksellers. —————, he declared, seemed to hardly like to speak my name'. Most disturbing to Yeats was the reason for the hostility of the Dublin booksellers: 'I am looked upon as heterodox is seems. *The Secret Rose* was strange to say particularly disapproved of, but they spoke with hostility of even *The Shadowy Waters*. Russell told me before I saw Bullen that clerical influence was he believed working against me because of my mysticism'.[25] Bullen had apparently gone from one bookseller to another making point-blank inquiries: 'Bullen found the Protestant booksellers little better', Yeats wrote, 'and asked me if T.C.D. disliked me. Magee, the College publisher, said "What is he doing here? Why doesn't he go away and leave us in peace?" He seems to have suspected me of some deep revolutionary designs'. Although 'Bullen was rather drunk when he told me these things', Yeats wrote to Lady Gregory, 'I asked his traveller, whom I saw on Monday, and got the same account'.[26]

Yeats was, of course, conscious of a shift of focus or interest in his own work, and he had weighed the consequences, though perhaps not in Bullen's terms: 'I imagine that as I withdrew from politics my friends among the nationalists will grow less, at first at any rate, and my foes more numerous. What I hear from Bullen only confirms the idea that I had at the time of *The Countess Cathleen* row[27] that it would make a very serious difference in my position outside the small cultured class.... Between my politics and my mysticism I shall hardly have my head turned with popularity'.[28] Although the hostility to his work in Dublin probably only made Yeats more determined than ever to print the truth as he saw it, Bullen would have been hard to convince. He was a business man, and he had £50 invested in Yeats's unfinished book. Sometime between May 1901, when he discovered the hostility to Yeats's 'heterodox' religious opinions, and December 1901, Bullen asked Yeats to substitute the volume of essays for the novel. A. P. Watt, Yeats's agent, 'strongly advised' him to accept, and he apparently did at a meeting with Bullen and Watt.[29] Yeats was urging Bullen to establish an office in Dublin and promote Irish books, his as well as others; and he probably thought that yielding to Bullen over the issue of his Rosicrucian novel would influence Bullen's decision.

It is significant, however, that Yeats did not abandon *The Speckled Bird*, choosing instead to rewrite with a drastically altered theme and plot: he had indeed 'awakened from the common dream'. Yeats himself both supports and denies my assumption about his 'impossible novel'. Some twenty-five years after the event, in *The Stirring of the Bones*, he recalled a visit to Coole Park in 1896 when he was already working on 'a novel that I could neither write nor cease to write which had Hodos Chameliontos for its theme. My chief person was to see all the modern visionary sects pass before his bewildered eyes, as Flaubert's Saint Anthony saw the Christian sects, and I was as helpless to create artistic, as my chief person to create philosophic, order.'[30] Since the outline and what I judge to be the early versions of the novel clearly do not have for theme 'Hodos Chameliontos' ('the Path of the Mixed Colours' on the Tree of Life), I suggest that Yeats's memory of chronology was bad, that he was thinking rather of what its theme became in the revised version which Bullen was hesitant to publish. Nor in fact does the hero of the typescript 'see *all* the modern visionary sects pass before his bewildered eyes' (my italics), though the section of the novel published by Bradford does bring together a rather heterogeneous group of occultists in a drawing-room situation reminiscent of that in Blake's *An Island in the Moon*. Although numerous sects and persuasions are mentioned, no real attempt is made to consider their various doctrines seriously.

Several of the characters are clearly recognisable or suggestive of people in the Theosophical Society and the Golden Dawn. One is especially interesting and may help to date the composition – an old clergyman searching for 'the elixir of life' who had 'tried it on a rabbit' which died as a result.[31] In a letter to Lady Gregory dated 20 January 1902, Yeats referred to this man (a colleague in the Second Order) and his experiment. Yeats called him 'my alchemist' and alludes ironically to the 'Elixir of Life' and its effect on rabbits.[32] Wade identifies him as the Rev W. A. Ayton, the minister who married Moina Bergson and MacGregor Mathers in June 1890.[33]

Among the others at the party who can perhaps be identified are Mr and Mrs Samuels. Yeats describes them as an unmarried American couple belonging 'to a spiritual community in America' who had come to England after 'one of them saw a vision telling them that they would find the divine truth here in London'. We see the couple through the eyes of Michael, the Yeats-figure of *The Speckled Bird* :

> They were both rather tall and thin, with dim emotional eyes, and when the one who had been called Mrs. Samuels spoke, it was the soft voice of the gushing American. She said, "But you mustn't think that we are really husband and wife; we call ourselves husband and wife for convenience in travelling. We wouldn't have been able to come at all if our friends hadn't subscribed when they heard of the vision. It was they who advised us to take the same name."[34]

This is surely a reference to a notorious American couple named

Edith and Frank D. Jackson. The older and much the larger of the two, Mrs Jackson had been married twice before and had assumed several aliases. She enjoyed being compared to Mme Blavatsky and had founded two occult societies in America: Koreshan Unity and Theocratic Unity. The Jacksons had come to London in 1899 posing as Theo and Mme Horos, then moved on to Paris, where they met Mathers. Mme Horos convinced him that she was Fräulein Anna Sprengel, the Chief of the Licht, Liebe, Leben Temple who was supposed to have authorised Westcott and Mathers to found the Isis-Urania Temple. For a time, apparently, she deceived Mathers, who wrote to Mrs Emery on 16 February 1900 that '"Sapiens dominabitur astris" is now in Paris, and aiding me with the Isis Movement'.[35] When Mathers discovered the deception, the Horoses moved their spurious occult establishment to Cape Town taking several manuscripts of the Golden Dawn from Mathers's library. Soon exposed again, they returned to London in late 1900, still posing as members of the Golden Dawn. On the basis of their acquaintance with Mathers, they sought membership in Isis-Urania, but were revealed as frauds. Since the story of their deception of Mathers was known in London, several members of the Second Order felt that Mathers, though no longer a member of Isis-Urania, should be warned about the Horoses. As Imperator, Yeats accepted 'the thankless task'. Mathers's angry reply to Yeats on 12 January 1901 makes it clear that he was aware of their imposture. Although he was astonished at the 'impertinence' of the rebel Yeats, Mathers did defend himself by outlining in some detail the deception and thievery of the Horoses.[36] On 23 October 1901, in a letter to the Spiritualist magazine *Light*, Mathers assumes the tone of prophet as he draws an ironic analogy between the deception of the Horoses and the rebellion of the Second Order: 'They soon quitted Paris for London, and again coincident with their presence more dissension arose in my Order there, culminating in severance of the discordant members from it'.[37]

The letter to *Light* is Mathers's effort to free his name from the stigma connected with the Horoses. On 26 September, they were arrested and tried for the rape of a sixteen-year-old girl who had been initiated into what they were calling the Golden Dawn. Since the trial (ending with their conviction on 20

December) received considerable publicity in London, it probably was at least partially responsible for the 'gloomy time' and 'bad spots' Yeats spoke of in the letters to Lady Gregory in January 1902; and it may have been the chief if not only reason for changing the name of the Order from Golden Dawn to Morgenröthe. Although we must wonder why the decision to change was so long in the making, the 'Manifesto' of 20 June 1902 perhaps refers directly to the notoriety created by the trial: 'We have taken this step owing to matters which happened at the end of last year and which rendered the retention of the letters G. D. inadvisable'.[38] Since the satiric section about various occultists begins at page 99 in the typescript of *The Speckled Bird*, some thirty pages after Yeats began to dictate, we can, I think, assume that it was written sometime after Yeats's discovery on 10 April of the ease with which he could dictate.

Of the remaining people at the meeting of the sects in Russell Square at least two besides Maclegan are important and probably represent Yeats's reflections on early associates in the Theosophical Society, which he joined in 1888 and remained in until he was asked to resign in August 1890:[39] Mrs Allingham and a lady who claimed to be 'all manner of great people'.

Mme Blavatsky was clearly the model for Mrs Allingham, 'about the only person who could get all the mystical sections together'. The record of Mme Blavatsky's remarkable success in uniting various esoteric sects under the umbrella of her Theosophical Society has already been told and need not be repeated here.[40] During the early 1880s there was considerable tension among several sects in the Society, particularly the groups headed by Anna Kingsford and A. P. Sinnett, representing the Christian orientation and the Buddhistic. When Mme Blavatsky and Col H. S. Olcott, the co-founder of the Society, arrived in London in March 1884, she 'peremptorily bade' Mrs Kingsford and Sinnett, who had quarrelled, 'to shake hands ... and let bygones be bygones for the sake of the universal brotherhood'.[41] Despite Mme Blavatsky's compelling magnetism, however, the tension continued until the Hermetic Society became first a separate lodge of the Theosophical Society and then an independent lodge with Mrs Kingsford as President. But the split-personality in the parent Society remained. By the

time Yeats joined the Theosophical Society it already contained
two groups with diverging viewpoints concerning the way to
truth : the one to 'proving the phenomena of spiritualism, table-
rapping, and the evocation of spooks';[42] the other concerned
with mysticism and Cabbalistic symbolism. Yeats 'joined the
Esoteric Section of TS' 'About Xmas 1888', as he recalled in
the brief 'Esoteric Section Journal' begun in October 1889.[43]
But Yeats expressed 'some doubt as to whether I could sign the
second clause' testifying to a belief in Mme Blavatsky's teachers; and on 20 December 1889, he recorded, 'I proposed scheme
for organization of occult research'. The scheme was accepted
a week later, and Yeats was made Secretary of the Research
Committee.

He was, then, not only clearly aware of the double vision in
the Society but also responsible for furthering the split. In the
struggle between the Sinnett branch and the Kingsford branch,
he clearly sided with her.[44] Although she and Edward Maitland
founded the Hermetic Lodge of the Theosophical Society in
April 1884, and then withdrew from the Theosophical Society
in December, Yeats must have known them and their well-
known book on esoteric Christianity, *The Perfect Way*; and
he included her in his sketches of the guests gathered at the
meeting of 'all the mystical sects'. Near the end of the evening
Mrs Allingham tries to introduce Michael to a lady who 'will
interest you so much ... she is very learned about Biblical
interpretation[45] and has quite a little following. . . . Dr. Clarkson
says that she was Mary Magdalen and then Faustina and then
Boadicea and all manner of great people. I don't know whether
it's true, but it's so interesting, and she's such a good woman
now. Do you know, I don't think she's ever flirted in her life,
and yet she's quite sure that she was Faustina. She can remember all about it'.[46] The information contained in this ironic
portrait must have come from Edward Maitland's monumental
two-volume record of *Anna Kingsford: Her Life, Letters, Diary
and Work*, published in 1896, the year Yeats began *The Speckled
Bird*.

According to Maitland, sometime after the beginning of his
spiritual collaboration with Mrs Kingsford, 'our illuminators'
gave her the 'spiritual or "initiation" name' of Mary 'as the
representative of the soul, the Biblical symbol for which is

Mary'.[47] In one of her books, edited by Maitland, Mrs Kingsford suggests that her illuminators must have had Mary Magdalen in mind. While 'under illumination', she had a vision of 'the events which occurred between the Crucifixion and the Resurrection': 'Jesus instructed his friends beforehand what to do. Joseph of Arimathaea was a friend of Mary Magdalen, and she procured him the requisite balms. I see her running with them through the sepulchre to the house. I have a most curious sensation, feeling as if, somehow, I were in Mary and were she'.[48] Maitland himself recorded that he had received an 'intimation', presumably from their illuminators, 'that I was to live with my colleague as John would live with Mary Magdalen, were the two to come back to tell the world what they knew of Jesus'.[49] But she was in communication with many spirits, and imagined herself at various times to be the reincarnation of several, including Anne Boleyn, Joan of Arc,[50] and 'Faustine, the Roman'.[51] Mrs Allingham was surely right in assuming that Michael should be interested in such a woman. And Yeats must have enjoyed his own ironic reference to Mrs Kingsford's unorthodox life with Maitland: 'I don't think she's ever flirted in her life, and yet she's quite sure that she was Faustina'.[52]

Since several of this motley crew assembled at the home of Mrs Allingham were obviously portraits of people Yeats actually knew, I rather imagine that all of them were. At any rate, they represent the impression they had made upon the fascinated but always sceptical Yeats as 'all the modern visionary sects pass[ed] before his bewildered eyes'.[53]

This section of *The Speckled Bird* is also valuable for the revelation of several important writers whose books Yeats had apparently read in those first exciting days of his introduction to 'all the mystical sections': Swedenborg, Kenneth MacKenzie, Fred Hockley, Thomas Lake Harris, Dante, Éliphas Lévi, and references to Irvingites, Martinists, and Cabbalists.[54] For the study of Rosicrucianism, Lévi is, of course, by far the most important name. He was greatly respected by occultists, and his many books perhaps represent the most significant existing body of literature on the 'doctrine and ritual of transcendental magic', to refer to the title of one well-known work.[55] Yeats was no doubt acquainted with these books, as he probably was

with an influential article about magic by Mackenzie in the
Rosicruciana, a magazine published by the Societas Rosicruciana
in Anglia.[56]

With the possible exception of Mathers, most of the sketches
of Yeats's fellow seekers in Book II are satiric, obviously representing sects and ideologies which he had explored and abandoned. But the portraits of Moina and MacGregor Mathers in
Book IV are sympathetic, though it is clear that Mathers is
to Yeats a great man gone to ruin. Yeats and Mathers apparently had quite similar interests in 1890, but Yeats must have
realised by 1900 that their religious and philosophical viewpoints were far apart. When he worked again on the end of
the novel, probably after April 1902, he planned to project
the two viewpoints in Michael and Maclagen as contrasts or
opposites:

> The difference of opinion about proper kind of symbolism
> between Michael and Maclagen must be accentuated. Mac-
> lagen had better be quite definitely a disciple of the Rosy
> Cross as that is embodied in the *Fama*. Michael should as
> definitely insist on the introduction of such a symbolism
> as will continue and make more precise the implicit symbo-
> lism in modern art and poetry. The antagonism must be
> made the antagonism between the poet and magician.[57]

Whether or not the actual disagreement was great, as it seems
here, this passage surely reveals a prime reason for Yeats's
discontent with the Second Order and with many of his colleagues. And he was 'doubtful', after summarising his plans
for portraying Mathers and his circle, 'if I should give any of
this, probably it would be better to confine the description in
this part of the book to the making of the order'.[58] Since some
of Yeats's frankest thoughts about the Golden Dawn and his
fellow members appear in the later part of *The Speckled Bird*,
its pages are certain to be studied with care by scholars and
critics, who will also be eager for the publication of the manuscript version.

It was perhaps not possible for Yeats to shape such frankly
autobiographical materials into satisfactory art. If he should
tell all, it would approach the scandalous; if he should tell too

little, it would seem like a puzzle to all but his colleagues in the Order. So at last it was abandoned – in part perhaps because he could not decide whether its theme should be magic or love. In the 'Abstract of Book IV', Yeats proposes to send his hero off to Persia to find if 'there is some way by which lovers who are divided in the flesh may meet in the spirit, some way of going out of the body and becoming one in dreams'.[59] Yeats would have intended it to be symbolic certainly that his hero should be leaving Maclagen on the station platform in Paris as he continues his quest for the mystery of existence, 'Hodos Chameliontos'. The poet and magician had parted company.

Yeats believed, of course, that he must find some means of combining his absorption with Maud and the Order if he was to achieve Unity of Being. One of the 'Private' notebooks expresses the hope that all may be brought 'back to the spiritual marriage of 1899', and a note on the following page, immediately above a letter from Maud, suggests how important the union of these disparate elements was to him : 'think meditation should be representative of initiation in the coffin of Father Rosy Cross. Must work out relation between this & mystic marriage'.[60] Perhaps he hoped to achieve in art what he could not achieve in life – an enduring union of these intractable contraries. Maud's withdrawal from the Golden Dawn must have been a severe blow, and *The Speckled Bird* is a record of his frustration and failure : for the only time in his creative life he left a major project unfinished.

He was more successful with *The Shadowy Waters*. Although the Dublin booksellers were hostile because of its mysticism, few of them, I suspect, could have explained what they found wrong with its doctrines. Clearly autobiographical, it records the spiritual marriage of Yeats and Maud in the characters of Forgael and Dectora. Although *The Shadowy Waters* is not wholly successful, as Yeats recognised in continuing to revise it for many years, he did not make the mistake of setting down the raw material of life as art. In fact, as he wrote in 1906, its plot 'was so overgrown with symbolical ideas that the poem was obscure and vague'.[61] Realising the problem, Yeats offered a clue to the meaning and an apology for the obscurity in the introductory poem, dated September 1900 :

And the images I have woven in this story
Of Forgael and Dectora and the empty waters
Moved round me in the voices and the fires;
And more I may not write of, for them that cleave
The waters of sleep can make a chattering tongue
Heavy like stone, their wisdom being half silence.

Addressing the 'immortal, mild, proud shadows', Yeats insists:

I only know that all we know comes from you,
And that you come from Eden on flying feet.

He is certain, despite the rhetorical question, that the visible world is merely an imperfect copy and symbolic of the invisible:

                    Do our woods
And winds and ponds cover more quiet woods,
More shining winds, more star-glimmering ponds?

The last stanza is one of Yeats's finest expressions of the ritualistic function of poetry:

I have made this poem for you, that men may read it
Before they read of Forgael and Dectora,
As men in the old times, before the harps began,
Poured out wine for the high invisible ones.[62]

But the invisible ones were unavailing with Maud. It was his most enduring vision that she should listen to their voices and cry out with Dectora:

                    I will follow you.
I have cut the rope that bound this galley to ours,
And while she fades and life withers away,
I crown you with this crown.
  . . . .
Bend lower, that I may cover you with my hair,
For we will gaze upon this world no longer.[63]

Unfortunately, reality rarely measures up to vision, and Maud was better suited for gazing upon this world than the other. She married John MacBride in February 1903, a kind of watershed in Yeats's life – not alone because of his discontent in love, but also because of his disillusionment with the Golden Dawn.

Two of the essays in *Ideas of Good and Evil* were apparently written in Ireland during the summer of 1901, soon after the great debate with the group. 'What is "Popular Poetry"?' hardly seems to reflect Yeats's preoccupation with the business of the Second Order, though one brief passage suggests his continued attempt to link peasants with poets and magicians: 'I learned from the people themselves, before I learned it from any book, that they cannot separate the idea of an art or a craft from the idea of a cult with ancient technicalities and mysteries. They can hardly separate mere learning from witchcraft, and are fond of words and verses that keep half their secret to themselves.'[64]

'Ireland and the Arts', perhaps written about the same time, has much more to say on the subject of art and the people. In one sense it is a companion essay to 'What is "Popular Poetry"?' Although Yeats did not print them together in *Ideas of Good and Evil*, they cast light on each other, the first concerned with the plight of art in Ireland from the viewpoint of the people, the other from the viewpoint of the artist, Yeats in particular. 'What is "Popular Poetry"?' ends on the pessimistic note that 'the counting-house had created a new class and a new art without breeding and without ancestry',[65] and 'Ireland and the Arts' begins with the same thought: 'The arts have failed; fewer people are interested in them every generation. The mere business of living, of making money, of amusing oneself, occupies people more and more, and makes them less capable of the difficult art of appreciation'.[66] There can be no doubt surely that Yeats's practical and religious experience in the Second Order had given him a new appreciation for and dedication to the arts. He had gone to Ireland in May tired, discouraged, and thoroughly disgusted with most of his colleagues; but he had the zeal of the missionary, and he renewed his hope for ultimate victory through faith in the peasant – in contrast to the middle-class people he had seen so much of in London during the months just past:

We who care deeply about the arts find ourselves the priesthood of an almost forgotten faith, and we must, I think, if we would win the people again, take upon ourselves the method and the fervour of a priesthood. We must be half humble and half proud. We see the perfect more than others, it may be, but we must find the passions among the people. We must baptize as well as preach.[67]

After his recent wrangle in London he was more conscious than ever before of 'the antagonism between the poet and magician'.[68] The new Chiefs in the Order were quite as absolute as Mathers had been but without his talent and imagination. He at least had faith in symbolic values, whereas his successors were literalists. 'In very early days', Yeats believed, 'the arts ... were almost inseparable from religion, going side by side with it into all life'. Now they have grown apart, the arts too proud and aloof in their quest of the perfect, religion too pedestrian and practical in its quest for power and sheer excitement. 'But here in Ireland, when the arts have grown humble, they [artists] will find two passions ready to their hands, love of the Unseen Life and love of country.'[69] 'In other words', he continued, 'I would have Ireland re-create the ancient arts' 'with subjects taken from his [the artist's] religious beliefs.'[70] Only in this way and perhaps only in Ireland is it possible to achieve once more the union of art and religion. 'An Englishman, with his belief in progress, with his instinctive preference for the cosmopolitan literature of the last century, may think arts like these parochial, but they are the arts we have begun the making of.'[71] Moreover, Yeats concluded ironically, the artist 'may, indeed, doubt the reality of his vision if men do not quarrel with him as they did with the apostles, for there is only one perfection and only one search for perfection, and it sometimes has the form of the religious life and sometimes of the artistic life.'[72] To Yeats, it was the function of 'art and scholarship' to 'make love of the unseen more unshakable, more ready to plunge deep into the abyss'.[73]

These are not, of course, new sentiments for Yeats, but he must have been more strongly convinced than ever before after the trying experiences he had undergone during the period of April 1900 to February 1901. 'Though there were times when he would doubt, as even the saints have doubted', Yeats believed that he 'had reawakened in himself the age of faith'.[74]

Those words were written about Shelley in 'The Philosophy

of Shelley's Poetry', an essay he planned as early as July 1899,[75] but did not publish until July 1900 in *The Dome*.[76] Part II, 'His Ruling Symbols', was not included in this first published version, and was presumably written after, probably not immediately after, that date. Since the tone and many ideas of Part II suggest that it was written about the time of 'Magic', that is early summer 1901, it has a special interest for this study. Cythna's recording of her 'wisdom upon the sands in "signs" that were clear elemental shapes' ('the key of truths which once were dimly taught in old Crotona')[77] is reminiscent of a dance in *The Speckled Bird* by means of which Mrs Maclagen wove 'symbols in honour of the divinity'. As Maclagen explained to Michael, 'the old symbols ... were made upon the temple floors by the feet of dancers'.[78] Years later, in Book I of *A Vision* (1925), Yeats recalled, perhaps unconsciously, both Mrs Maclagen's dance and Cythna's 'signs' in the dance of Kusta ben Luka's students which recorded 'some great secret' in the desert sands by 'the marks of their feet'.[79]

Although Yeats could find no evidence that Shelley had given 'any deep study' to the occult 'doctrine of symbols or signatures', he was certain that Shelley had brooded over 'the traditions of magic and of the magical philosophy'. Recalling the opening section of 'Magic' and thinking more of himself than Shelley, Yeats observed that 'our little memories are but part of some great Memory that renews the world and men's thoughts age after age'. 'Shelley understood this', Yeats insisted, 'but whether he understood that the great Memory is also a dwelling-house of symbols, of images that are living souls, I cannot tell'. He was certain, however, that Shelley 'expected to receive thoughts and images from beyond his own mind',[80] and he discovered, not surprisingly, that many of these symbols were those with which he had been preoccupied in the Golden Dawn: rivers, fountains, wells, caves, cups, looms, honey, gates, towers, stars, sun, and moon. Although many if not all these symbols are traditional and might have been known to both Shelley and Yeats from a wide variety of sources, it is significant that Yeats cites sources frequently consulted by his Order – especially the Neoplatonists in the translations of Thomas Taylor.[81]

In the justly famous ending to his essay Yeats draws a

distinction between the kind of worship one might have expected of Blake and Shelley if they had lived in ancient times, and concludes that Shelley might have found some one image or picture which 'would lead his soul, disentangled from unmeaning circumstance and the ebb and flow of the world, into that far household where the undying gods await all whose souls have become simple as flame, whose bodies have become quiet as an agate lamp'. It is obvious, I suppose, that those lines say more about Yeats than Shelley. Particularly revealing in the context of the disorder in his life from early 1900 through most of 1902, they are perhaps the most eloquent expression in his prose of an unfulfilled yearning to be 'lost in a ceaseless reverie, in some chapel of the Star of infinite desire'.[82]

The opening of 'The Happiest of the Poets' sounds almost like a continuation of the essay on Shelley. Although the happy poet is Morris, Yeats begins by discussing Rossetti, whose 'genius like Shelley's ... follows the Star of the Magi, the Morning and Evening star'. In Yeats's opinion happiness in the normal sense was not possible for Shelley and Rossetti because they sought unattainable ideals; they were, he said, 'among those that would have prayed in old times in some chapel of the Star'. Like Yeats (as he enjoyed thinking of himself), Rossetti 'desired a world of essences, of unmixed powers, of impossible purities', and 'he painted as though he had seen the flame out of whose heart all flames had been taken, or the blue of the abyss that was before all life'.[83] These descriptive lines and others like them suggest in metaphorical terms the power of magic as Yeats conceived it. In the troubled years after the spiritual marriage with or physical loss of Maud and during the disillusionment over the quarrels in the Second Order, Yeats sought for 'some moment of intensity when the ecstasy of the lover and of the saint are alike, and desire becomes wisdom without ceasing to be desire'.[84]

There was, of course, another side of Yeats. As a worshipper of 'natural abundance', he was like Morris and Blake 'glad to be alive'. And like them – on some days at least – Yeats 'would have prayed under the shadow of the Green Tree, and on the wet stones of the Well, among the worshippers of natural abundance'.[85] Both images were to Yeats projections of 'an "energy" that is not the less "eternal delight" because it is half of the body'.[86] If this sounds more like the late than the early Yeats, we may be reminded of how crucial these years were to his development. In one sense at least 'The Happiest of the Poets' clearly reveals not only what Yeats sought in religion but what he found in Rosicrucianism that was missing in traditional Christianity. Morris's Well and Green Tree project a faith diametrically opposed to the Wilderness and the Dry Tree of the early Christians. As one of 'the greatest of those who prepare the last reconciliation when the Cross shall blossom with roses', Morris was to Yeats a member of the brotherhood striving to achieve the 'reconciliation of Paganism and Christianity' which he spent a lifetime seeking. After his frustrating experiences with Mathers and the groups in the Second Order, Yeats must have been convinced that only poets and artists can 'carry the burdens that priests and theologians took from them angrily some few hundred years ago'.[87] But he did not resign from the Order, though he must have been unhappy and disillusioned.

NINE

The Poet's Prophecy Fulfilled

From other Tarots I have done & these I come to this con-
clusion: Very shortly some terrible trouble will take place
in the Bristol Temple (L.O.E.). The evil will appear there
with redoubled force – F.R. will I think probably die –
success will be abandoned – by L.O.E. & those supporting
her & possibly the whole Order practically broken up. It
also looks as if some final decision would be arrived at,
probably for reconstruction, about the latter end of June.
Very few will be left; probably all the Priests will resign
& Dr. Hammond.

If this is true, then it is what you told me two years ago
– 'That this trouble was permitted so that the Order might
be purified & only the earnest students left to carry on.' It
is very curious.

MISS CHRISTINA MARY STODDART to YEATS (21 March 1921)

After the great struggle of 1901 Yeats was, I think, never again
so involved in affairs of the Order. But he remained an active
member when the name was changed from Golden Dawn to
Morgenröthe in June 1902.[1] Demon Est Deus Inversus and
Festina Lente were included in the active list of 'Lords & Ladies
of the Portal 5=6' which accompanied the Manifesto of 26
June 1902.[2] But Yeats must have been unhappy that several
old and good friends were no longer active: among those who
had 'died or resigned during the past 18 months' were five of
the rebels who had fought so hard to legalise groups, and three
of them had been intimate associates of Yeats for many years
– Mrs Emery and Mr and Mrs Hunter. Yeats patched up the
friendship with Mrs Emery, continuing to correspond with her
until her death in 1917; but he was surely saddened at the
changes in the Order, though he had helped to bring some of

them about. He was deeply concerned over the bickering, disputes, and political manoeuvring in a religious society representing ideal brotherhood and dedicated to the quest for truth. But he remained in the Order, perhaps in part because he had been the prime mover in the struggles of 1900 and 1901 and in part because the Order meant so much to Uncle George Pollexfen.

Although the internecine battles in the Order were not over, Yeats did not assume a leading role in subsequent disputes. He had apparently made a serious effort to disengage himself from administration, and he confided to Lady Gregory on 3 January 1903 that 'it has been a good year with me too – a very good year'.[3] He was, I suppose, thinking that calm had come to the Order with the new Constitution of June 1902, which re-established a government with three strong Chiefs at the head similar to the original government of 1888. Unfortunately, peace was temporary. Although Felkin, Bullock, and Brodie-Innes, the new Chiefs, pleaded with the Second Order 'to permit no discord to mar our harmony' and sought to convince the members that 'unity of will is the occult condition precedent to a realisation of our aspirations',[4] forces of disruption were at work, and another split occurred the following year. Waite was the leader of a revolt at the Annual Meeting in 1903. According to the account in *Shadows of Life and Thought*, when Brodie-Innes presented 'his Constitution with histrionic magnificence', Waite objected to one clause after another and sought to amend most of them. Fearing that the draft might pass and Brodie-Innes be declared Chief, Waite proposed 'the rejection of the second draft Constitution *in toto*, with the result that this also lapsed for want of the requisite majority'. Waite then proposed that 'those who regarded the Golden Dawn as capable of a mystical instead of an occult construction should and had indeed resolved to work independently, going their own way'. Although only a minority sided with Waite, the Third Annual Meeting since the expulsion of Mathers 'dissolved in chaos ... with Brodie-Innes in a state of white rage'.[5]

As the leader of the rebels, Waite set about reorganising the Golden Dawn – for the third time, it should be noted, since April 1900:

Immediately after I arranged that the Hermetic Society, as the G∴ D∴ was called in the outer world, should continue its Meetings at Mark Masons' Hall; and joining forces with Blackden the Rite went on, as if no revolutions had occurred. The Triple Headship was restored by co-opting the Rev. W. A. Ayton as a co-Chief, he being Senior Adept among us.[6]

According to King, who is unsympathetic to Waite, 'The new Temple abandoned all magical work, abolished examinations within the Second Order and used heavily revised rituals designed to express a somewhat tortuous Christian mysticism'.[7] If King is correct – and I have no reason to doubt, Yeats must have been appalled at the turn of events : Waite and his group were in effect denying the validity of the philosophic premises that Yeats had struggled to establish in 'Is the Order of R.R. & A.C. to remain a Magical Order?' I have found no reference in Yeats's unpublished papers or in the published letters of 1903 to the issues involved or to the General Meeting at which the split occurred. If he had been in London, he surely would have been present at an annual meeting; and if he had been present, he surely would not have remained silent.

After this revolt, according to Waite, 'For two or three years we heard practically nothing of any opposing parties'.[8] But he is writing long after the event, and he may be wrong. Some time after his expulsion in April 1900, Mathers attempted to organise an independent temple. Unfortunately, little is known of its history. Howe refers to it briefly as 'Dr. Berridge's Temple', and comments that Westcott was active in it.'[9] Waite also has little to say about Dr Berridge's 'experiment with an active Temple in London, under the Mathers obedience'. He points out that 'it held meetings at Portland Road', and he remembers having been 'approached by discontented Members, who told me strange stories about a parlous state of affairs, of gross neglect and mismanagement, and of the verminous condition of the robes used in the Grades. In the end I heard vaguely that the new Temple had flickered out, and before long Berridge himself passed away, whether before or after MacGregor Mathers I do not know'.[10] Since Mathers did not die until 1918, four years after Waite had closed Isis-Urania, he obviously either knew nothing about

Dr Berridge's group or did not choose to comment.

Waite is also vague about the group that remained faithful to Felkin, Bullock, and Brodie-Innes in the Amoun Temple of Stella Matutina:

> I believe that it was founded subsequently to the abortive attempt of Berridge, and it did not recognize Mathers. It was claimed further that Felkin had no official connection with Brodie-Innes and that he was working alone, so far as government was concerned. Whence he pretended to derive authority I never heard, his appointment to a ruling position by vote at successive Annual Meetings having lapsed obviously at the end of the third year.[11]

Waite's group announced its intention of seceding in a manifesto dated 24 July 1903, and he wrote to Brodie-Innes on 1 August that his group was unwilling to negotiate with Brodie-Innes and Felkin (Bullock had resigned).[12] These two groups were poles apart ideologically. In a series of questions to Waite on 8 September, Brodie-Innes pointed out the basis for their differences. He suggested that Waite's group did not believe in the Third Order or 'the existence of magical powers', that they insisted on being excused from examinations, and that they wanted to 're-edit the Rituals'. Finally, Brodie-Innes observed, 'What is meant by a "mystical trend" and by the "lower occultism" is obscure'.[13] Waite replied on 7 November, denying the 'legal standing' of Brodie-Innes and Felkin and insisting upon the right to the properties of the Temple. Waite wrote again to Brodie-Innes on 18 November, rejecting explicitly the suggestions about 'The Third Order', 'Revision of the Rituals', and 'Progress by Examination'. Since these issues were basic to the Order as it was conceived by Mathers and defended by Yeats in the quarrel of 1901, compromise was apparently impossible. But Yeats tried. According to a letter Waite wrote to Felkin on 1 January 1904, Yeats had suggested 'they should use a common Temple for the Outer Order and for Second Order purposes share private rooms, but Waite could not agree to this'.[14]

By the end of 1903, apparently, there was no solution but separation. Felkin and the majority withdrew, founded the Amoun Temple, and named their branch the Stella Matutina.

'After lengthy negotiations', according to Howe, 'in April 1907 Felkin signed a concordat which was intended to govern the relationship between his own and Waite's Temple'.[15] To many of the Adepti, especially those who had been members for many years, the choice between the two groups must have been difficult. Though Yeats was no doubt disturbed over such a serious break with the past, he surely did not hesitate: he could not approve any group that denied the validity of magic and eschewed the necessity of examinations for progress. Like Mathers and Mrs Emery, but for a different reason, Waite's group proposed to abandon discipline, order, and hierarchy – that is, in effect, the whole Cabbalistic system of Degrees. That, to Yeats, was unthinkable. So he chose to affiliate with Felkin's group. The struggle for loyalties no doubt became fierce at this stage, and many members must have been genuinely distressed over having to make a choice which frequently separated friend from friend. For many of them the philosophic issues were not clear-cut, as they were to Yeats and Uncle George. An unpublished letter (dated 21 December 1905) from Pollexfen to Pamela Coleman Smith[16] will suggest the dilemma many of them must have faced. In answer to an inquiry from Miss Smith for astrological information 'as to her partnership affairs', he concluded with a comment on her 'reference to the Order. Owing to my being so far away from London I am not sufficiently active in the matter to influence others as to what they should do. But both I myself and my nephew – WBY – after fully considering the matter decided to remain with those who are with Dr. F——.' Yeats was surely one of those trying 'to influence others as to what they should do'.

Although Yeats maintained a strong interest in the Stella Matutina for most of the remainder of his life, as we shall see, few records have been preserved. When the Secret Chiefs chose to relay messages to Felkin through the mediumship of his wife by means of automatic writing,[17] Yeats must have been reminded that MacGregor and Moina Mathers had received their information by a similar method: 'These teachings were built up by D.D.C.F. from instructions received clairvoyantly by Vestigia (Mrs. M.) from certain Powers calling themselves "THE HIDDEN AND SECRET CHIEFS" and believed by D.D.C.F. to be our THIRD ORDER.'[18] And Yeats surely had both couples in mind when his communicators transmitted to him through the automatic writing of his wife the teachings that were to become *A Vision*.

Felkin realised, of course, that his continued influence would depend on the faith he could instil in his colleagues that further teaching and the rituals for more advanced degrees would be conveyed by the Secret Chiefs – or their instruments the Sun Masters – through him. In 1909, according to Miss Stoddart's 'Investigations', 'we find promises that when the time is ripe this THIRD ORDER would indicate where the genuine Rituals and it may be M.S.S. could be found'. Since the rituals for all the degrees through $5 = 6$ had come through Mathers many years before, Felkin was under considerable pressure to produce further rituals; and he appealed to Brodie-Innes, who had renewed his friendship with Mathers and was serving as 'Deputy Archon Basileus' of the Amen Ra Temple in Edinburgh. Some time after August 1913, Brodie-Innes replied:

> I have stacks of MSS. and teachings going to far further lengths than I used to think possible.... All the teaching I have got I will gladly pass on to you on the same conditions as I have received it.... My commission as such comes from the Third Order – or not to make ambiguity of these words from those Higher Adepts whom I so term – and I can pass them on to such as acknowledge my authority and position. This of course involves also recognition of Mathers, who has committed his authority to me.[19]

The dependence on Mathers may have been irksome, but Felkin's need was urgent, and he accepted.

Among the Adepti ready to receive the Degree of $6 = 5$ was Yeats, who may well have been the senior member of the Second Order by this time. Having advanced to the level of Theoricus Adeptus Minor, $5 = 6$, on 10 July 1912, Yeats had apparently studied the new manuscripts and was advanced to the Degree of $6 = 5$ on 16 October 1914. He preserved a typed copy of the 'Impression of $6 = 5$ Ceremony, Postulant Frater D.E.D.I.',[20] written I imagine by Felkin or his wife, who may have been the only other Adepti to have achieved the $6 = 5$ at this time. Although I have not examined a ritual of this Degree, the 'Impression', especially the part of the Ceremony concerned with 'the ringing of the 36 Bells', suggests that Felkin (or Mathers, if indeed the material came from him) had sought for something novel. Even Mathers's ingenuity may have been failing.[21]

The year 1914 is important in the history of the Golden Dawn in London. By this time, the Amoun Temple had won the battle for numbers, and Waite capitulated: 'In 1914 I put an end to the Isis-Urania or Mother Temple, owing to internecine feuds on the authenticity of documents. A few persons attempted to carry on by themselves, but it proved a failure.'[22] Two years later (in July 1916), when Felkin founded three new temples, one to accommodate the dispossessed group from Isis-Urania, he estimated that 'there are some fifty or sixty members of the Temple which used to be ruled by Waite, also a number of members of the Anthroposophical Society who are seeking admission'.[23] Less than a year before, according to a record located by Howe, there were 123 members in the Stella Matutina.[24] One of these was Georgie Hyde-Lees. Although I do not know the date of her admission, it was probably in 1914. On 23 October, exactly one week after Yeats's attainment of the Degree of $6=5$, she signed a receipt for a copy of 'The Address on the Pillars', one of the 'Knowledge Lectures'.[25]

Felkin too was busy in 1914. Although by his own account he had received notes for Rituals $6=5$, $7=4$, and $8=3$ when he visited the continent in 1913, he and Mrs Felkin returned to 'receive further grades and instructions' in 1914. They planned also to visit the old vault of Christian Rosenkreuz in southeastern Austria. Unfortunately, 'the War intervened and they were forced to return to England about the end of August'.[26] In Germany they had been accompanied by Miss Stoddart, whose 'Investigations' and *Light-Bearers of Darkness* are important but not always reliable accounts of the Stella Matutina. Her letters to Yeats over a period of several years discuss major issues in the Order and cast some light on his attitudes and convictions in the last years of his membership.

After founding the new temples in 1916, Felkin moved to New Zealand, where he had founded the Smaragdine Thalasses Temple in 1912.[27] Although he continued to rule the temples in England, troubles soon developed in the Order, and the

senior Adepti must have been reminded of similar problems
when Mathers attempted to rule from Paris. Although the
records of activities in the Stella Matutina from 1916 to 1919
are very scant, some few observations may be made, chiefly
on the basis of Miss Stoddart's 'Investigations'. After Yeats
and Miss Hyde-Lees were married on 21 October 1917, they
remained involved and important members of Amoun, the
Mother Temple. As an elder statesman, he was a trusted advi-
ser to Miss Stoddart, the Rev Will Reason (Semper Sperans),
and the Rev F. N. Heazell (Evocatus Paratus), the co-Chiefs. 'In
March 1917', according to Miss Stoddart, 'we suddenly began to
receive astral messages through a member who had been for
some years under F.R.'s [Felkin's] special and private training.
... At the end of 1918 I.F.C. [Miss Stoddart] had reason to
suspect that all was not well and stopped these messages for a
time communicating her doubts to various members'. Yeats was
surely one of these members. The messages were to lead up to a
special 'Initiation' of three people, one of whom 'was to have
Inner vision (mediumistic)'. When Miss Stoddart discovered
'suddenly without further warning' that she had been chosen to
receive 'this Initiation at the Tenebres service on Thursday 17
April, the evening before Good Friday', she 'sensed evil', became frightened, and 'refused to have anything to do with it'.[28]
Unfortunately, Miss Stoddart does not tell who was attempting
to conduct this initiation, though she does suggest, in *Light-
Bearers of Darkness*, that it was a black mass presided over by
'the false "Christ" or Lord of Light and his Twelve Brethren',
who were clothed 'in black habits with cowls over their
heads'.[29] When she wrote to Felkin requesting advice and an
explanation, he replied ironically on 19 July 1919:

> Have you ever made any attempt at reconstruction in the
> World...? I think it would be better if instead of fearing
> imaginery BLACK ROSICRUCIANS in Germany or elsewhere
> you would consciously endeavour to co-operate with the
> true ROSICRUCIANS who do undoubtedly exist and are
> seeking to guide Central European thought into the LIGHT,
> you would then belong to the GREAT WORK for the World
> and would have nothing to fear from that source.

In response to that Miss Stoddart observed in her 'Investigations': 'Consider the state of the World at this moment.!!'[30]

The affairs of the Stella Matutina were likewise in a bad state: 'Before Dr. Felkin had left England, and up to the closing of the Temple in 1919', Miss Stoddart recalled in 1930, 'the Order was rent by dissensions, jealousies, underground whisperings, and open strife and rebellion...'.[31] The closed temple was Amoun,[32] but the work continued, presumably in Miss Stoddart's home at 56 Redcliffe Gardens. From this address, over a period of some two years she wrote a series of letters to the Yeatses explaining the problems of the Order as she saw them and requesting their advice and support. The first letter, dated 1 December 1919 and addressed to Nemo (Mrs Yeats), suggests that the Yeatses were supplying Miss Stoddart with materials for rituals or examinations: 'I find it won't after all be possible to get up Mrs. Erskine's $5=6$ this week so I won't bother you for any more grades until you come up in January'.[33] The Yeatses were in Oxford but planning to sail from London to America on 6 January.[34]

The remainder of the letter reveals more of Miss Stoddart's personal problems than of the Order's. It also illustrates the respect Yeats continued to receive from his colleagues in the Order: 'I need not tell you how much you & D.E.D.I. have helped me in all this beastly trouble. Just at first I felt so absolutely stranded with no one at all capable of giving me any sound advice or making any suggestion as to how to fight these devils'. Miss Stoddart's determination to be 'quite sure of our foundations' and to eliminate 'all that is not purely Order teaching' must have reminded Yeats of Miss Horniman's determination over similar issues more than eighteen years before.[35] In the search for allies Miss Stoddart had proposed, and surely with Yeats's knowledge and approval, that he should be appointed Chief: 'By January', she wrote, 'I hope to have heard from F.R. [Felkin] in answer to my proposal to ask D.E.D.I. to be Ruling Chief in place of Mr. Reason who wishes to resign.... Then I firmly believe F.R. will leave us to ourselves'. But Felkin was too canny. He replaced Reason with Dr William Hammond (Pro Rege Et Patria),[36] explaining his rejection of Yeats in a letter of 21 July 1920: 'Unfortunately Yeats will not do, as he has already been offered and refused, also I may tell you privately that I have heard that he or his wife have been talking too freely in America about the Order and its present troubles. He never was very reticent'.[37] Since Yeats did not return from America until late May or early June,[38] the news of his indiscretion must have travelled fast. More likely, Felkin had invented the rumour. I have not, unfortunately, been able to discover when the position was 'offered and refused'.

The letter to Nemo contains one other tantalising reference: Miss Stoddart has heard that one or two of Bernard Hamerton's Oxford friends may want to join the Order, and she hopes to bring one of them to London in January when the Yeatses come through on the way to America. In closing, she mentions an evening spent with an old acquaintance, Mrs Cecilia Macrae: 'Vincit & I sat talking until 7 o'clock on Sat. I had to invoke ∇ [water] over her & she over me!! Many thanks, Yours, I.F.C.' Having joined the Golden Dawn in May or June 1891, Mrs Macrae (Vincit Qui Se Vincit) had been in the Order almost as long as Yeats. She signed the petition to reinstate Miss Horniman in December 1896, but as a member of Mrs Emery's first group she opposed Yeats and Miss Horniman in the quarrel of 1901.[39] Surprisingly, her motto does not appear on the list of 26 June 1902.[40] Sixteen months after the exciting evening with Miss Stoddart, V.Q.S.V. was made a member of a committee to sit in judgement on her friend. I will return to that episode.

Yeats was away from England for most of 1920 and perhaps had not kept up with developments in the struggle between Miss Stoddart and Felkin. But when he returned to Oxford in October, after a tonsillectomy in Dublin and a visit to Coole Park, Yeats was soon involved in Miss Stoddart's affairs. Needing advice and sympathy, she wrote to him on 9 November, enclosing a copy of a letter to the Fratres and Sorores of Amoun from Felkin's daughter, Ethel (Quaero Altissima), who was attempting to resolve 'the crisis in the London Temple'. She had just returned from a trip to the continent for a consultation with Dr Rudolph Steiner,[41] founder of the Anthroposophical Society and a widely respected occultist; and she had arranged for Dr Carnegie Dickson (Fortes Fortuna Juvat) to visit Steiner 'to get the necessary teaching & advice to enable the present chaos to be grappled with'. Miss Felkin pretended also that she had asked the Ruling Chiefs to allow Miss Stoddart, who was very anxious to check Felkin's claims, to accompany Dickson to the Continental Centre: 'I am sorry to have to tell you', she wrote to the Adepti, 'that I was unable to get permission for a second representative to go nor was I able to get permission for the G.H.S.I.F.C. [Greatly Honored Soror Il Faut Chercher] to go tho I especially asked for this'. She concluded her brief letter by assuring the Adepti that if Frater F.F.J. (Dickson) is unable or unwilling to go 'I have been instructed how to act & in any case will communicate with you at once as soon as I know'. Miss Stoddart was suspicious. She discovered that Miss Felkin had received a coded cable from her father, and she presumed that 'it contained fresh instructions from F.R. definitely limiting the introductions to Dr. Dickson & again refusing to give me one. He must think I know too much & will insist on investigating also that the other Chiefs do not support him but back me up in my rebellion!'

Miss Stoddart explained to Yeats at that point that 'Dr. Dickson is son of Dr. Dickson[42] of Edinburgh one of the early members'. She pointed out that Dickson was 'only $5 = 6$' (advanced degrees were now common apparently) and had done all his work in Edinburgh under Brodie-Innes. She concluded that Dickson 'knows little or nothing of the trouble & has taken no part in the work except while F.R. was in London he acted as Hiero for six months'. The last is a reference to Dickson's brief tenure as one of the three Chiefs of The Secret College which Felkin founded in 1916. Indeed, Felkin may have persuaded him to come to London for this service. But The Secret College, 'restricted to members of the Societas Rosicruciana in Anglia',[43] was not successful. Although I have not discovered how long it existed, its demise was probably the reason for Dickson's return to Edinburgh. At any rate, he was one of Felkin's trusted lieutenants. 'He and his wife both worked with the A.B.S.[44] the Arab group', Miss Stoddart explained to Yeats; also 'he holds I understand most of F.R.'s papers re the ⊙ [Sun] Order & Masters'. She thought Dickson's designation a mere ploy and wondered 'what F.R.'s next move will be'.

Although Dr William Hammond, also a former Chief of The Secret College, urged her to resign, Miss Stoddart felt that her work would not be complete until she had exposed the evil and broken 'its obsessing power', so she planned to 'hold on':

> My position is this: while wishing to prevent F.R. re-estab-
> lishing the Order as a basis for this teaching of his, which
> I am afraid I consider very evil, I on the other hand feel
> we have no foundations. Our Rituals & teachings are all
> perhaps, perhaps not, [evil] & so mixed up with astral in-
> structions & teachings that to me there is no soundness
> in them. I don't say 'tis all evil but how to sift the good
> from the evil is beyond me.
>   Some of the Rituals are beautiful I admit but that does not
> sanctify them in my eyes.

Although she professed a desire 'to study occultism', she had
'lost all faith in the Order ... & without faith the Order is
nought but a valley of dead bones'. Moreover, her faith could
not be restored without proof from Felkin of the authority he
claimed to hold from the Third Order. Troubled, obviously
unsure of her ground and hoping for support, she concluded
with a plea: 'I would like to know what you feel about it all'.
   We too would like to know what Yeats thought about all
this, and indeed we may some day if his replies to Miss Stoddart's letters are discovered. Although he was clearly in sympathy with her problems, he was obviously not active in the
routine affairs of the Order. He was already planning *A Vision*,
his record of 'strange adventures' for 'a handful of fellow students, who are dead or estranged'. The dissension in the Amoun
Temple must have reminded him, in a moment of truth, that
although 'few ... who belonged at all intimately to our circle
abandoned the study ... the lives of most in so far as they are
known to me have been troubled & unhappy because [of] it'.[45]
In November 1920, possibly the week before the letter from
Miss Stoddart I have just quoted, Yeats composed 'All Soul's
Night', the Epilogue to *A Vision* and a celebration for three of
those dead friends mentioned in one draft of the Dedication
'To Vestigia': W. T. Horton, Florence Farr Emery, and Mac-
Gregor Mathers. In contrast to Yeats, who 'wished for some
system of thought which would leave my imagination free to
create as it would', these 'fellow students' were 'looking for
spiritual happiness & without any practical aim for some form
of unknown power'.[46] If Yeats felt that he had a 'different

object' from that of these once 'intimate friends', how much more estranged must he have felt from the Felkin circle?[47]

But he continued to listen to Miss Stoddart, though he was not an active participant, being, I think, 'Wound in mind's pondering'.[48] On 18 March she sent him the copy of another memorandum from Miss Felkin. The tone of Miss Stoddart's letter makes clear that Yeats was no longer well informed about the continuing struggle or even the people occupying some of the offices. 'Herewith Q.A. again!' she began. 'This I am quite sure has been drawn up & typed by Mr. Heazell one of the Chiefs!! ... We are no longer Ruling Chiefs to the S.M. only of the A.T. (Amoun Temple)! I am also quite sure that the Priests Fr. Fitzgerald, Mr. Hamerton & Mr. Heazell are the instigators along with Dr. Dickson & possibly L.O.E.'[49]

Miss Felkin's memorandum 'To the Three Ruling Chiefs of A.T.' (dated 17 March) emphasises 'two points which were raised at the meeting on March 14th'. First, she insists that 'while the Temple is closed' she can work only with the Chiefs who 'are co-operating with the whole O[rder] thro' F.R.'s Link' – that is, with the Third Order. Therefore, she implies, she cannot give Miss Stoddart an introduction to the Continental Centre. Also, she proposes to call a meeting to determine the loyalty of all members, and she demands access to the papers of the Order – in particular, the list of members and their addresses, the Sun 'Master M.S.S.' and 'F.R.'s personal papers left in the safe'. Second, she points out that although Felkin's expulsion of Miss Stoddart was suspended until after the meeting of 14 March to allow her an opportunity to state her case, it is still in effect, and she therefore has no authority to retain office. Miss Felkin concludes with a request of the Three Chiefs for a vote of the members to determine whether or not 'a majority of them support I.F.C. in her action'. Yeats surely must have been reminded of Mathers's expulsion of Miss Horniman twenty-five years before. But times had changed: Mathers did not wait for a vote, and his decree was accepted, on the surface at least, by all the members.

Miss Stoddart was probably correct in her evaluation of Miss Felkin's motivation: 'They are determined to get rid of me & I am afraid they wish to stop investigation & know that the Continental Centre is an unknown quantity not easily proved'. She was aware also that Miss Felkin had been soliciting votes from most of the members, who knew little 'about the Constitution', according to Miss Stoddart. 'There are', she continued, 'no personal papers of F.R.'s in the safe unless she means the Anna Sprengel letters'. She is referring to an attempt he had been making in 1910 and 1912 to authenticate the Sprengel letters supposedly written to Westcott.[50] Miss Stoddart assumes that Miss Felkin 'probably wishes to cover up F.R.'s mistake about her [Anna Sprengel]'.

The remainder of the letter is concerned with Miss Stoddart's attempt to ascertain whether or not 'F.R. has the authority he claims'. She had asked a recently admitted member named H. Collison, who had 'joined the Stella Matutina with a watching brief from Steiner',[51] to ask Steiner about the 'supposed Continental Centre' as well as the qualifications of the Felkins as occultists. Collison's 'Notes',[52] which I will mention again, illustrate the kind of irrelevant arguments which must have convinced Yeats that he should leave the Stella Matutina. 'It almost looks'', Miss Stoddart concluded her letter of 18 March, 'as if he [F.R.] had again been deceived'. Yeats may have wondered at this stage who and how many were being deceived.

Three days later (on 21 March 1921) she wrote to Yeats again, ostensibly to send four pages of Tarot divinations she had completed the day before but also to continue the discussion of troubles in the Order, hers in particular. She referred again to Miss Felkin's memorandum, which 'is full of indefinite statements & no bed-rock facts. It is in fact an abrogation of the intellect & a call to "Faith"'. She informed Yeats also of a report of the meeting (on 14 March) which Heazell had made to Hammond, who apparently was not present. Describing Heazell's report as 'incorrect in parts & completely Felkinite', she pointed out his mistakes: (1) he said that she had spoken of 'the solar influence (& *because solar therefore evil*)'; (2) he said that she had 'no supporters except Mr. Yeats & possibly Mrs. Yeats'; (3) he implied that she was 'the obstructionist by persistently refusing to resign'. 'Dr. Dickson', she said, 'made an earnest appeal for peace and unity'. But Hammond wanted her to resign, and he looked so worried that she was feeling 'cruel-hearted' in being stubborn. 'If I were to resign', she added, 'I would resign my office under F.R. I would

not resign from the Order as it does not belong to F.R.' She
was willing to give up 'F.R. & his teachings' because she had
decided that he had no real authority. She had shown Collison's
notes to Hammond, who was 'too upset to appreciate them',
and she told Yeats to 'keep those I sent to you'. Although Miss
Stoddart was obviously disturbed, she assured Yeats that she
did not 'think we need worry in the matter', then added, pro-
phetically: 'I believe the whole thing is going to be broken
up ... & I would hold the properties until they paid me my
dues'. She may be referring to the fact that the Order had been
using her home at 56 Redcliffe Gardens as a meeting place since
the closing of the Amoun Temple in 1919.

Her prophecy about the break-up of the Order was based
on Tarot divinations. Although those enclosed for Nemo had
been prepared only the day before (on 20 March), she had
apparently been making them successfully for some months:
'All my Tarots have worked out during this time of trouble
altho' sometimes at the moment I did not always read them
aright or quite understand them'. She was confident, therefore,
in offering the Yeatses her 'Tarots' on 'What is to happen
to various people during the next 3 months in connection with
the Order'. Mrs Yeats is strangely absent from her list of
divinations, but most of the principals in the controversy of
recent months and one for the Order as a whole were included.
All but three of the people were identified by the initials of
their mottoes, in the following order: I.F.C. (Miss Stoddart),
Fr Fitzgerald, Q.A. (Miss Felkin), Dr Dickson, D.E.D.I. (Yeats),
A.B.S. (Ara Ben Shemesh), Q.L. (Mrs Felkin), L.O.E. (Miss
Hughes), F.R. (Felkin), Dr Hammond, Order. Two brief notes
are interesting: at the conclusion of her own Tarot Miss Stoddart wrote, 'Compare this with D.E.D.I.'s'; beside the one for
the Order she wrote, 'I think this means foolish actions'. At
the end of the Tarots she appended her predictions, the most
important of which appears to be based on an observation by
Yeats:

From other Tarots I have done & these I come to this conclusion.
    Very shortly some terrible trouble will take place in the
Bristol Temple (L.O.E.); the evil will appear there with re-

doubled force. F.R. will I think probably die – success will be abandoned – by L.O.E. & those supporting her & possibly the whole Order practically broken up. It also looks as if some final decision would be arrived at, probably for reconstruction, about the latter end of June. Very few will be left; probably all the Priests will resign & Dr. Hammond.

If this is true, then it is what you told me two years ago, 'That this trouble was permitted so that the Order might be purified & only the earnest students left to carry on.' It is very curious.

It is in character, I think, for Yeats to have made such a prediction about good coming out of evil. His continued membership in the Order despite quibbling over doctrinal differences, struggles for power, and numerous splits is nothing short of remarkable. Tending always to champion the underdog, he was the peacemaker and recognised seer almost from the beginning, after 1900 certainly. Although there is every reason to believe that he might have made such an optimistic statement to Miss Stoddart 'two years earlier' (that is, in 1919), he must have had doubts about both people and issues in the 'war' of 1921.

He must have declined her plea for his active participation almost at once. She wrote again on 29 March 1921.

Very many thanks for your letter. I quite agree with both yours & Nemo's decisions. The Turban & carpet slippers would finish you both I am quite sure. F.R. likes such things & what they represent & evil powers find them useful.

Miss Stoddart had considered organising a new branch. The Yeatses apparently had discouraged further fragmentation, and she agreed 'that we cannot split members & properties & so form a new Order'. Recalling the advice from Yeats she had quoted in her last letter, Miss Stoddart observed that 'nothing but a second deluge will do any good. We want a clean new Order & new members with F.R.'s and all Felkin influence out of it. A complete break up & fresh soil'. Without Yeats's letters to her we cannot, of course, know precisely what he advised. He had apparently suggested patience: 'As you say', she wrote, 'we must await developments & passive resistance is the best game until Q.A. leaves'. But Miss Stoddart was restless, not having 'heard from Dr. Hammond for nearly a fortnight'. In the meantime, however, she had asked Mr Sandrieux, 'a cultured man & a business man',[53] 'to talk matters over' with Hammond, who had gained 'more confidence' by the conversation. To strengthen Hammond's courage, she had also asked Sandrieux 'to try & get Collison to write out certain of Steiner's statements giving date & place of interview & signing it as witness'. The remainder of the letter rehashes old issues: the question of Felkin's 'authority as sole Head in Gt. Britain' and the authenticity of 'M.S.S. received by E.O.L. in 1910'.[54] She assured Yeats, who had no doubt been fearful over her mental condition, that she was 'in a more philosophic frame of mind now & do not intend to let anything they may say or do upset me'. Yeats was probably amused or concerned or both, when she added: 'tho' I may be justly angry & do a bit of swearing if necessary'. She promised in conclusion to let him 'know if any further developments arise' and offered the flattering observation that 'your fine philosophy would be lost on the great majority of the present members; it is a philosophy for thinking men & women not for blind followers of the blind'. By this time surely Yeats must have agreed that the blind were in control.

Four days later (on 2 April 1921) Miss Stoddart wrote again, to report that Sandriuex had seen Collison, who had promised, 'after much persuasion', to make a signed statement 'giving details of his conversation with Steiner in Holland'. Collison had insisted, however, that 'the previous notes' (Appendix U) be destroyed because he wanted to omit the 'personal references' to the Felkins. Miss Stoddart asked Yeats to return the notes and promised to send him a copy of Collison's statement. He did not return the notes, and she may not have sent him a copy of the statement. If she did, Yeats did not preserve it with her correspondence, as he probably would have. Fortunately, Howe discovered a copy of the statement in the form of a letter to Sandrieux dated 8 May 1921. According to Collison, Felkin had attended one of Steiner's ceremonies in Munich and had received instruction but no grades; Steiner had refused to make Felkin his 'sole representative in England'; Steiner had warned that 'self-deception is very possible' 'under the old form of clairvoyance' practised by Felkin's group; Steiner had observed ironically that 'the Order is decorative and useful to those who need it and are able to distinguish between mere ornament and reality'.[55] About this time, according to Howe, who does not cite the source of his information, Yeats suggested to Miss Stoddart that she write to Edouard Shuré, the author of *Les grands initiés*, for information about Anna Sprengel. Shuré informed Sandrieux (in a letter dated 8 August 1921) that he had 'never heard of Miss Anna Sprengel, supposed to have died in 1893'.[56]

On 15 April 1921 Miss Stoddart wrote to inform Yeats that Miss Felkin had called a meeting of the Second Order at Dickson's house for 23 April. She had issued a plebiscite asking for votes, and had threatened the Order if they 'did not obey her demands at once'. Miss Stoddart and her allies held that the proposed meeting and plebiscite were unconstitutional. She also reported that she had seen Collison, who reported that Steiner had said 'to send over *any* sensible person with whom he could talk the matter over & he would give them advice'. 'Up to date', Collison added, 'no sensible person had been sent'. Miss Felkin had apparently made two unsatisfactory journeys, and now informed the Order that 'it was definitely settled that Dr. Dickson was to go abroad & receive instruction (& no one else) so as to enable him to grapple with the chaos in the Order'. They may have questioned Dickson's capacity to bring order out of chaos, but they had no doubt that chaos existed.

Although Yeats was a patient man, he was surely bored by this time hearing the same issues and details repeatedly discussed. But he must have been interested in news of an old fellow student. Miss Stoddart reported that 'Dr. Hammond saw Wynn Westcott & had a talk. He agrees very much with us & advises us to hold on & give up nothing. He seems to think that Dr. Dickson is backing Q.A. possibly as a means to an end later on!'

Again Yeats responded quickly. Six days later (on 21 April), Miss Stoddart wrote a hurried note to him which opens with 'Many thanks for your letter'. Her object was to send him 'a copy of the Plebiscite' and inform him that she had refused 'to address & forward [the forms] to various members one being to you'. Both the meeting and the plebiscite, she insisted again, were unconstitutional. She added in a postscript that 'Q.A.

sails 5th May I hear tho' not from her'.

The enclosed copy (in Miss Stoddart's hand) of the notice was headed 'Private & Confidential for Present Inner Members only'.[57] It invited members to 'attend if possible: if quite impossible a reply to Dr. Dickson marked personal indicating the course favoured by yourself is desired'. The members were informed that 'the matters to be decided are whether' they support the rebel Chiefs, support F.R., or want a deputation to investigate his authority.

Miss Stoddart's copy was probably sent to Yeats on Thursday. By the time he received it, most likely, the meeting had already been held. On Saturday, 23 April, at 3 p.m., twelve members met at the home of Dickson to decide the future of the Amoun Temple. Ten other members who could not attend expressed 'their sympathy with the objects of the Meeting'. Yeats was, I think, neither present nor in sympathy, but he probably did receive copies of a ballot and an explanatory statement which Miss Felkin and some few of the twelve present had perhaps already seen. The ballot at least they must have come prepared to distribute.[58] Both sheets are marked 'Strictly Private', and the ballot, headed 'Saint George's Day: 23rd April, 1921', proposed a resolution in support of Felkin and listed four alternative courses of action which all Inner Members were to be offered. In brief the choices were these: (1) 'to continue ... under the Constitution drawn up by F.R.'; (2) 'to follow the lead of certain other Members or Ex-Members, independently and without the farther ... co-operation of F.R.'; (3) 'to go into abeyance for a period of one, two, or three years'; (4) 'to resign' and 'return all ... Order Manuscripts, Papers, Implements, etc.'

The explanatory statement accompanying the resolution and choices was authenticated by the motto initials of three members of a committee 'appointed to carry out the wishes of the Meeting': F.F.J. (Dickson), S.S. (Brodie-Innes), and V.Q.S.V. (Mrs Macrae). The committee was charged to 'discuss, and if necessary investigate, the Continental source of F.R.'s authority and teaching – making use of the introductions granted by him for that purpose'. The intent of that charge was to meet the objections of Miss Stoddart, though she was excluded from the continental delegation and obviously would have remained dissatisfied. In conclusion, hoping to allay suspicion and gathering doubts, the committee attempted to reassure the rebels:

> Its members earnestly desire the 'SUMMUM BONUM' – the Greatest Good of the greatest number; and they wish to avoid any such reproach as is embodied in the words: – 'Ye have taken away the key of knowledge: ye entered not in yourselves, and them that were entering in, ye hindered'.

They also invited 'any alternative and helpful suggestions ... either on the lines indicated, or in any other direction'.

But the Stella Matutina was now thoroughly divided. When Miss Stoddart wrote next to Yeats, on 10 May 1921, Miss Felkin had departed, and her 'little group is not feeling quite sure of its position'. Miss Stoddart speaks of 'the other side', and suggests that some people are uncertain which side to choose. Among the vacillators was Heazell, one of the Chiefs. Although Hammond and Miss Stoddart were planning to draw up a 'short statement to be sent out to all Inner Members', they wanted to know Heazell's attitude before revealing their strategy. They were willing to ask the 'Higher Grade members' for advice, but 'the acting must be done thro' the Ruling Chiefs'. In effect, they were opposed to action by the committee. In the meantime, Miss Stoddart was eager to circumvent the opposition: 'As soon as possible after hearing from Mr. Heazell', she informed Yeats, 'I will get the meeting arranged for the Chiefs, yourself & Mr. Sandrieux'. At this time clearly Yeats was still an important member of the Inner Order.

Whether or not this meeting ever occurred I cannot discover. Yeats was away from Oxford most of the summer – at Shillingford from April to June, at Thame until September,[59] then back at Oxford for the winter. Little apparently transpired in the affairs of Amoun during the summer. On 18 November 1921 Miss Stoddart wrote a long and informative letter to Yeats, intending apparently to summarise the events of recent months. She had just received a letter from Hammond with a draft of the statement to members she had mentioned in her letter of 10 May. Yeats had been working behind the scene. Miss Stoddart told him that the note had been 'drawn up from suggestions made by you'. She had postponed writing to Yeats until she could get the statement written out for Hammond's signature. 'I am', she said, 'sending it out to all Inners & Outers, 67 in all & all had to be written by hand. I sent them off to Dr. Hammond this morning & as soon as he returns them I will send them out'.

Although I have not been able to locate a copy of this statement, it is clear from Miss Stoddart's comments that Yeats had tried to heal the breach. 'As you have worded it', she said,

> there is nothing I cannot accept for altho' I hold that F.R. & Q.L. got in touch with something besides Steiner still I believe it was neither genuine nor safe & had nothing to do with us. It is a great relief to me that our position has been so clearly defined – they won't like the "mystification" – I haven't said much but it has been no easy or pleasant position for me – the scapegoat has many a time longed to do a bit of butting – but I knew the game was rather to watch, wait & will. However I feel that our patience with Dr. Hammond has not been useless. When I started to write out the copies there was for a short time decided opposition which however disappeared as I quickly ignored it & continued writing.

In the meantime, Miss Stoddart had heard from Miss Imrie that she had seen Yeats and shown him a copy of a 'letter sent out by Mrs. Vir [?] Jones to the Outers'.[60] Unfortunately, I have not seen this letter, which may have prompted Yeats to urge Hammond to action: 'I am very glad you went along to him', Miss Stoddart said, 'for I couldn't get him to move'. Fearful that sending details 'to the members would be unwise', she was confident 'now that the short statement is being sent out' that they could 'ignore F.R. as he has ignored us'.

During these months of accusation and quarrel the ordinary business of the Stella Matutina must have stood still. The properties of the Order were in the home of Miss Stoddart, who held them on the technicality that she should receive rent ('not that I want it'): 'The opposition say that I am holding on to the properties, as if I had stolen them! & they can't get the Order restarted'. 'Dr. Dickson', she informed Yeats, 'had appealed to Brodie-Innes to help him (to get the papers & properties) against us but B.I. refused to have anything to do with the matter'.

In the meantime, Miss Stoddart continued her 'Investigations into the Foundations of the Order'. As a result of her urging, Sandrieux had inquired of Vigilate (Mrs Helen Rand), whose memories of 'early Order matters ... were largely a confirmation of what I already knew or suspected'. In fact, of course, Miss Stoddart was merely seeking confirmation of conclusions she had arrived at months before. Although she told Yeats that she would 'try & enclose a copy' of Mrs Rand's observations, she apparently did not. Miss Stoddart was persistent in her search for the 'truth'. She asked Sandrieux to 'try to get some information' from Mrs Mathers, who had returned to London after MacGregor's death (20 November 1918), and suggested to Yeats that he inquire of Miss Horniman ('I suppose you never come across her now?').

Many members were restless that no business was being conducted in the Order. 'Mr. Bennett who is now Dean of Chester has written to me', Miss Stoddart informed Yeats: 'It may be that like many others he is disappointed that nothing has been done'. Mrs Erskine was also disturbed at the inactivity, and 'the Edin[burgh] people (three only) are getting restive wondering why nothing is being done & wanting a branch Temple of their own'. Amen Ra was apparently closed; Brodie-Innes and Dickson had transferred to Amoun. Collison and the Hunts, who are mentioned here for the first time, had also 'drawn away', and it seemed to Miss Stoddart 'more than time a statement should be sent out'. She was pessimistic but determined to pursue her course:

> Whatever may eventually happen I mean to hold on & investigate in every possible way giving the Order every possible chance before finally deciding. Honestly I don't see much hope for it but I am certain we are being helped by some strong good forces.

A month later (on 17 December 1921) Miss Stoddart revealed for the first time in the correspondence Yeats preserved her conception of the evil forces opposing them. She thanked Yeats for some clippings on the 'Jewish Peril', a subject about which she was to become, if she were not already, completely obsessed:

I knew about them and I am afraid I used the word "Protocol" without due consideration for I really referred to the articles in the Morning Post (2 I think) on the Illuminati & kindred Secret Orders, also to the chapter on Illuminism in Mrs. Webster's "World revolution." The Jewish Peril I don't refer to for the "Illuminati" did not encourage Jews & only admitted them by special permission. We I believe have a few if any Jews among our members & the Cipher M.S.S. evidently fear Jesuits for in it we find 'Avoid Roman Catholics but with pity.'"[61]

In the next paragraph Miss Stoddart quotes Weishaupt, the founder of the secret society known as the Illuminati, to illustrate the lack of faith she has in 'the messages etc. which have come thro, supposedly from our Superiors': 'One must speak sometimes one way, sometimes in another, so that our real purpose should remain impenetrable to our inferiors'.[62] 'It was', she confided to Yeats, 'only when it was almost too late to draw back that I suspected the truth'. The truth, as she outlined it, was that the Second Order was to become the centre of a vast network of subversive activities. With the Amoun Temple as the parent organisation, the movement was to develop first in London and then spread over the world. She expected 'a number of inspired messengers (of Light)' to appear in London and 'lead the people'. Before this could happen, however, 'much had to be done in the Vault & among the members preparing them in some way – more initiations probably!'[63] If she had not thought all this so serious to herself and her associates, she wrote, 'I would have said it was all futile & foolish mummery'. Obviously about to break down from a serious persecution complex, she confided to Yeats that she had 'received a last frantic message from the "Brethren" saying that if I did not choose to walk by the path appointed I would have to ascend the Mountain thro' much suffering & tribulation!' She was aware, of course, that her vague fears would not convince the members: 'We have to stick to the dry hard material facts & of these we have few. Indeed it is the lack of these facts that is one of the weak points of the Order & its foundations'. By this time, I imagine, most of her colleagues would have agreed that there were few facts to support her wild conclusions. She was also aware, apparently, that even Yeats's patience was wearing thin: 'I won't say any more', she wrote in conclusion, 'as you must be pretty fed up with it all'.

At this point she shifted completely to say how much she was enjoying *Four Plays for Dancers*. She had seen *At the Hawk's Well*, she compared *The Dreaming of the Bones* and *The Only Jealousy of Emer* to 'beautifully set dream jewels', but she could not 'yet quite grasp' *Calvary* and 'must think it over'. In the context of my discussion the brief concluding paragraph – her last words to Yeats so far as I know – is especially significant:

> I am, as always, deeply interested in your "Phases of the Moon." I suppose by the "Robartes Papers" you mean your philosophy. I too with the Old Arab worship more "His Chance" than "His Choice."

It is not surprising, of course, that an occultist like Miss Stoddart should have had some insight into the meaning of the developing cosmic myth which was to become *A Vision*, though we could wish to know what 'Robartes papers' she had seen in December 1921. If she is recalling the 'learned Indian' of 'All Souls' Night' who discourses on 'Chance and Choice' in 'the soul's journey', the fusion with the 'Old Arab' is suggestive. She may have seen in him a literary portrait of Ara Ben Shemesh, Felkin's Arab teacher; and she was obviously convinced that Yeats had found a persona in Robartes. One could wish that she had commented further on the occult symbolism and philosophy she apparently recognised in *Four Plays for Dancers, The Wild Swans at Coole, Michael Robartes and the Dancer*, and *Four Years*, three of which were published in 1921. Since Miss Stoddart would have known, for example, that 'we ought as far as we can to seek the correspondences to our own planet throughout nature both on the material and astral planes', she would not have been astounded or even surprised at a poem like 'The Cat and the Moon', which follows 'The Phases of the Moon' in *The Wild Swans*. She might even have known that Mrs Felkin's 'animal is the cat – whose dilating pupils correspond to the waxing and waning moon', and she probably recalled that Yeats's 'alternative symbol would obviously be the Lamp of the Kerux',[64] disguised in 'The Phases' as 'The lonely light that Samuel Palmer engraved'. At any rate, she clearly enjoyed recognising allusions to teachings of the Second Order in the art of her strongest supporter during a time of tribulation.

Unfortunately, there are no further letters from Miss Stoddart in the Yeats papers. We can assume, I think, that matters continued to get worse in the Second Order, and that her paranoia was increasingly aggravated. She wrote to Hammond on 5 April 1922 that 'the history of the Order consists of a long series of mystifications, the one following and overlapping the other'.[65] On 15 June she issued her 'Investigations into the Foundations of the Order and the Source of Its Teachings'.[66] 'On the same day', according to Howe, 'she compiled a list of the names and addresses of the forty-five people who were members of the Stella Matutina's Second Order'.[67] Although she named Yeats as 'Imperator', I can find no evidence that he was actively participating in the administration of the badly fragmented Order.

I have not found the date of his formal resignation, if indeed he offered one; but he must have given up any significant connection in 1922. During the spring he gave up the house at Oxford and settled in Dublin, having purchased a home at 82 Merrion Square in February. During 1921 and 1922 he had been engaged in the composition of *The Trembling of the Veil*, Book I of which contains the well-known portrait of his old friend Mathers.[68] Moina Mathers was greatly incensed when she discovered Yeats's book: 'I have read your "Trembling of the Veil"', she wrote on 5 January 1924. 'I had expected some kind of a shock, but not quite such a violent one as I have received'. Quoting from memory apparently, she objected to 'the passage relating to our War prognostications' and to the statements that *'he was to die of melancholia'* and that he was *'self-educated, unscholarly, though learned'*. In fact, Yeats said that 'Mathers had learning but no scholarship, much imagination and imperfect taste....'[69] She accused Yeats of implying that Mathers's 'influence on your group as well as on his entourage generally was pernicious'. If so, she continued, 'why did you *in our recent conversations* propose to send me certain of your following to be taught in S.R.'s school' (my italics). This observation is, I think, significant: it suggests that the Stella Matutina was definitely defunct by the end of 1923 if Yeats had proposed to send certain of his 'following to be taught' in some other school, particularly in her version of the Golden Dawn, which she called Alpha and Omega when it was organised by her and Brodie-Innes.[70] Mrs Mathers assured Yeats that 'every portion of the A.O. (G.D.) curriculum ... has come to us directly or indirectly through S.R.M.D....' There is another minor but interesting point to be made. In the Dedication 'To Vestigia' of *A Vision* (1925) Yeats stated that 'when the first draft of this dedication was written, I had not seen you for more than thirty years, nor knew where you were nor what you were doing....'[71] If he were being precise, as he usually was, he had already written the Dedication before the 'recent conversations' (no later than 1923) mentioned in her letter.

Clearly, at any rate, they had renewed an old friendship which, Moina said, 'this awful book of yours' has destroyed: 'I can never meet you again or be connected with you in any way save you make such reparation as may lie in your power'. Yeats wrote to her on 8 January, in a letter I have not seen, offering to make amends. She replied on 12 January that she would 'go through your book carefully ... noting the few passages that I think can be altered without disturbing your character study in any fundamental way'. She asked also for the name of a friend who must have been named as the cause of 'this misunderstanding' about Mathers's melancholia. She insisted that his 'superb mental work' had 'reached its height on the day of his death in 1918'. Obviously appeased by Yeats's concessions, she closed with a reference to 'the pleasure I had in meeting you again. I suppose I was so pleased to see you that the past for the moment had receded'.

On 4 February she thanked him for a letter of 28 January and suggested that she would like to discuss the 'few notes' she had made on *The Trembling of the Veil* 'with you personally' if he were coming to London soon. She offered also 'to go into the G.D. matter that has been under so much discussion, though a certain portion must remain private to yourself, for the present'. She was grateful to him for 'writing to me as you have done', and expressed the hope that he could meet some of

Mathers's 'friends & pupils of recent years'. Whether or not Yeats travelled to London for these discussions I do not know. Since he was in Dublin and 'just returning to work on *A Vision*', as he wrote to Edmund Dulac on 28 January,[72] Moina's offer to discuss Golden Dawn matters may have been prompted by a request from him. When she wrote to him next, on 24 June 1926, it was in reply to a request from him about Sapiens Dominabitur Astris (Anna Sprengel). Yeats noted at the top of this letter : 'Answered, to be kept with Mathers letters if found'. Some weeks later (on 14 July) Moina wrote again about S.D.A., this time offering to 'look up my husband's papers bearing on your citation from one of his letters'. Yeats may have been quoting Mathers's letter of 16 February 1900 in which he had written to Mrs Emery that ' "Sapiens dominabitur astris" is now in Paris, and aiding me with the Isis movement'.[73] Mathers is referring here to Mme Horos, who, according to Moina, 'we never believed in ... for one moment'. Moreover, she added in the letter of 14 July, Mathers did not believe in either the German S.D.A. (Anna Sprengel) or the American S.D.A. (Mme Horos), though he did consider Mme Horos 'a learned adept and reputable person'. 'I have answered this matter as well as can be done in a few words', she concluded, 'and I hope that you have now understood'. So ends Yeats's correspondence with the clairvoyant and talented Moina Bergson Mathers, whose 'beauty' and 'learning' and 'mysterious gifts were held by all in affection' when Yeats and his fellow students 'met nearly forty years ago in London and in Paris to discuss mystical philosophy'.[74]

Why Yeats was inquiring about Mathers's opinion of the authenticity of either Anna Sprengel or the pretender is not easy to determine. It is possible, though unlikely I think, that Miss Stoddart had appealed to her friend Yeats, as she had in November 1921, for assistance in obtaining information from old Order members still in London. It is much more likely that he merely wanted the truth. Having recently completed *A Vision* and the revised *Autobiographies* with its long note on 'The Hermetic Students' and an altered sketch of Mathers, he must have had the Golden Dawn much on his mind. The note on 'The Hermetic Students' makes clear that Yeats had been inquiring about the origin of the Order from Moina Mathers, 'the only survivor from that time', and that he was giving 'these few facts' with her permission. However, he continued,

> ... I have not submitted to her my account of her husband because I did not think it right to ask her either to condemn or to accept my statements. She was shocked at the account in the first edition, and apart from one or two errors of fact I have omitted nothing of it, though I have added new passages.[75]

A minor but interesting change was made in the observation about Mathers's education: from 'Mathers had learning but no scholarship' to 'Mathers had much learning but little scholarship'.[76] A much more important change was an addition about 'a Society which sometimes called itself – it had a different name among its members – "The Hermetic Students"'. 'I was', Yeats recalled, 'initiated into that Society in a Charlotte Street studio, and being at a most receptive age, shaped and isolated'. He described Mathers as 'a born teacher and organiser. One of those who incite – less by spoken word than by what they are – imaginative action'. He was 'generous of time and thought'.[77] That, essentially, was Yeats's concession to Moina.

Talking in 1926 like one who had been long away from active participation in the Order, Yeats defended the authenticity and the substance of the rituals, then added: 'I do not know what I would think if I were to hear them now for the first time, for I cannot judge what moved me in my youth'.[78] Although he had now disengaged himself, it is important to keep in mind that Yeats never disavowed the Hermetic Order of the Golden Dawn (or its successors by changed titles), that in fact he remained steadfastly convinced it was the only satisfactory religious Order in his experience. Basing its symbolism and ritual upon the metaphysical assumption that 'things below are as things above' and its system of Degrees on the Cabbalistic tree of life, the Golden Dawn offered an ideal resolution to a visionary artist who conceived the phenomenal world as merely symbolic of the invisible or real world. Although he apparently resigned or withdrew in 1922,[79] Yeats continued to live and create by the cosmic faith expressed in the doctrines of the Golden Dawn. The concluding lines of his explanatory note in *Autobiographies* suggest Yeats's sadness over leaving an Order continually disrupted by the fantasies of the psychotic and the quarrels of the power-mad:

> All creation is from conflict, whether with our own mind or with that of others, and the historian who dreams of bloodless victory, wrongs the wounded veterans. My connection with the 'Hermetic Students' ended amid quarrels caused by men, otherwise worthy, who claimed a Rosicrucian sanction for their own fantasies, and I add to prevent needless correspondence that I am not now a member of a Cabbalistic Society.[80]

He had endured more than his share of conflict – some in his own mind surely – as well as fantasies and quarrels. Over a long period of time – from 1890 to 1922 certainly – he had been called upon consistently to resolve the squabbles and reorganise the chapters. The memorandum of 23 April 1921 may have been the last straw. Although it is hard to imagine Yeats resigning after staying through so many upheavals, he may have decided that he had reached the limit of endurance; or he may have accepted an 'abeyance' which extended to the end of his life rather than the one, two, or three years suggested in the memorandum; or he may have believed, as he had suggested to Miss Stoddart in 1919, that 'the earnest students [would] carry on'.

Or more likely perhaps, he decided simply that the Order had served its purpose, that he had learned from it all he could, and that he was no longer obligated to teach his friends what he knew of symbolic truth. At any rate, he thought the time had come to set the record in order, and he had been engaged on the mythopoeic history of his religious quest for many months: *A Vision* contains the essence of his reading in, thinking about, and experimenting with 'mystical philosophy' for a period of 'nearly forty years', as he suggests in the Dedication. Although this is not the place for a detailed explanation or defence of that assumption, it should be remembered that the Dedication is addressed 'To Vestigia' and the Epilogue is 'All Soul's Night',[81] which was written in 1920, two years after Mathers's death while Yeats was still involved in the affairs of Stella Matutina. All the people mentioned in both Dedication and Epilogue had been members of the Golden Dawn. Besides Moina Mathers in the Dedication there are Florence Farr Emery, W. T. Horton, Allan Bennett, and 'a learned brass-founder ... who visited us occasionally'.[82] In 'All Souls' Night' Horton and Mrs Emery share the spotlight with Mathers, who also appears in a rejected passage of the Dedication. Among the manuscript materials of *A Vision* are a draft of an Epilogue 'To Vestigia' and two considerably different versions of the Dedication. It is, I suggest, important to note the great care Yeats took not only to 'enshrine my old chums in a decent edifice' (the words are Conrad's) but also to inform Vestigia that *A Vision* is his continuing effort 'to prolong or to amend conversations that took place before our five-and-twentieth year'. Even more explicit perhaps is the observation that 'this book has been written because a number of young men and women, you and I among the number, met nearly forty years ago in London and in Paris to discuss mystical philosophy'. 'Though much had happened', he continued, 'since we copied the Jewish Schemahamphorasch with its seventy-two Names of God in Hebrew characters, it was plain that I must dedicate my book to you'.[83] As he looks back to 'that phantasy' of their early study, he has now decided that it 'did not explain the world to our intellects which were after all very modern, but it recalled certain forgotten methods of meditation and chiefly how so to suspend the will that the mind became automatic, a possible vehicle for spiritual beings'.[84] In the typescript copy Yeats ended Part I of the Dedication at this point, then added a significant sentence in the galley proofs: 'It carried us to what we had learned to call Hodos Chameliontos'.[85] These sound like the words of a man who is justifying or explaining some important judgements or decisions of the past. If indeed Yeats resigned from the Order in 1922 or became inactive, his change in status may very well have stimulated him to complete the book that was in effect an outgrowth of his visionary meditation on the mystical philosophy of the Golden Dawn. Many, perhaps most, of his 'old fellow students' had been searching for 'some form of unknown power', whereas he was searching for symbols and ways of thought that would enable him to create 'the one history, and that the soul's'.[86] These words are reminiscent of an observation about Mathers in the note, perhaps written about this time, on 'The Hermetic Students': 'Though he did not show me the truth, he did what he professed, and showed me a way to it, and I am grateful....'[87]

Yeats was, of course, first and always a creator and not simply an occultist, a theologian, a historian, or a philosopher, though he was a complex combination of all these. His vision was necessarily symbolic and must be projected in the concreteness of the art object. As he explained apologetically, *A Vision* was, therefore, intended for two groups: those who have 'some interest in my poetry' and 'my old fellow students'. 'If they will master what is most abstract there and make it the foundation of their visions, the curtain may ring up on a new drama'.[88] The prophetic tone of the Dedication makes clear that when he finished the typescript and signed it 'W.B.Y. Capri February 1925', he was looking back on a thirty-five year period as though it were a closed chapter in his life. *A Vision* is a monument to that greatly exciting time; it records a turning point in his life. Although he believed that he might have written an immeasurably richer book in another year and indeed expected 'someday [to] complete what I have begun', he felt compelled to 'put it out of reach' so he could 'write the poetry it seems to have made possible'.[89]

He was a little sad, I suspect, and more than a little nostalgic as he reviewed the golden years of the Rosicrucian quest, but he had no serious regrets. By the time he recorded the 'moments of exaltation' he had experienced in writing 'All Souls' Night', he had forgiven the bickerings and quarrels among his 'old fellow students' 'who claimed a Rosicrucian sanction for their own fantasies'.[90] He had forgiven because they seemed in retrospect to have served a necessary though not always clear function. Nevertheless, they had shown him the way to truth. As he reviewed the whole of his experience, therefore, he understood that names and personalities were insignificant parts of the cosmic plan:

> But names are nothing. What matter who it be,
> So that his elements have grown so fine
> The fume of muscatel
> Can give his sharpened palate ecstasy
> No living man can drink from the whole wine.[91]

As he wandered in ecstatic delight along the cliff-side at Capri, he envisioned all the past as part of a whole completed to February 1925. Even the 'worst part of life', those awful months from April 1900 to February 1901, became a part of the cosmic process; and he could murmur, as he had 'countless times': 'I have been part of it always and there is maybe no escape, forgetting and returning life after life like an insect in the roots of the grass'.[92] What better tribute could be offered to the memory of his old friends among 'The Hermetic Students'?

Epilogue

Unfortunately, as Yeats might have expected of a book about his esoteric philosophy, 'the splash' of *A Vision* was 'very far off and very faint', like that of stones he had dropped into 'a certain very deep well' as a child.[1] By March 1926 only AE and Frank Pearce Sturm had responded at all.[2] Almost as soon as he finished *A Vision*, Yeats began planning a revised and much different version. Having learned in the Golden Dawn that 'much of the confusion of modern philosophy ... comes from our renouncing the ancient hierarchy of beings from man up to the One', he 'dream[ed] of doing nothing but mystical philosophy and poetry'.[3] In particular, he read Plotinus in the translation of his friend Stephen MacKenna. The point is that he read and thought about 'mystical philosophy' for the remainder of his life. Although he told Lady Gregory in April 1928 that he was 'at work on the final version of *A Vision*',[4] he continued to revise and expand it until October 1937,[5] only fifteen months before his death.

After March 1922 Yeats was in London for short visits only, and he made no attempt to keep in touch with 'old fellow students' of the Second Order, but he heard from or came in brief contact with some few who ought to be mentioned. After the exchange of letters with Moina Mathers, Yeats may not have kept up a correspondence with any Adepti of the early days. In November 1923 he had received a letter from Charles Rosher (Aequo Animo)[6] congratulating him on the Nobel Prize Award. Rosher spoke of 'the days when we used to meet' and asked in a postscript, 'Is your friend Pollexfen still going?' He obviously had not seen Yeats for many years and apparently knew little of affairs in the Second Order. He informed Yeats that he was starting a review, to be called *The Pharos*, 'a *popular* Hibbert – dealing with Philosophies, Religions, Art, Literature, Music, Hygiene, Ancient Wisdom & Modern Outlook'; and he took 'the liberty to enclose a few MSS. of verse' for Yeats's criticism. If Aleister Crowley's judgement that Rosher 'wrote some of the worst poetry I have ever read'[7] was sound, Yeats may have been too embarrassed to respond to his old friend's request for 'criticism, pro or con'. In fact, Yeats did not indicate on the letter, as he frequently did, that he had answered it.

Several years later, in a letter to Olivia Shakespear (dated 13 October 1929) Yeats spoke of a trip 'to the west of England to look up a little group of Kabalists'. He refers no doubt to the Hermes Temple in Bristol, which he must have been invited to visit. Fifteen months later he received a letter (dated 25 January 1931) from a Frater of Hermes, E. Yarrow Jones (Taot'an), who had written to him at the suggestion of Miss C. E. Hughes, an original Chief of the Temple: 'L.O.E. . . . tells me that you wished to know of any dream or vision of an arrow being shot at a deer'.[8] The remainder of Jones's letter is an account of his vision, which had occurred while he was being helped 'to accomplish a Tattwa' by L.O.E. and F.E.T.:[9] Yeats must have been especially excited at the description of 'a Blake-like figure of the Ancient of Days leaning out from heaven & drawing a bow in the direction of a dappled stag'. Jones informed Yeats in a postscript that he had received his address from Edmund Dulac, whose 'present state of nervous & bodily prostration' almost 'completely incapacitated' him. A minor artist and illustrator himself,[10] Jones reminded Yeats that Dulac had taken him 'once or twice to see you & Ezra Pound' – some time in the past obviously.

In the letter of 13 October Yeats informed Olivia that he had one other obligation in England besides the visit to Hermes: '. . . I must meet an old Kabalist in London and must accept his date for lunch or dinner – a sign that the great work is almost finished and that I want to give it to the right people. In private life he [is], I think, a Hegelian professor – how surprised his pupils would be'.[11] The almost finished great work is, I assume, *A Vision*.

Yeats had planned to arrive in London on 23 October for a visit of three weeks. During the time, however, he caught a very bad cold, became seriously ill, and was forced to postpone the departure for Rapallo.[12] A stranger in London now, he turned for medical advice and assistance to an old friend from the Stella Matutina, Dr W. E. Carnegie Dickson. Having X-rayed Yeats's chest and prescribed medicine for him, Dickson urged Yeats 'to follow the rather careful life' he and a medical colleague thought best – or necessary – for him. 'My dear Frater', Dickson wrote on 12 November 1929, 'I had a good long talk with Mrs Yeats this afternoon, as to regimen and treatment, and I am very glad that you have such a capable "better half" to look after you!' The old friends had apparently found time to talk about the past. 'When you are quite fit again, I shall look forward to having another gossip with you on the matters in which we are mutually interested – if not before you go abroad, certainly after you come back from Italy.' Dickson made it clear that he would not accept fees from ' "Brethren", either Masonic or otherwise',[13] and suggested instead that Yeats should 'send me one or two of your books with a not too formal inscription of your "kind regards" on the fly-leaf!'

Dickson corresponded with the Yeatses in January, perhaps about his health; and he wrote again on 3 March 1930 to find 'how things went with you'. But the real object of his letter, addressed to both Yeatses, was something far more momentous. Dickson and his wife had been asked to help consecrate a 'Meditation Room' in an Anglican vicarage in the north of London. When he entered the room, Dickson had 'a very curious surprise experience! … there, sitting at the east end of it, as an altar, was the old I.U.T.P…s [Isis-Urania Temple Pastos], with Vesty's paintings on it all complete!!!' The vicar explained to his astounded guest that it had been given to him by Mrs Helen Rand (Vigilate) when she died the year before. 'You will remember', Dickson reminded the Yeatses, 'that the old properties had been stored at Whiteby's [?] in Mrs. F's [Felkin's?] name – & that, when she died suddenly, they were transferred to the names of V. [Mrs Rand] and M.W.Th. [M. W. Blackden], who then became adherents of S.R. [A. E. Waite], & these between them annexed & carried them off from their rightful owners'.[14] It is indeed surprising to find that many of the properties had remained all those years with Waite, who 'regarded the Golden Dawn as capable of a mystical instead of an occult construction',[15] and in effect denied the magical tradition. 'When S.R.'s group "bust up" ', Dickson wrote, most of the properties were consigned to the incinerator – the old G. D. Library was sold ... – but V. stored the P. ...s and, as I say, left it to my friend the parson in whose meditation room it is now reposing as an altar! To-day he has written me a letter making it over to me – so it has come back after many adventures & vicissitudes to the faithful remnant of the old group! Without our seeking it! I hope it is a symbol of renewed life & activity & *harmony* in the old order.

With these sentiments Yeats would no doubt have agreed, though he must have been sceptical, after all the crises he had participated in, that 'renewed life & activity & *harmony*' were possible. We would like to know, of course, whether or not 'the faithful remnant of the old group' had maintained an active organisation in London[16] and whether or not Yeats had remained in contact with it.

He must have been a little sad to be reminded how 'The old order changeth, yielding place to new', though he understood that 'God fulfills Himself in many ways'.[17] But he must have been pleased, perhaps even thought it symbolic, that Dickson should also have found in the vicar's Meditation Room 'a copy of your "A Vision", which I promptly borrowed from him & am now reading with interest. I remember hearing of its coming out at the time', he added, then apologised for not having purchased a copy, and concluded : '... so this is the first time I have seen the book – and, as I say, I am much interested therein – including the dedication!' Although Yeats was no doubt delighted that a member of the Order had discovered his visionary odyssey of 'The Way of the Soul between the Sun and the Moon', he was perhaps no longer so optimistic as he had been in 1925 that 'if they will master what is most abstract there and make it the foundation of their visions, the curtain may ring up on a new drama'.[18] More likely, I think, from the perspective of his 'mountain top about five miles from Rapallo',[19] he imagined that the curtain was coming down. And he surely agreed with the valedictory observation of his old fellow student that 'It's a funny world'.

Notes

CHAPTER I

1. Quoted in 'The Pathway', *The Collected Works of William Butler Yeats* (Stratford-on-Avon, 1908) VIII, 192. Hereafter cited as *Collected Works*.

2. Ibid., VIII, 191.

3. Allan Wade, *A Bibliography of the Writings of W. B. Yeats* (London: Rupert Hart-Davis, 1968) p. 358. Hereafter cited as *Bibliography*.

The article, as it appeared in *The Speaker*, was called 'The Way of Wisdom', a somewhat more descriptive title than 'The Pathway', which it became in 1908.

4. For the sake of convenience I plan to use the generic title Golden Dawn throughout this study unless it is important to draw attention to significant changes or distinctions for gradation in the name.

5. *The Permanence of Yeats* (New York: Collier Books, 1961) pp. 311, 309. A more recent example is Harold Bloom's comprehensive study *Yeats* (New York: Oxford University Press, 1970), which has no entry for Golden Dawn, Rosicrucianism, or Theosophical Society in the index.

6. *The Letters of W. B. Yeats*, ed. Allan Wade (New York: Macmillan, 1955) p. 211. Hereafter cited as *Letters*.

7. Ibid., p. 210.

8. *Collected Works*, VIII, 191.

9. Ernest Boyd, *Ireland's Literary Renaissance* (London, 1923) pp. 213-14. Boyd considers the foundation of the Dublin Lodge of the Theosophical Society in 1885 as important to the Renaissance as 'the publication of Standish O'Grady's *History of Ireland*, the two events being complementary to any complete understanding of the literature of the Revival' (pp. 241-15).

10. Richard Ellmann, *Yeats: The Man and the Masks* (New York: Macmillan, 1948) p. 41. Hereafter cited as Ellmann.

11. Ibid., pp. 42-4.

12. During 1885 and 1886 several of Yeats's Indian and Arcadian poems as well as three poetic dramas appeared in *The Dublin University Review*. Their subject matter and atmosphere were influenced by his studies in theosophy and other esoterica. (See *Bibliography*, pp. 19-22, for details of publication.)

Johnston's article appeared in the issue for July 1885 (pp. 144-6). The source of most, if not all, of Johnston's information in Sinnett's *Esoteric*

Buddhism, especially Chapter II, 'The Constitution of Man'.

13. *Collected Works*, VIII, 191.

14. Ibid., VIII, 196.

15. Ibid. In 'The Way of Wisdom', the early version, this sentence read: 'nor am I quite certain that any among us has quite awoke out of the dreams he brought among us'. (Quoted in Harbans Rai Bachchan, *W. B. Yeats and Occultism* [Delhi: Motilal Banarsidass, 1965], p. 33); Bachchan concludes that the revision represents a 'change' in Yeats's thinking that 'had taken twenty-four years' (pp. 33-4), but makes no attempt to analyse the change.

16. Ibid.

17. Edward Maitland, *Anna Kingsford: Her Life, Letters, Diary, and Work* (London, 1913) II, 185-7. Hereafter cited as Maitland, this two-volume monument to a strange and unusual woman illuminates the struggle between two factions of the Theosophical Society and many related groups and sects. First published in 1896 by John M. Watkins, a member of the Golden Dawn, the book was no doubt well known to Yeats, as were other books by Maitland and Mrs Kingsford.

18. Ibid., II, 188. Maitland's or Mrs Kingsford's italics.

19. Ibid., II, 257-8.

20. *Autobiographies* (London: Macmillan, 1956) p. 173. The Society for Psychical Research had sent Richard Hodgson to India in June 1885 to investigate reports that Mme Blavatsky was a fraud. Johnston was in the audience when Hodgson denounced her after his return to London, according to Ellmann, who concludes that Yeats did not join the Theosophical Society because he was 'shaken by Hodgson's charges' (p. 62).

21. Ibid., p. 174.

22. See Denis Donoghue (ed.), *W. B. Yeats Memoirs* (London: Macmillan, 1972) p. 281. Appendix A is a complete transcription of 'Occult Notes and Diary, Etc.', now in the National Library of Ireland, MSS. 13570. The 'Occult Notes' are also in Ellmann (pp. 65-7) with slight differences.

23. Maitland, II, 153.

24. Ibid., II, 154.

25. Donoghue, p. 281.

26. Maitland, II, 147.

27. Donoghue, p. 281. Yeats listed four alternative explanations of the Masters: '(1) They are probably living occultists, as HPB says, (2) They are possibly unconscious dramatizations of HPB's own trance nature, (3) They are also possibly but not likely, as the mediums assert, spirits, (4) They may be the trance principle of nature expressing itself symbolically' (p. 281). Yeats refers to this diary entry in *Autobiographies*, p. 186.

28. Ibid., p. 282.

29. Ibid. Ellmann transcribes 'renewed' as 'reviewed'.

30. *Letters*, p. 137.

31. Ibid., p. 150.

32. Ibid.

33. *Autobiographies*, p. 181.

34. Ibid., pp. 181-2.

35. Ibid., p. 182.

36. Ibid. This part of *Autobiographies* was first published as *Four Years* (Dublin: Cuala Press, 1921).

37. Ellic Howe, *The Magicians of the Golden Dawn: A Documentary History of a Magical Order 1887-1923* (London: Routledge and Kegan Paul, 1972) p. 55n.

38. Donoghue, p. 282.

39. *Letters*, p. 236. Wade's note outlines briefly the basis of the quarrel between Judge and Mrs Besant.

40. Yeats preserved the printed invitation requesting him to be present for initiation into the 'Order of the G. D. in the Outer. Isis-Urania Temple, No. 3', at 17 Fitzroy St. on 'Friday the 7th day of Mar. 1890'. The information in the first set of quotation marks is printed at the top of the form and followed by the mottoes and offices of the three Chiefs: V. H. Frater Magna Est Veritas, 5=6, Imperator. V. H. Frater Sapere Aude, 5=6, Praemonstrator. V. H. Frater S'Rioghail Mo Dhream, 5=6, Cancellarius. These three – W. R. Woodman (who died in 1891), Westcott, and Mathers (usually identified as Deo Duce Comite Ferro) – organised the Isis-Urania Temple. Although the warrant for its founding is undated, it is supposed to have been signed on 1 March 1888. According to a letter from Ellic Howe, 'the source for this information is a postcard from Westcott to Dr R. W. Felkin dated 5 April 1912'. Felkin became Chief in 1901.

At the bottom of Yeats's invitation a pen-note in Mathers's hand instructed him to 'ask for M. Mathers & the Hermetic Students' meeting'. Some twenty-nine years later, probably when he pasted the invitation in the back of a notebook devoted to Golden Dawn matters, Yeats wrote: 'My admission W. B. Yeats Dec 28 1919'.

41. *Autobiographies*, p. 183.

42. Maitland, II, 186-7.

43. Ibid., II, 257-8. Mohini Chatterji lectured in the same series.

44. The year before Mrs Kingsford's death, when she was already quite ill, Mathers dedicated his translation of *The Kabbalah Unveiled* (1887) to her and Edward Maitland: 'I have much pleasure in dedicating this work to the authors of *The Perfect Way*, as they have in that excellent and wonderful book touched so much on the doctrines of the Kabala, and laid such value on its teachings. *The Perfect Way* is one of the most deeply occult works that has been written for centuries' (quoted in Maitland, II, 169). In the Preface to *Esoteric Buddhism* (1883), A. P. Sinnett had paid a similar tribute to the authors of 'a remarkable book published within the last year or two, "The Perfect Way" ... as showing how more roads than one may lead to a mountain top'.

45. See Howe, especially pp. 34-44, and Francis King, *Ritual Magic in England 1887 to the Present Day* (London: Neville Spearman, 1970) pp. 39-46.

46. This brief account of twenty-four typed pages is dated June 1922. If not an active member at this date, Yeats obviously was still interested

in the affairs of the Order. See Chapter 9 for further details about the termination of his membership. The copy of 'Investigations' I am quoting here is signed by Il Faut Chercher (Christina Mary Stoddart), about whom I will speak later. See Appendix U.

47. See Howe, pp. 1-25, King, pp. 193-4, and Arthur Edward Waite, *Shadows of Life and Thought* (London: Selwyn and Blount, 1938) pp. 218-19, for further details about the Cypher MSS. and for conjectures about their origin.

48. V.O.V. and S.A. are initials of mottoes for membership in the Golden Dawn. For many of these identifications I am indebted to Geralde Yorke, whose typescript of 'Key Mottoes of Members of the Hermetic Society of the Golden Dawn' relates mottoes to names and to temples in the Order. Still others are identified in Howe's *Magicians of the Golden Dawn*, to which my study is also deeply indebted. Mr Howe has read portions of my manuscript and generously responded to numerous inquiries. Since I have included as many names and mottoes as I can identify in Appendix X, I have thought it superfluous to repeat them frequently in the text.

49. See Howe, pp. 26-33, for details.

50. See 'Suspect Documents', Howe, pp. 1-25, for a careful evaluation of the discovery and use of the Cypher MSS. The title of the chapter indicates Howe's conclusion. He suggests that 'Soror S.D.A. was a mythical person' invented by Westcott (p. 7).

51. See Howe, Plate IV, facing p. 21.

52. Since I must refer frequently to these grades or degrees, I will explain them briefly here. Although Golden Dawn became the generic term for the entire structure, it referred at first to the five degrees of the First or Outer Order: $0°=0°$ (Neophyte), $1°=10°$ (Zelator), $2°=9°$ (Theoricus), $3°=8°$ (Practicus), $4°=7°$ (Philosophus). The Second or Inner Order (to become known as Ordo Rosae Rubeae et Aureae Crucis) contained three degrees: $5°=6°$ (Adeptus Minor), $6°=5°$ (Adeptus Major), $7°=4°$ (Adeptus Exemptus). The Third Order, ruled by the Secret Chiefs, also contained three degrees: $8°=3°$ (Magister Templi), $9°=2°$ (Magus), $10°=1°$ (Ipsissimus). (Hereafter, for the sake of convenience, I will omit the symbol for degree.) As Howe has pointed out (p. 16), all these degrees except $0=0$ and $10=1$ correspond to degrees in the Societas Rosicruciana. They also correspond to Cabbalistic branches or regions on the Sephirothic Tree of Life. (See Virginia Moore, *The Unicorn: William Butler Yeats' Search for Reality* [New York: Macmillan, 1954] p. 134, for a useful discussion of these and other symbolic correspondences in the degrees.)

53. I have reproductions of two manuscripts of this lecture: one, copied by Frederick Leigh Gardner, is in the library of Gerald Yorke; the other, copied by George Pollexfen, is in the library of Senator Michael B. Yeats. Both mention the death of Mme Blavatsky (1831-91), and are obviously revisions of the original. Since both copies I have consulted identify Westcott as Q.S.N. (Quod Scis Nescis), his motto initials in the Societas Rosicruciana which appeared on the Warrant,

he perhaps had not yet chosen a new motto. If so, it may have been written almost immediately after the founding of the Isis-Urania Temple.

54. I am quoting from a copy of the Pollexfen MS.

55. One, 'Pernelle the wife and fellow worker of Nicholas Flamel', was especially interesting to Yeats. He headed a section of *The Green Helmet and Other Poems* (Dublin: The Cuala Press, 1910) 'Raymond Lully and His Wife Pernella', then called attention to 'AN ERROR' by means of an erratum slip: 'By a slip of the pen when I was writing out the heading for the first group of poems, I put Raymond Lully's name in the room of the later Alchemist, Nicolas Flamel' (Wade, *Bibliography*, p. 96). Since Maud Gonne is the subject of all eight poems in this section, it is clear that Yeats was drawing a symbolic analogy between himself and Flamel, Maud and Pernella. During the months when these poems were written Yeats and Maud underwent a series of mystical visions (from June 1908 to January 1909). These experiences, which he referred to as a 'spiritual marriage', were recorded in an unpublished notebook opening with 'At Paris with P.I.A.L.' (see Moore, pp. 197-8). P.I.A.L. stands for Per Ignem Ad Lucem.

56. See notes 17 and 44.

57. The thought that the achievement of *summum bonum* was possible appealed to Yeats. He used the phrase three times in contexts which suggest that he was remembering its significance in the 'Historic Lecture'. In *The Speckled Bird*, Yeats's unfinished novel, a character modelled on MacGregor Mathers criticises the protagonist, modelled on Yeats: 'I have come to recognize that you are not a magician, but some kind of artist, and that the *summum bonum* itself, the potable gold of our masters, [is] less to you than some charm of colour, or some charm of words.' (I am indebted to William H. O'Donnell for bringing this to my attention. His forthcoming edition of *The Speckled Bird* (Dublin: Cuala Press, 1974) will be especially useful to students and scholars interested in Yeats's occult investigations.) From this direct allusion to alchemical teachings of the Golden Dawn, Yeats extended the symbolic significance of the *summum bonum* to accommodate his own theories of philosophy and art. In the Dedication 'To Vestigia' of *A Vision* (1925) Yeats maintained that the members of the Golden Dawn 'differed from ordinary students of philosophy or religion through our belief that truth cannot be discovered but may be revealed', and he illustrated his point by reference to a 'learned brassfounder' who 'was convinced that there was a certain moment in every year which, once known, brought with it 'The Summum Bonum, the Stone of the Wise' (pp. x-xi). Six years later in the Introduction to *The Words upon the Window-pane* he used the phrase to describe the difference between Berkeley's thought and Spinoza's: 'Berkeley's declaration, modified later, that physical pleasure is the *Summum Bonum*, Heaven's sole reality, his countertruth to that of Spinoza'. (*The Variorum Edition of the Plays of W. B. Yeats*, ed. Russell K. Alspach [New York: Macmillan, 1966] p. 965.) The distinction Yeats is drawing similar to that being made in the

'Historic Lecture' between the concretion of 'our own Hermetic Society of the GD' and the abstraction of 'the Eastern School of Theosophy and occultism'.

58. See Francis King, *Astral Projection, Ritual Magic and Alchemy* (London: Neville Spearman, 1971) pp. 91-6, for the entire text and 'Supplementary Notes'. This lecture is Flying Roll No. XVI. Students of the Golden Dawn will be grateful to King for publishing the Flying Rolls. Unfortunately, he included only twenty of the thirty-six in the 'Catalogue of Flying Rolls'.

59. Ibid., p. 92.

60. (London, 1887) pp. 64-196. Waite wrote on the title page that his history was 'founded on their own manifestoes, and on facts and documents collected from the writings of initiated brethren', but he did not become a member until January 1891 (Howe, p. 71).

61. King, *Astral Projection*, p. 94.

62. Ibid., p. 95.

63. Howe, p. 49. These figures include the membership of four temples in England (Isis-Urania, Osiris at Weston-super-Mare, Horus at Bradford, Amen Ra at Edinburgh) and, after 1894, Mathers's temple in Paris (Ahathoor). Howe has prepared a very convenient table showing the initiations from 1888 until 1896.

64. Howe, p. 34.

65. So Moina Mathers wrote in July 1926 in the Preface to a new edition of *The Kabbalah Unveiled* (London: Routledge and Kegan Paul, 1954) p. xiii.

66. By his own account in a letter to F. L. Gardner (dated 17 March 1897), Westcott was forced to resign his position in the Golden Dawn when 'state officers' discovered that he 'was a prominent official of a society in which I had been foolishly posturing as one possessed of magical powers – and that if this became more public it would not do for a Coroner of the Crown to be made shame of in such a mad way. So I had no alternative' (Howe, p. 165).

67. *The Kabbalah Unveiled*, p. ix. See also Howe, p. 170.

CHAPTER 2

1. Howe, p. 127.

2. Ibid., p. 133. According to a section on 'The Hidden and Secret Chiefs' in the typescript of Miss Stoddart's 'Investigations', Mrs Mathers received the teachings of the Secret Chiefs in a manner reminiscent of that by which Mrs Yeats received the automatic script which became the source material for *A Vision*:

These teachings were built up by D.D.C.F. from instruction received clairvoyantly by Vestigia (Mrs. M.) from certain Powers calling themselves 'THE HIDDEN AND SECRET CHIEFS' and believed by D.D.C.F.

to be our THIRD ORDER. These Chiefs we are told on good authority before giving further teachings demanded of D.D.C.F. and Vestigia an obligation swearing absolute faith and belief in these Chiefs and the teachings and instructions that were to be given by them. Only on these conditions would the teachings be given. Vestigia did not wish to take this obligation but she was over ruled and complied.

3. Ibid., p. 132.

4. Ibid., p. 134.

5. Ibid., p. 135.

6. That is, 'Care et Very Honored Soror Fortiter et Recte'.

7. That is, Sapere Aude (Westcott), Levavi Oculos (Percy W. Bullock), Sapientia Sapienti Dono Data (Mrs Florence Farr Emery), Resurgam (Dr Berridge), Anima Pura Sit (Dr Henry Pullen Burry), Vigilate (Mrs Helen Rand), Non Sine Numine (Col James Webber Smith), Sub Spe (J. W. Brodie -Innes), and Shemeber (Mrs Pamela Carden Bullock). For the sake of consistency I have capitalised all mottoes throughout this study unless they are uncapitalised in quotations.

8. I am indebted to the Library of the Warburg Institute for permission to quote from this letter to Miss Horniman in the extensive collection of books, manuscripts, journals and letters of the Aleister Crowley papers. Unfortunately, this magnificent collection of occult materials, chiefly by and about Crowley and his circle, is not yet catalogued. Howe also quotes the letter with some omissions and slight changes (pp. 135-6).

9. Howe, pp. 137-8.

10. According to Ellic Howe (in a letter to me dated 10 July 1971), 'Annie Horniman terminated her financial allowance to Mathers in July 1896 with a final payment of £75'. (I am much indebted to Mr Howe for many factual details including several identifications of Order members.) An unpublished letter from Gerald J. Yorke to Allan Wade (dated 15 November 1951) observes that 'she was making him an allowance of (I believe) some £420 a year'. (All students of the Golden Dawn are deeply indebted to Yorke, who is perhaps the best-informed living authority on the Order.)

11. See Chapter 1, note 40.

12. *Autobiographies*, p. 184.

13. *Memoirs*, p. 281.

14. *Letters*, p. 297.

15. Ibid., p. 298. See also *Autobiographies*, pp. 335-6, for Yeats's recollections of Mathers in Paris: 'At night he would dress himself in Highland dress, and dance the sword dance, and his mind brooded upon the ramifications of clans and tartans. Yet I have at moments doubted whether he had seen the Highlands, or even, until invited there by some White Rose Society, Scotland itself.' In 1900 when Mathers sent Crowley to London as his envoy, he too wore a highland costume.

An extended passage in the *Autobiographies* (pp. 335-42) appears to be a record of several vivid experiences during a visit to Paris in

April-May 1898. Although Yeats, as usual in the *Autobiographies*, gives no dates, he speaks of being 'eager for news of the Spanish-American war' at a time when he was 'under [Mathers's] roof' (p. 338). The war broke out in April.

16. When Yeats wrote 'a first rough draft of Memoirs made in 1916-17', he was very tolerant of Mathers's weaknesses and eccentricities: 'I found him a gay, companionable man, very learned in his own subject, but [without] the standards of a scholar' (*Memoirs*, pp. 19n, 74). Some years later, after Mathers's death (in 1918), Yeats's evaluation was much harsher in *The Trembling of the Veil* (London: T. Werner Laurie, 1922): 'Mathers had learning but no scholarship, much imagination and imperfect taste, but if he made some absurd statement, some incredible claim, some hackneyed joke, we would half consciously change claim, statement or joke, as though he were a figure in a play of our composition' (p. 73). In 1926, as a result of an exchange of letters with Mrs Mathers, Yeats altered the first sentence to read 'Mathers had much learning but little scholarship' (*Autobiographies*, p. 187), and included a long note 'about the origin of "The Hermetic Students" with Mrs. Mathers's permission, but I have not submitted to her my account of her husband because I did not think it right to ask her either to condemn or to accept my statements. She was shocked at the account in the first edition ...' (*Autobiographies*, p. 576).

He was in fact recalling her very words: 'I have read your "Trembling of the Veil" ', she wrote on 5 January 1924. 'I had expected some kind of shock, but not quite such a violent one as I have received....' See Chapter 9 for further details.

17. *Letters*, p. 210. See also pp. 208-9.

18. Ibid., p. 230.

19. Yeats and Maud's project for a Celtic Castle of Heroes has, of course, been frequently discussed (e.g. in Ellmann, pp. 120 ff.), and details need not be repeated here. Yeats dreamed of making the Castle in Lough Key 'an Irish Eleusis or Samothrace'. In part at least as a result of years in occult societies, he felt 'the need of mystical rites – a ritual system of evocation and meditation.... I meant', he wrote in the 'Autobiography', 'to initiate young men and women in this worship, which would unite the radical truths of Christianity to those of a more ancient world, and to use the Castle Rock for their occasional retirement from the world.... My own seership was, I thought, inadequate; it was to be Maud Gonne's work and mine. Perhaps that was why we had been thrown together. Were there not strange harmonies amid discord?' (*Memoirs*, pp. 123-4). Although Maud was to be his chief help, Yeats sought to involve several others in the development of the Celtic Mysteries, notably George Pollexfen, George Russell, William Sharp (or his alter ego, Fiona Macleod), the Matherses and several of Yeats's intimate friends in the Golden Dawn, notably Miss Horniman, Mary Briggs, and Mr and Mrs E. A. Hunter (see numerous references in *Letters*, pp. 293-300).

Yeats was, I think, most preoccupied with his project during 1897 and 1898. During those months he corresponded with Moina Mathers, who was enlisting the aid of people in Paris, especially an editor named Bailly. (An unpublished letter from Moina to Yeats dated 16 March 1897 observes that Bailly 'is very anxious to communicate with you on the Celtic Religious movement.... He says that the whole nearly of the french press are ready to help in this matter'.) Among the Yeats papers is preserved a record of three most unusual experiences concerned with his Celtic mysteries. The first, headed 'Celtic Vision: Explorations', is dated 29 December 1897. With D.E.D.I. as 'Conductor', a group of six Fratres and Sorores of the Golden Dawn embarked upon a visionary journey 'to get the talismatic shape of the Gods done' (*Letters*, p. 265). Yeats and his colleagues achieved this end by calling the names of various Celtic heroes and gods who gave different signs when their names were called. Mary Briggs (Per Mare Ad Astra), the recorder, drew sketches of them as they presented themselves to the group. The records of two other visionary Explorations (both in January 1898) are preserved, and there is some indication in the letters and in unpublished notebooks that many others were conducted.

More significant perhaps is a considerable body of miscellaneous material now deposited in the National Library of Ireland. These papers (140 pages by my count) are chiefly drafts of rituals for the Celtic Mysteries. Some parts are typed with occasional revisions in Miss Horniman's hand. A large number of the manuscript pages are also in her hand, some in Yeats's, some in Mary Briggs's, and a few in a hand I cannot identify. Several pages devoted to descriptions of Irish divinities are in the same hand as the recorder of the Celtic Visions of December 1897 and January 1898. These descriptions are probably the result of the effort to visualise 'the talismatic shape of the Gods'. If so, Wade's date of '1896 or later' for the letter containing this phrase is perhaps wrong. Two chance dates among the papers suggest a later date for the work on the materials in the National Library. One note alludes to some activity with F L [Festina Lente, George Pollexfen] 'during year 1899'. Another records on 26 December 1898 that 'F L had a bad cold & felt ill fitted for divination'. These divinations are preserved elsewhere in the Yeats papers under the heading of 'Visions of Old Irish Mythology'. They were conducted in Sligo over a period stretching from 13 December 1898 to 8 February 1899. In the narrative for 13 December Yeats twice mentions having conducted similar experiments with PIAL (Maud) only a few days before.

20. *Letters*, p. 182. Yeats was no doubt responsible for her admission. According to a list of motto initials and names compiled by Gerald Yorke, she achieved the degree of 4=7, the highest degree in the Outer Order. The fact that she had not attained the degree of 5=6 perhaps explains why she was not present at Yeats's Celtic Explorations.

21. *A Servant of the Queen* (London: Victor Gollancz, 1938) pp. 259-60. Unfortunately, she does not record dates connected with her

experience in the Golden Dawn.

22. She refers to Mathers's translation of a French manuscript published as *The Book of the Sacred Magic of Abra-Melin the Mage, as delivered by Abraham the Jew unto his son Lamech, A.D. 1458* (1898). It was reprinted by the L. W. de Laurence Company, Chicago, in 1932, 1939, and 1948.

23. *Letters*, pp. 313-14.

24. '"Meditations upon Unknown Thought": Yeats's Break with MacGregor Mathers', *Yeats Studies*, No. 1 (1971) 175-202.

25. On 17 March 1897 Westcott wrote to F. L. Gardner that he was forced to resign 'owing to my having recd. an intimation that it had somehow become known to the State officers that I was a prominent official of a society in which I had been foolishly posturing as one possessed of magical powers – and that if this became more public it would not do for a Coroner of the Crown to be made shame of in such a mad way. So I had no alternative – I cannot think who it is that persecutes me – someone must talk'. Apparently, Mathers had betrayed him (see Howe, pp. 165-70).

26. See note 2.

27. See Appendix A for this and other letters and documents quoted here which bear directly upon the quarrel with Mathers. Sapiens Dominabitur Astris was Fräulein Anna Sprengel, Chief of Licht, Liebe, Leben Temple Number 1 of the Golden Dawn. A somewhat mysterious German woman whose name played an important part in the development of the Order, she probably died in 1893. In 1926, in answer to an inquiry from Yeats, Moina Mathers insisted that she and MacGregor did not consider S.D.A. a reliable person being 'convinced from the first that the M.S.S., as well as certain facts connected with the Order in her possession, had been obtained by illegal methods' (unpublished letter dated 14 July 1926). In fact, Mrs Mathers declared, 'This woman was an American and not a German' (letter dated 24 June 1926). Mathers was deceived for a time by a woman posing as S.D.A. I will return to this episode in a later chapter.

See Howe, especially Chapter 1 ('Suspect Documents') for a careful examination of the role of Fräulein Sprengel in the establishment of Isis-Urania: 'The myths perpetrated in the 'Historic Lecture for Neophytes' ... reinforce my contention that Soror S.D.A. and G.D.'s alleged German connection was invented by Westcott' (p. 25).

28. Although Howe's attempt 'to reconstruct how the Soror S.D.A. correspondence might have been produced' is highly conjectural, it is convincing (see pp. 13ff.).

29. Actually, he identified only nine in the letter of 3 December to Miss Horniman. See note 7.

30. See *Letters*, pp. 282-3, on the petition for her reinstatement. The letter to Gardner returning the petition was signed F.L. (Festina Lente). Both Gerald Yorke and Mrs Yeats informed Allan Wade that Festina Lente was Yeats's motto in the Outer Order, but it surely belonged to George Pollexfen. Yeats was visiting Pollexfen at the time of the return

of the petition to Gardner. According to Howe, there is no evidence that Yeats signed the petition. If not, he obviously abstained because he did not want to upset Mathers. Pollexfen would not have been similarly inhibited, and he probably signed at Yeats's urging. Also the correction at the end of the letter sounds more like Pollexfen than Yeats: 'Please note My address is simply Sligo and not Rosses Point'. The very next letter in Wade, written about the same time according to Yorke and mailed from Sligo, is signed D.E.D.I., not F.L., and directs Gardner to reply 'c/o Geo Pollexfen Sligo'. See Chapter 4, note 6.

According to an unpublished letter from Miss Horniman to Gardner (dated 23 November 1896), she had gone to Florence (apparently for an extended stay, as she was learning Italian), and had been replaced by Gardner as instructor of beginners in the Outer Order.

I am indebted to Gerald Yorke for permission to cite this letter and other papers in his possession concerning the Golden Dawn. Among the most important of these papers to this study is a record of a series of visionary experiments on the planets conducted by Gardner and Miss Horniman from 12 September to 3 December 1898. These experiments are very similar to the Celtic Explorations Yeats had been conducting only a few months before, and to the Divinations he was conducting in Sligo during December 1898.

The point is that although Miss Horniman had been expelled from the Order she was making use of its teachings to conduct symbolic experiments with her successor, who most likely continued to work for her reinstatement.

31. Crowley's own record of this encounter follows the main outlines of the Committee's report, though his emphasis and interpretation are, as might be expected, greatly different from theirs: 'My arrival in London as the envoy extraordinary and plenipotentiary of Mathers put the cat among the chickens. My identity was very soon discovered and a typhoon began to rage in the teacup. The rebels resorted to all sorts of lawless and violent acts, and spread the most stupidly scandalous stories, not only about me, but about the few others who remained loyal to Mathers.... To this day I cannot understand how people like W. B. Yeats should not have repressed such methods in the sternest way and insisted that the fight be fought with fair weapons.' (*The Confessions of Aleister Crowley: An Autohagiography* [London: Jonathan Cape, 1969] pp. 196-7. Hereafter cited as *Confessions*.) Crowley's account is unreliable but always entertaining. Compare also Howe, Chapter 15, 'The Battle for Blythe Road'. This account supplements my article cited in note 24, which also reproduces the letters quoted.

32. See *Confessions*, pp. 195-6, for further details about Crowley's recollections, including the list of questions that were to be asked of members of the Second Order.

33. *Letters*, p. 340. See also Howe, who points out that Crowley learned from Mrs Hunter in a letter dated 25 March 1900 that 'the Second Order in London did not recognize his recent $5°=6°$ initiation in Paris' (p. 208).

34. In a note appended to the first edition of *Autobiographies* (London: Macmillan, 1926), Yeats informed his readers that 'I am not now a member of a Cabbalistic Society' (p. 473).

CHAPTER 3

1. See Appendix B for the full text of this letter from SSDD to Sub Spe. See also Howe, pp. 250-1, for a paper on 'The Group as I knew it, and Fortiter'.

2. Yeats also listed dates of two other 'events for rectification'.

3. In 1898 or 1899 (Yeats was not quite sure of the date when he tried to recall exactly in later years) Yeats achieved an uneasy resolution of his desire for Maud in what he was to call their 'mystical marriage'. One of the unpublished 'Private' notebooks recording extended mystical experiences he shared with Maud in 1908 recalls on the opening page the spiritual marriage of some ten years before: 'June ———— at Paris with P I A L on Saturday evening (20th) she said something that blotted away the recent past & brought all back to the spiritual marriage of 1899. [8 appears to be written over the final 9.] On Sunday night we talked very plainly. She believed that this bond is to be recreated & to be the means of spiritual illumination between us. It is to be a bond of the spirit only & she lives – now on she said – for that & for her children.' (See Moore, p. 197, for a slightly different transcription and further comment.) On the following page, beside a letter of 26 June from Maud which is glued to the page in its envelope, Yeats noted: 'think meditation should be representative [?] of initiation in the coffin of Father Rosy Cross. Must work out relation between this & mystic marriage'. Another notebook records that he was 'much with M G over 98 celebration in summer of 1898' and tries to recall exact date of their spiritual union: '? date of Spiritual Marriage. It was in 99 certainly'. In fact, of course, Yeats's resignation was temporary, the fascination of Maud remaining strong until his marriage in October 1917.

4. *A Servant of the Queen*, p. 318.

5. Ibid., p. 319. During the night apparently MacBride planned a trip to America to seek funds from the Clan-na-gael, a militant organisation of Irish-Americans, for the resistance movement in Ireland. In a few weeks MacBride wrote to Maud urging her to come to America to help him. Her going no doubt had much to do with Yeats's unhappiness in early 1901. (See pp. 319-24 for Maud's account of the American tour with MacBride.)

6. Ibid., p. 308.

7. Ibid., pp. 328-9.

8. Ibid., pp. 329-30. According to Maud's record, Yeats implored her to marry him, to 'give up this tragic struggle and live a peaceful life'. She replied: 'Willie, are you not tired of asking that question? How

often have I told you to thank the gods that I will not marry you. You would not be happy with me.' When he replied 'I am not happy without you', she responded in words well known to most students of Yeats: 'Oh yes, you are, because you make beautiful poetry out of what you call your unhappiness and you are happy in that. Marriage would be such a dull affair. Poets should never marry. The world should thank me for not marrying you.' She was, of course, writing long after the fact; but there is no reason to doubt that she was essentially right about both his unhappiness and his making great art of it, as 'Adam's Curse' was to prove.

9. Ibid., p. 334.
10. Ibid., p. 323.
11. *Letters*, p. 352.
12. Moore, *Unicorn*, p. 134.
13. Quoted in Ellmann, p. 188.
14. *Letters*, pp. 339-40.
15. Ibid., p. 340.
16. Ibid., pp. 341-2.
17. Ibid., p. 342.
18. The 'Statement' consists of two printed sheets summarising the 'List of Documents' against Mathers and Crowley by the Committee of 7. Since the 'Statement' contains additional information about subsequent developments, it was obviously prepared and distributed after the 'List'.

19. The 'Statement' concludes with the following:

The Executive elected for the present year are:
Moderator, Sapientia Sapienti Dono Data
Scribe, Fortiter et Recte
Warden, Hora et Semper
Instructor in Divination, Vigilate
    „   *Clairvoyance*, Deo Date
    „   *Tarot & Chess*, Silentio
    „   *Ceremonial*, Ma Wahanu Thesi
    „   *Symbolism*, Aequo Animo
    „   *Mystical Philosophy*, Demon est Deus Inversus
    „   *General Instruction*, Dum Spiro Spero

These officers, in order of appearance, are Mrs Emery, Miss Horniman, E. A. Hunter, Mrs Helen Rand, Dorothea Hunter, Reena Fullham-Hughes, M. W. Blackden, Charles Rosher, Yeats, and Henrietta Paget.

20. *Letters*, p. 344.
21. Ibid., pp. 341-2.
22. Ibid., p. 346.
23. Ibid., p. 262n. According to Lady Gregory, a presentation of plays in London by the Irish National Theatre Society (in May 1903) prompted the support of the Theatre by Miss Horniman (*Our Irish Theatre* [New York: Capricorn Books, 1965] pp. 38-9). Lady Gregory

may not have been aware of Yeats's association with Miss Horniman in the Golden Dawn.

24. See Howe, Chapter 10, for an account of 'The Petition', including a list of signatories, those who refused to sign, and one 'On the fence' – Dr R. W. Felkin (pp. 143-4).

25. *Letters*, pp. 282-3. See also Chapter 2, note 30. When Miss Horniman petitioned to return to the Second Order on 26 April 1900, Yeats took credit for her reinstatement: 'With the unanimous consent of all the working members, though with much regret, as I knew that it would look like bad taste to invite the return of a member he had expelled, almost in the hour of S.R.M.D.'s own expulsion, I invited Soror Fortiter et Recte to return to the Order and to become its Scribe. We had all perfect confidence in her business capacity.' (See Appendix G for the full text of this open letter to the Second Order.)

26. See *Letters*, pp. 479, 490, 493, 499-500, 535, 542, 544. Her interest in the Abbey must have waned considerably with the opening of her Manchester Repertory Theatre on 25 September 1907. From the time of Yeats's refusal (in early 1908) to allow her to present his plays in England until the withdrawal of her support from the Abbey in 1910 their relations were somewhat strained. One sentence from an unpublished letter to Shaw will illustrate: 'Miss Horniman is quiet just now but I thought she was going to bring us to an end'. (From the papers of Senator Yeats, with whose permission it appears here.)

27. Unpublished letter (dated 27 February 1901) in Yeats papers addressed to 'Care et V.H. Fratres et Sorores'. This letter is signed by Fortiter Et Recte, Sub Spe, and Demon Est Deus Inversus.

28. Copy of unpublished letter (dated 17 January 1901) in Yeats papers. See Appendix B.

29. Compare remarks in Appendix C. This unpublished letter from Miss Horniman to F. L. Gardner written in Florence and dated 23 November 1896 (only eleven days before her expulsion by Mathers) suggests that Mrs Emery was even then proselytising among the members of the Order: 'What a time of it you must give S.S.D.D. She wants me to study Egyptian too, but I find one new language enough at a time and am hard at work at Italian'. Gardner was for many years a kind of Order librarian who instructed beginners. I am indebted to Gerald Yorke, through the kind offices of Miss Kathleen Raine, for a copy of the letter.

30. Some light is cast on her invitation by a passage in the Azoth Lecture prepared for aspirants taking the examination of the Degree 4=7: 'The symbol of Venus on the Tree of Life embraces the whole Sephiroth, and it is therefore the fitting Symbol of the Isis of Nature. Hence also its circle is always to be represented larger than that of Mercury – ♀ ☿'. I quote from a 'copy made by F. L.' (George Pollexfen) which had originally been 'Presented & copied by SSDD 5=6 Cancellaria'.

31. I refer to this unpublished letter in the Yeats papers with the permission of Senator Yeats.

Yeats's letter must have been written after Mrs Emery posted her notice in the Order rooms inviting those who had attained 'the grade of Theoricus'. If so, however, Yeats and Miss Horniman must not have seen the notice before his letter to Mrs Emery. On the other hand, she may have invited only the Theorici in the notice but have accepted or even sought Zelators in secret. Yeats most certainly had grounds for his accusations.

Through the kindness of John Kelly, who will edit a comprehensive collection of Yeats's letters for Oxford University Press, I have a transcript of this letter made by Wade but not included in his edition of the letters. Wade's suggested date of May 1900 is surely wrong. In the context of the great break of 1901, this letter is significant. The first part is in Miss Horniman's hand and marked 'copy' on the first page. Since the second part (about half) is in Yeats's hand and much of it scratched over, there is some doubt that it ever reached Mrs Emery. Yeats might have thought his threats and cajolery too blunt or obvious. Since, however, Yeats would not have sent a letter to Mrs Emery in Miss Horniman's hand, she may have been copying it for a typist, and the typewritten copy may have gone to Mrs Emery.

32. By 'theatrical project' Yeats may have had in mind the new direction he was planning for the Irish Literary Theatre. He and George Moore had finished *Diarmuid and Grania* in December 1900, and it was performed on 21 October 1901 with an English company. Yeats announced that this production was to be the last for the Irish Literary Theatre. He definitely had a new development in mind, and Moore was probably advising, as they were planning to collaborate on *Where There Is Nothing* (1902), but they quarrelled, and Moore was left out when the Irish National Theatre Society was formed in February 1903.

33. If we can judge correctly by Yeats's letters, the project of the New Irish Library did originate with him. He was perhaps justifiably indignant that it should have been carried out under the direction of Charles Gavan Duffy, T. W. Rolleston, and Douglas Hyde. See *Letters*, pp. 188, 200; *Autobiographies*, pp. 199-200, 224-8, 328; and *Memoirs*, pp. 81-5.

CHAPTER 4

1. *Bibliography*, p. 63.
2. *Letters*, pp. 402-3.
3. Ibid., p. 403.
4. See Appendix D. All quotations from 'The Scribe's Account of the Executive Difficulty' are from the typed copy, which follows the handwritten copy carefully. There are numerous revisions, including several attached insertions, in the long-hand version, preserved in the Yeats

papers, which apparently Yeats did not see before it was typed or he surely would have commented on some of them.

5. Ma Wahanu Thesi was Marcus Worsley Blackden. The typed copy consistently has *Wahaun* for *Wahanu*, suggesting that Miss Horniman did not do the typing. I have corrected typing errors throughout.

6. George Pollexfen died on 26 September 1910. In an upstairs room of his house in Sligo his niece Lily Yeats 'found neatly arranged the objects that symbolized his life', prominent among which were 'books on astrology, symbolism and such. His masonic orders all are there – and all in perfect order'. (See William M. Murphy, *The Yeats Family and the Pollexfens of Sligo* [Dublin: Dolmen, 1971] pp. 43-4.) Since two large notebooks of his horoscopic materials and many of the Golden Dawn instructional manuals and rituals Pollexfen had copied are now in the Yeats papers, I presume they are the materials described by Lily.

Also preserved in the Yeats papers is a strange account by an unnamed recorder of a kind of visionary quest for the dead Pollexfen. It is dated 1 October 1910 and set 'in the Temple, with Vault erected for the initiation of Frater F.F.J. [Fortes Fortuna Juvat, Dr George Dickson or his son Carnegie]'. According to the recorder, Frater F.R. [Fenime Respice, Dr Robert W. Felkin] told me of the Death of Frater F.L. and asked me if I would observe whether he was anywhere about in the Temple'. Not finding him in the Temple, the narrator 'asked to be told where he was'. He was directed to follow a bird which plunged downward obliquely through a large body of water and various dark passages. The narrator discovered Frater Festina Lente stretched out on a floor surrounded by 'members of the R.C. [Rosy Cross] Order'. After looking at him 'for a few minutes ... a voice said, "Do not disturb him – this is the best place for him, the Vault would not be suitable – he is resting – apart from earth vibrations – at the right time he will arise – but that time is not yet." So I left him', the narrator concludes, 'and returned to the Temple.' The date identifies F.L. almost certainly as Pollexfen. Yeats attended his funeral on 28 September and was in Dublin the following day (see *Letters*, pp. 552-3), so he might have been back in London on 1 October. But I assume that he did not participate in the visionary quest or his presence would have been noted by the recorder, to whom F.L. was 'personally unknown'. See Chapter 2, note 30.

7. It may be well to keep in mind the different steps (or Degrees) which the aspirant or candidate was obligated to climb on the 'ladder into heaven'. In addition to the grade of Neophyte (0=0) there were four grades in the Outer Order: 1=10 (Zelator), 2=9 (Theoricus), 3=8 (Practicus), 4=7 (Philosophus); three in the Inner Order: 5=6 (Adeptus Minor), 6=5 (Adeptus Major), 7=4 (Adeptus Exemptus); and three in the Invisible Order: 8=3 (Magister Templi), 9=2 (Magus), 10=0 (Ipsissimus). The last three were usually considered unattainable by any but the Secret Chiefs of the Order. See Howe, p. 16, and Moore, p. 134.

8. 'As he had plenty more to bring forward' was inserted as a revision, possibly an after-thought, in the manuscript.

9. The manuscript makes an interesting change: from 'putting a stop to an irregular initiation' to 'arranging properly a proposed irregular initiation'.

10. In the manuscript 'painfully' replaces 'terribly' and 'up in my mind.... on their behalf' is an insertion.

11. Deo Date was Mrs E. A. Hunter. She participated in two of Yeats's Celtic Explorations. See Chapter 2, note 19.

12. Too long for insertion on the crowded page, these lines are written on a small piece of paper, marked with an asterisk, and attached to the manuscript.

13. Yeats's only comment upon this unusual proceeding is 'cross examination continued'.

14. This observation and Mrs Emery's remark are on a separate slip of paper – an after-thought, apparently.

15. Someone, Yeats most likely, changed 'Tombs' in the typescript to 'Tomb'. The reference is to the symbolic tomb of Christian Rosenkreuz, a central object in most of the rituals.

16. After denial to admission to the Second Order, Crowley kept his motto (Perdurabo) and founded a similar secret order which he called Argenteum Astrum. As editor of its official organ, *The Equinox*, Crowley had an outlet for his own eccentric literary productions and for occasional vituperative comments about 'my crapulous contemporaries'. Yeats, of course, was one of these. Crowley gave his work an 'extended criticism' in *The Equinox* (Vol. i, no. ii, p. 307), and insisted that Yeats was jealous of his superiority as a poet. A 'black, bilious rage ... shook him to the soul', Crowley wrote years after their quarrel. 'What hurt him was the knowledge of his own incomparable inferiority'. Crowley described the members of the Second Order in London as 'an abject assemblage of nonentities', 'vulgar and commonplace'. With the exception of Mrs Emery, 'they were utterly undistinguished either for energy or capacity' (*Confessions*, pp. 165-6, 177).

17. Dr Berridge was a well-known but eccentric physician who was intensely loyal to Mathers. His quarrel with Miss Horniman in 1896 was at least partially responsible for her expulsion by Mathers (see King, *Ritual Magic*, pp. 52-3). In a libel case brought by George Cecil Jones against De Went Fenton (editor of *The Looking Glass*), Dr Berridge testified that he had warned Crowley, apparently in April 1900 when Crowley 'was over here as an envoy on official matters concerning the Order', that 'they accuse you of unnatural vice'. (Jean Overton Fuller, *The Magical Dilemma of Victor Neuburg* [London: W. H. Allen, 1965] pp. 184-5.) Writing about the trial in his *Confessions*, the incensed Crowley called Mathers 'a notorious rascal' and Berridge 'an ill-reputed doctor on the borders of quackery' (p. 642).

18. After the reorganisation in 1900, she was assigned the duty of instruction in Tarot and Chess.

19. Yeats marked through the *s*, inserted *was* above *were*, and observed in the margin that 'motion about groups then passed'.

20. Municipal Astronomer in Charge of the Observatory in Edinburgh and Imperator of the Amen Ra Temple in Edinburgh. He was also known as Veritas Et Lux. See Howe, p. 70n.

21. 6 February, I presume, since that is the date recorded at the end of the 'Account'.

22. In the margin Yeats wrote: 'discussion on elections at end of meeting'.

CHAPTER 5

1. See Appendix E. The handwriting is not Miss Horniman's.

2. I quote from typescripts of this and other unpublished open letters in the Yeats papers. I have changed some few spellings and marks of punctuation in these letters. Copies of these letters are also in Gerald Yorke's papers.

3. See Chapter 3, note 19, for further details. The new structure is outlined in 'R.R.A.C. in London. Second Order Bye-Laws', dated 1900 (Appendix N).

4. The source of Westcott's information is a basic document of Rosicrucianism, the well-known *Fama Fraternitatis*, which ends appropriately with 'Sub umbra alarum tuarum, Jehova'. The *Fama* was available in a book by a fellow member of the Order: A. E. Waite, *The Real History of the Rosicrucians* (London, 1887), pp. 64-84. In 1903, according to Francis King, Waite (Sacramentum Regis) and Blackden withdrew from the Second Order and set up their own temple, retaining the name of Isis-Urania (*Ritual Magic*, pp. 94-6). Although Waite was a member of the Second Order during the time of the troubles in 1900 and 1901, he did not apparently take an active part in the altercations.

A prolific writer and translator, he was influential, especially in the early years of the Golden Dawn. His *Book of Black Magic and of Pacts* led Crowley to seek admission to the Order. After being denied admission to the Second Order, however, Crowley satirised Waite unmercifully, describing him as one of 'my crapulous contemporaries' in *The Equinox* (Vol. I, no. v, 1911, p. 133). See also *Confessions*, pp. 16, 197. Waite's autobiography, *Shadows of Life and Thought*, discusses various changes in the Second Order and many of the people involved in this study. Although Waite is pontifical and sometimes unreliable, his book contains valuable source material for students of the Golden Dawn and similar organisations in London.

5. King, *Astral Projection*, p. 96. See pp. 91-6 for the whole of 'Flying Roll No. XVI'.

6. See Appendix F.

7. *Letters*, p. 344.

8. Ibid., p. 340.

9. Ibid., p. 341.

10. Ibid.

11. Someone other than Yeats or Miss Horniman or the writer of the salutation has made several minor verbal changes and added some punctuation to the typescript. I have kept the verbal changes and insertions but dropped occasional marks of punctuation.

12. See Mrs Emery's account in Appendix B.

13. This is a reference to Mrs Hunter, who was for a time in 1900 Secretary of the Isis-Urania Temple. Her husband (Hora Et Semper) was Warden, one of the three administrative offices under the new Constitution of 1900. Mrs Emery (Moderator) and Miss Horniman (Scribe) were the other two administrators. The remaining members of the Council, Yeats included, were instructional. See Chapter 3, note 19.

14. He changed 'well intentioned' to 'friendly'.

15. See Appendix G.

16. 'The chief of the faint rumours', according to Yeats, 'is that they re-affirm the harmlessness of their "groups" and blame your Scribe for suspiciousness and for a passion for red tape.'

17. Among the Yeats papers there is a considerable file of her letters to him after she moved to Ceylon in 1912 to accept a position as Principal of Ramanathan College for Hindu Girls. According to Yeats, in the words of 'All Souls' Night', she

> Preferred to teach a school
> Away from neighbour or friend
> Among dark skins, and there
> Permit foul years to wear,
> Hidden from eyesight, to the unnoticed end.

It may be, of course, that these lines (written three years after her death in 1917) reveal more of Yeats's motivation than of Mrs Emery's.

In the typescript entitled 'Investigations into the Foundations of the Order ...', there is a curious reference to the head of Mrs Emery's College for Hindu Girls.

F.R. wrote to the Chiefs Nov. 1, 1919 : –

'If it had not been that Ramanathan had been used to aid me I am doubtful if I would ever have got into connection with the Continental Order at all.'

Ramanathan is an Indian and has a native girls' school in Ceylon. He does not belong to our Order. He comes from a family of hereditary Eastern Mystic Teachers.

Since this typescript was compiled by Christina Mary Stoddart (Il Faut Chercher), a friend of Yeats, I assume that he must have directed Dr Felkin (Finem Respice) to Ramanathan.

18. See Appendix N.

19. The italicised words were filled in with a pen by Miss Horniman.

20. See Appendix H.

21. The italicised words are inserted in ink by the writer who made the insertions in the 'First Letter'. All italicised words in the remainder of the letter are in the same hand. Although I am not certain of the reason for leaving them blank when the letter was typed, I presume that Yeats thought the typist should not see them.

22. 'A member of this Order who is now expelled once boasted that he had done no less', Yeats inserted parenthetically. He was, I think, referring to Aleister Crowley, who claimed great magical powers. See *Confessions, passim.*

23. The handwriting is not Yeats's.

24. See Appendix I.

25. Some light is cast on the reference to the Grail by a paper written in late 1902, apparently, by Dr Felkin about 'The Group as I knew it, and Fortiter':

> Now the original Egyptian Group only lasted from the summer of 1898 to 1901, when we had a meeting and we were told that the Egyptian had retired from the Group and the Group as it was then constituted was brought to an end, the reason being that he was changing his place on the higher planes and could no longer work with us ... so the second Group was formed having the Holy Grail on the central pillar (Howe, p. 251).

26. In her 'preface to the New Edition' (dated July 1926) of *The Kabbalah Unveiled*, Mrs Mathers wrote: 'The general constitution of the teaching, the skeleton of the work, was handed to him by his occult teachers together with a vast amount of oral instruction. The object of the establishment of this school was similar to that of the foundation in ancient times of centres for the Celebration of the Mysteries. The literature of this school, with a few exceptions, was written by my husband under the direction of these teachers, based upon the ancient mysteries, chiefly those of Egypt, Chaldea and Greece, and brought up to date to suit the needs of our modern mentalities. It is a system eminently suited to Western occultism, which a man can follow while living the ordinary life of the world, given that this is understood in its highest sense. Dr. Woodman and Dr. Wynn-Westcott aided in the administrative side of this school and its teaching to a certain extent' (pp. viii-ix). After Westcott resigned in 1897, Mathers 'entirely reorganized the school under orders, and further teachings were given him' (p. ix). See Chapter 2, note 2, for a somewhat similar account of Moina's role in the reception of knowledge, and compare Howe, pp. 130-1.

27. I am uncertain about all the words in the parentheses except 'consider' and 'money'.

28. Servio Liberaliter was Miss Kate R. Moffat, a member of the Amen Ra Temple in Edinburgh; Urge Semper Igitur was Mrs Henry Pullen Burry, whose husband (Anima Pura Sit) was also a member.

29. Symbolised in the number 1, the true Kether is the crown of

existence in the Cabbalistic ladder of perfection. It is represented in
the perhaps unattainable grade of 10=1 in the Third Order, and is sometimes described as Macroprosopus or The Vast Countenance, also as
The White Head or The Ancient One. It represents the spiritual world in
contrast to the material world. If it were possible of attainment, the title
conferred would be Ipsissimus. See *The Kabbalah Unveiled, passim*, but
especially pages 20, 28, 51, and charts opposite.

Again, Dr Felkin's paper on 'The Group' is helpful:

> The objects of the Group were: to concentrate forces of growth,
> progress and purification, every Sunday at noon, and the progress
> was 1st, the formulation of the twelve workers near but not in 36
> [Blythe Road]; 2nd, Formulation round London; 3rd, Formulation
> round the Earth; 4th, Formulation among the Constellations. Then
> gradually reverse the process, bringing the quintessence of the greater
> forces to the lesser. The process was to take about an hour (Howe,
> p. 250).

30. She refers to 'Ritual W: Minutum Mundum'. The Diagram
consists of ten circles, representing the Cabbalistic Sephiroth, connected by lines. 'The First Diagram of M M' in the study manual for the
students of 5=6 'Sheweth the Sephiroth in the colours of the Queen
and the Paths in the colours of the King'. The 'Minutum Mundum' was
the first section of the 'Liber Hodos Chamelionis', a title which Yeats
borrowed for one section of *The Trembling of the Veil*. In his explanation of the title Yeats avoids revealing how well he knew the 'Minutum
Mundum': '... and I was lost in that region a cabbalistic manuscript,
shown me by MacGregor Mathers, had warned me of; astray upon the
Path of the Chamelion, upon Hodos Chameliontos' (*Autobiographies*,
p. 270).

Yeats was surely excited over the prospect that the Book of the Path
of the Chamelion could teach 'the knowledge of the Colours of the
Forces which be behind the Physical Universe'. The study manual opens
with an injunction which Yeats never forgot, though he may not have
read it first in the manual: 'Study then well that saying of Hermes
"That which is below is like that which is above ..." '. This well-known
sentence from the famous Smaragdine Tablet is the metaphysical basis
for the teaching of the Golden Dawn: 'Kether is in Malkuth, and Malkuth is in Kether'. That is, Primum Mobile or Kether (10=1) is in the
Elements or Malkuth (1=10).

Yeats's 'Hodos Chameliontos' is primarily concerned with various
mystical experiments he conducted with George Pollexfen. They were,
of course, making use of knowledge acquired in the Order, chiefly from
Mathers.

31. Sub Hoc Signo Vinces was Mrs F. A. Brodie-Innes, Cancellarius at
Amen Ra. She refused to sign the petition for Miss Horniman's reinstatement in December 1896.

32. In the typescript D.E.D.I. is followed by 'sometimes', which is
crossed out.

33. Yeats had, I suppose, been in Ireland much of the summer of 1900. In the 'Second Letter to the Adepti', he speaks of advising Miss Horniman after her return to the Order and 'before I went to Ireland', and he later implies that much had happened in the interval between his departure and his return. During his stay in Ireland, he and George Moore collaborated on *Diarmuid and Grania* (see *Letters*, p. 347).

34. Thomas joined the Societas Rosicruciana in Anglia on 17 December 1877 (Howe, p. 32). Maud Gonne left the Golden Dawn because she considered it too closely related to Freemasonry (*A Servant of the Queen*, p. 259).

35. Miss Horniman also made notes 16 and 17 at the end of the sentence concluding 'by him alone'. Although the numbers are crossed out in the letter, she did make comments in her handwritten notes. For (16): 'Ma Wahanu Thesi to his letter of Jan. 25th about his "motions" and "slight amendment" adds this P.S. "I am writing to V.H.S. S.S.D.D. in the matter of these motions"'. For (17) see note 36 below.

36. Miss Horniman made a note marked *A* but also identified as number (17): 'As Sapientia after setting aside the regular Order business proposed to take Ma Wahanu Thesi's "motions" first and then took the Election scheme instead, I feel that I was justified in considering that they had some connection'.

37. Miss Horniman again made a dual identification, *B* and (18), for her note: 'I had already decided on resignation from the Twelve Seniors and not to stand again for office. The meeting on Feb. 1st caused me to determine to do this before the elections, at the first opportunity'.

38. Yeats made no comment here, but Miss Horniman noted under *C* and (19): 'I refer to the Examination Book which shews, or should shew when Implements are consecrated'. To Yeats and Miss Horniman, this issue was especially important. The study for advancement in the Order was carefully outlined by Stages. According to the 'Regulations for the Conduct of the Progress of a Member through the Zelator Sub Grade of the $5=6$ Grade of Adeptus Minor' (revised in 1895 by Mathers and Westcott), the aspirant must consecrate his magical implements in the 'First Stage' of five stages. Numbers 6, 7, and 8 of instructions for the 'First Stage' direct the aspirant to receive Ritual D (Lotus Wand), E (Rose Cross), F (Sigils from the Rose), and G (Fire Implements); and to *make* as well as *consecrate* the Lotus Wand, Rose Cross, Sword and Four Elemental Implements 'after approval by the Chief Adept in charge'. Moreover, 'The Adept *must* pass Examinations marked A., B. and C. at the end of this First Stage'. The 'B–Elemental' examination (one of eight) was concerned solely with the Magical Implements, and the 'Regulations' were clear:

Part I Written and Part II Viva Voce in presence of Examiner. No Part at Home.
Subject – *The Magical Implements, Sword, Cup, Wand, Dagger, Pentacle, Lotus Wand.* The construction, constitution and symbolism

of these. Rules for their use. The dangers of imperfect construction and ignorant use. Ceremonies of Consecration. Formulae of Invocation.

All these implements as well as various manuals of instruction concerning their construction, symbolic meaning, and consecration are among the Yeats materials in the Library of Senator Yeats. Yeats passed Part I in 1895 (see Chapter 6, note 10).

39. Among the Yeats papers is another typescript of this letter (with some slight differences) which is signed in ink.

40. For convenience, I identify these people again in the order of appearance on the page: Mrs Florence Farr Emery, Mrs Helen Rand, Mrs E. A. Hunter, Miss Reena Fullham-Hughes, Mrs Henrietta Paget, E. A. Hunter, M. W. Blackden and Robert Palmer Thomas.

41. In the approximate centre of the postscript there is a large almost complete circle (an inch and a half across) enclosing a kind of half circle. If it was drawn by Yeats, it may project his graphic representation of 'chaos' – or the circularity of their argument. At any rate, it appears to be something other than a random mark.

42. See Appendix J.

43. It should be observed that Yeats had not yet achieved the grade of Theoricus Adeptus Minor (T.A.M.). According to an entry in one of his 'Private' notebooks (see note 38 above), he passed the last test and was certified for the grade by Dr Robert W. Felkin (Finem Respice) on 10 July 1912. Part of the certification is in Yeats's hand, part in Felkin's. Because he had passed the A, B and C examinations seventeen years earlier (in June 1895), this date is puzzling, suggesting certainly that there was some substance to the accusation that he did not attend regularly. It also illustrates how involved the examination system was in the form originally conceived by Mathers.

CHAPTER 6

1. See Appendix K. I am indebted to Senator Yeats for permission to reprint the essay from the copy I use here. I have discovered reproductions of three separate copies of the pamphlet. The copy owned by the Henry E. Huntington Library and Art Gallery has a special interest. It had been owned by John Quinn, who purchased it from Mrs Emery. Allan Wade records the note from the Quinn sale catalogue:

> [Yeats] has never acknowledged the authorship of this article. It was written as a member of a magical socitey in London, and when there was a split in the society, this copy was bought by Mr. Quinn from Miss Florence Farr, the actress-author, also a member of the society, against Mr. Yeats' rather strenuous opposition. No copy of this brochure has ever been offered at public sale, and it is one of the rarest of Yeats' writings in existence. (*Bibliography*, p. 54)

Across the top of the title page someone, possibly Mrs Emery, wrote 'Yeats, Wm B'. Because this copy contains numerous annotations by her, it has a special value for my explication, and I am grateful to the Huntington Library for permission to quote these notes at appropriate points of my discussion.

Mrs Emery's annotations were transferred by Mrs Jeanne Robert Foster, Quinn's secretary, to a typed copy of Yeats's essay which is a part of 'The Jeanne R. Foster – William M. Murphy Collection', and I am indebted to Prof Murphy for permission to refer to this copy here. Mrs Foster wrote '*Rare*' across a blank sheet of paper attached to the typescript, then added: 'Yeats was the head of an occult the R.R. & A.C. This article for members of the order was given me by W. B. Yeats. The longhand emendations were Yeats suggestions & emendations copied from *his* original. JRF. March 1901'. This note is puzzling in several particulars: (1) the annotations are certainly not Yeats's; (2) since Mrs Foster did not meet Quinn until November 1918, she could not have copied them from Quinn's copy before that date; (3) also, if Yeats gave her the typescript, she must have received it after that date; (4) if so, I cannot imagine why he gave her a typescript rather than a printed copy; (5) in fact, I cannot imagine Yeats's giving anyone outside the Order a copy. Therefore, I can only conjecture that Mrs Foster made the typescript and copied Mrs Emery's notes before the sale of the copy to the Huntington Library. Moreover, Mrs Foster's note, cited above, was probably made many years after the event.

2. A Second Order Diary for 1892-3 records the following: '*Fri. 20 Jan.* "Portal for Demon est Deus and Obligation and 1st Point Adept. S.S.D.D. left at 7 o'clock'. The initiation was completed on 21 January (Howe, p. 97; see also p. 102).

3. The first of Mrs Emery's annotations refers to (4): 'which of the Seniors would be allowed to arrogate this power to himself even if he wanted to undertake it'.

4. The Societas Rosicruciana was founded in 1866 by Robert Wentworth Little, who supposedly based the teachings, rituals, and Grades of the Society on some old papers he had found. Although Little was a student of occult lore, especially the books of Éliphas Lévi, the Societas was in fact Rosicrucian in name only. Dr W. R. Woodman succeeded Little as Supreme Magus in 1878, Westcott became the Secretary General, and Mathers was on the High Council. (See Howe, Chapter 2, 'The Rosicrucian Society of England', and Moore, *Unicorn*, p. 129.)

5. Quoted from an unpublished letter in the Yeats papers.

6. Quoted by Moore, *Unicorn*, p. 131. The quotation comes from *The Perfect Way* (1882), a book Yeats probably read (see *Letters*, p. 97). It was written by Anna Bonus Kingsford and Edward Maitland, about whom I will have more to say in a subsequent chapter. A revised and enlarged edition of *The Perfect Way* was published in 1887.

7. See Appendix A for the full text of this letter, and Chapter 2 for consideration of its significance to the quarrel.

8. See Chapter 3, note 19, for the identities and offices of the other nine.

9. Letter 'To the Twelve Seniors' dated 2 February 1901 (see Appendix E).

10. Those who achieved 'Theoricus' usually attached the initials 'T.A.M.' to their Order mottoes. Yeats did not reach this Degree until 1912 according to a certification in one of his notebooks. On two successive pages Yeats has written the following certification for A, B, C, and D examinations: 'I the undersigned do this day certify that I have duly examined D E D I & am satisfied with the attainments which I have been shown'. A and B are certified by Non Omnis Moriar (Westcott). C and D have no certification, but Yeats noted below C that he had 'passed this (Part I) in June 1895'. E contains an added clause, a signature and a date in the hand of Dr Robert W. Felkin: 'and that he is now T.A.M. Finem Respice July 10th 1912'. In Yeats's papers there is also a typed certification signed by 'Finem Respice T.A.M. Chief':

ORDO R.R. et A.C.

I, the undersigned, hereby certify this 10th day of July in the year 1912 that having investigated the V.H. Frater D.E.D.I.'s papers and certificates, he is now a T.A.M. in the Order.

On a sheet of his personal note-paper Felkin wrote hastily: 'Certificate enclosed. I return end of the month & will then send addresses &c which you need. FR 7/10/12'. I am not therefore sure whether 10 July is the date of the examination or of Felkin's reading of it. But I am certain that Yeats considered both the date and the attainment important.

The subject of E is Magic, the examination for which was divided into three essential parts: (1) *Talismans* and *Flashing Tablets* their formation and consecration; (2) *Ascending in the Planes*; (3) *Vibratory Mode* of pronouncing Divine Names. (See chapter 5, note 38, for further information about the 'Regulations'.)

11. The copy of the manual I cite came from the library of George Pollexfen. It bears the date of 28 May 1894.

12. No. 19 in the Pollexfen manual is concerned with 'The Meaning of the *Moon Luna* on the *Tree of Life*. . . .' Years later as he was compiling notes and composing *A Vision*, Yeats combined this conception with that of the phases of the moon and the Lightning Flash in two rough diagrams headed 'WBY's flash' and 'GHL's flash'. Since the following page of the loose-leaf notebook in which the diagrams appear is devoted to a brief analysis of their flashes in terms of the phases of the moon, my guess is that they were drawn soon after his marriage to Georgie Hyde-Lees, who is referred to as 'GY' in the analysis. The card-file index which Yeats prepared at one stage in the composition of *A Vision* (1925) contains a card headed 'Lightning Flash (Jan 5 1918)'. At the top of one flash is written 'Mine', at the other 'George'. Another card, filed under 'Symbols', relates the number in the sketch of the flash to both the Phases of the Moon and the Tree of Life. One note explains that this

is 'Blake's form', another that 'numbers refer to lightning flash' and a third that the flash represents 'Daimonic descent into Spiritual Memory'.

13. I presume that Yeats is referring to the 'Obligation of Adeptus Minor 5=6' which all must take. His 'private' notebook dated 28 June 1893 opens with this Obligation, which apparently he had memorised. It begins, 'I Demon Est Deus Inversus do bind myself that I will to the utmost lead a pure and unselfish life, and will prove myself a faithful and devoted servant of the order [;] that I will keep secret all things connected with this order & its secret knowledge from the whole world, equally from him who is a member of the first order of the G. D. as from an uninitiated person, & that I will maintain the veil of strict secresy between the First and Second Order'. The entire Obligation contains ten parts each headed by the Hebrew letters (for Kether to Malkuth) signifying the ten Degrees. I have quoted three parts but not more than fifteen per cent of the whole.

This extensive notebook appears to be a workbook for progress examinations. Since the handwriting is easier to read than usual, I imagine that it was to be examined by Yeats's superiors. For further information about it, see my article 'From Zelator to Theoricus: Yeats's "Link with the Invisible Degrees"', *Yeats Studies*, No. 1 (1971) 80-6.

14. Peck was a city official of Edinburgh and Imperator of the Amen Ra Temple. Since his name appears often during these troubles, he must have been on an extended visit to London.

15. See *The Kabbalah Unveiled*, Plate IV, facing p. 30, for an elaborate 'Table showing the relations of the Sephiroth with the Four Worlds, etc.' For a fuller discussion, see also Israel Regardie, *The Tree of Life* (New York: Samuel Weiser, 1972) pp. 89, 96. Among the Yeats papers there is a copy of the Lecture for 2=9 to 3=8 which has different arrangements of the metals 'in respect to the Ten Sephiroth'. Two separate diagrams designate iron as the symbolic metal of Tiphereth and Mars its planet. The copy was loaned to George Pollexfen on 28 July 1894.

16. Mrs Emery objected: 'This is no question of incarnate life'.

17. Mrs Emery noted that 'a clock is a more interesting piece of mechanism than a cartwheel'. Yeats was thinking of a factory rather than a cart. He may have been recalling the image in Blake's *Jerusalem* of 'wheel without wheel, with cogs tyrannic' which drive the 'Loom of Locke'. Years later Yeats recorded his dislike of Locke in the ironic lines of 'Fragments':

> Locke sank into a swoon;
> The Garden died;
> God took the spinning-jenny
> Out of his side.

18. Mrs Emery wrote 'Why?' in the margin.

19. Although Crowley was to become much more notorious, to Yeats he was already 'a person of unspeakable life' (*Letters*, p. 342). In recent years a considerable bibliography has grown up about Crowley's circle. The interested reader should begin with his *Confessions*. More important

for the study of his relationship to the Golden Dawn is *The Equinox*, an occult periodical which he edited and wrote most of during the years from 1909 to 1913 and briefly in 1919. Considerable detail about Crowley's 'magick' (as he spelt it) may be found in John Symonds, *The Magic of Aleister Crowley* (London: Frederick Muller, 1958) and *The Great Beast* (London: Rider, 1951). Among the many other books which devote some space to Crowley, two recent ones are of special interest to this study: Jean Overton Fuller's *The Magical Dilemma of Victor Neuberg* and Francis King's *Ritual Magic in England 1887 to the Present Day*. Exciting but less reliable is *Light-Bearers of Darkness* by Christina Mary Stoddart (under the pseudonym of 'Inquire Within') (London: Boswell, 1930). All these sources rely heavily upon Gerald Yorke, one of Crowley's trustees. Most of his astonishing collection of materials (both published and unpublished) by Crowley and various members of his coterie is now deposited in the Library of the Warburg Institute.

20. Mrs Emery's note is merely petulant: 'frailties should be trodden underfoot not gathered up'.

21. More than twenty years later, in a rejected Epilogue for *A Vision* addressed 'To Vestigia', Yeats referred to a statue of the goddess Isis in the corner of her drawing room.

22. G. R. S. Mead (ed.), *Select Works of Plotinus*, trans. Thomas Taylor (London: G. Bell and Sons, 1929) p. 322. First published in 1895, Mead's edition was no doubt well-known to Yeats. In *A Vision* (1925), he finds a different use for Plotinus's famous image: ' "The Divine returns to the Divinity" through the *Celestial Body*, and to invert *Plotinus* "the Lonely returns to the Lonely" in the dream of the *Passionate Body*, for mother, murderer and huntsman are alone' (p. 226). In April 1909 Yeats attributed these quotations to Proclus when he chose them as an epigraph for his 'Preface to the First Edition of John M. Synge's *Poems and Translations*' for the Cuala Press: 'The Lonely returns to the Lonely, the Divine to the Divinity'. He may have been thinking of a favourite poem by his friend Lionel Johnson, 'The Dark Angel', which ends with these lines:

> Lonely, unto the Lone, I go;
> Divine, to the Divinity.

23. Yeats may be recalling the 'gate' in Blake's lovely lyric which introduces Chapter 4 of *Jerusalem*:

> I give you the end of a golden string,
> Only wind it into a ball,
> It will lead you in at Heaven's gate
> Built in Jerusalem's wall.

The word *gate* serves a significant symbolic function in Boehme, a favourite of both Blake and Yeats.

24. *A Vision* (London: Macmillan, 1937) p. 291.

25. Quoted in Moore, *Unicorn*, p. 155.

26. Published in 1887, *The Real History of the Rosicrucians* is an assemblage of 'facts and documents collected from the writings of initiated brethren'. In addition to the *Fama Fraternitatis*, *The Real History* also contains *The Confession of the Rosicrucian Fraternity* and *The Chymical Marriage of Christian Rosencreutz*, both basic to the study of the development of Rosicrucianism. The *Fama* is the best known source of information about the discovery of the tomb of Christian Rosenkreuz, its dimensions and its contents. On the door of the entrance to the tomb was written 'Post CXX Annos Patebo'. As the product of the numbers 1 to 5 multiplied in sucession, 120 has symbolic significance. So too have the contents, the shape and the internal dimensions. According to the account in the *Fama*, when the discoverers of the tomb opened the door, 'there appeared to our sight a vault of seven sides and seven corners, every side five foot broad, and the height of eight foot. Although the sun never shined in this vault, nevertheless, it was enlightened with another sun, which had learned this from the sun, and was situated in the upper part in the center of the sieling.' Each of the seven sides was divided into ten squares on which were inscribed symbolic 'figures and sentences'. In the centre of the vault was an altar, and under the altar was a brass plate covering the pastos containing the 'whole and unconsumed' body of Christian Rosenkreuz (pp. 76-8). It hardly needs saying, I suppose, that every object, every dimension, every book and every inscription has symbolic significance which many of the Golden Dawn rituals are designed to reveal to the aspirants.

27. King, *Astral Projection*, p. 113.

28. *Real History of the Rosicrucians*, pp. 443-4.

29. On 3 July 1901 George Moore sent Yeats 'a little scenario which you may be able to develop'. This was the scenario for *Where There Is Nothing*, which they planned as a collaborative effort. See Charles J. Burkhart, 'The Letters of George Moore to Edmund Gosse, W. B. Yeats, R. I. Best, Miss Nancy Cunard, and Mrs. Mary Hutchinson' (unpublished dissertation, University of Maryland, 1958) pp. 265-8. Also see Jack W. Weaver, 'An Exile Returned: Moore and Yeats in Ireland', *Eire-Ireland*, III (spring 1968) 40-7, and ' "Stage Management in the Irish National Theatre": An Unknown Article by George Moore?' *English Literature in Transition*, IX (1966) 12-17. See my essay 'The Reconciliation of Paganism and Christianity in Yeats' *Unicorn from the Stars*', *All These to Teach: Essays in Honor of C. A. Robertson* (Gainesville: University of Florida Press, 1965) pp. 224-36.

30. *Variorum Edition of the Plays*, p. 710.

31. Ibid., p. 712.

32. The reference to Blake comes at the end of his note in a sentence concluding as follows: '. . . with our old lyricism so full of ancient frenzies and hereditary wisdom, a yoking of antiquities, a Marriage of Heaven and Hell' (p. 713). The hereditary wisdom, the yoking of antiquities, and the Marriage of Heaven and Hell perhaps cast some

light on Yeats's conception of his own prophetic role. See *Blake: Complete Writings*, ed. Geoffrey Keynes (London: Oxford University Press, 1969) p. 825, for his description of the poet as 'Secretary' in a passage Yeats liked to quote.

33. See *Bibliography*, pp. 52-4, for the known details of publication. Since Yeats had little money in 1901, I assume that Miss Horniman paid for the publication of the essay and the 'Postscript'.

34. Ibid. See Appendix L for this rarest of Yeats items. I am indebted to the University of Kansas Libraries for a reproduction of the copy from the Library of P. S. O'Hegarty, the distinguished Irish historian and book collector.

35. See Appendix M.

36. See postscript of Appendix I.

CHAPTER 7

1. *Letters*, p. 349.

2. *Essays and Introductions* (London, 1961) p. 107.

3. Ibid., pp. 96, 98.

4. *Bibliography*, p. 64.

5. Ibid., p. 53.

6. *Letters*, p. 352.

7. Ibid., p. 353.

8. Ibid., p. 357.

9. Ibid., p. 363.

10. See Appendixes N and O.

11. Howe, p. 143.

12. *Letters*, p. 359. The essay he promised to write, 'Speaking to the Psaltery', was finished by 5 April and published in *The Monthly Review* for May 1902 (*Letters*, p. 369).

13. Ibid., p. 363.

14. Ibid., p. 364. If, as he seems to be, Yeats is referring to his work on the rituals for the Celtic Mysteries, the date of this letter (13 January 1902) is significant: some two or three years after the period of most intense activity on the Mysteries, this date as well as the tone of the observation to Lady Gregory suggests that he had been working steadily at his project and that he still intended carrying it to a satisfactory conclusion. (See Chapter 2, note 19, for further information about the Celtic Mysteries.)

Yeats may have been referring also to work on the rituals of the Golden Dawn. There is some evidence that he had planned with Miss Horniman (who also helped with the Celtic Mysteries) to rewrite many, possibly all, the rituals. Among the notebooks in Senator Yeats's library is a carefully revised manual for 1=10 Degree of Zelator bearing the initials F.E.R. and dated January 1901. Also among the papers is a part of the same ritual revised in Yeats's hand. He was chiefly concerned with stylistic changes. One example will illustrate. The manual reads:

'Not as yet canst thou bear the dazzling radiance of that Light. Return for thou canst not pass by.' Yeats's revision reads: 'Your eyes cannot yet bear that dazzling image. Return then for you cannot pass me by.' Miss Horniman's version retains the biblical pronouns: 'Thine eyes cannot bear that dazzling image. Return for thou canst not pass by.' Although Yeats was not correcting her revised version, it seems likely from this one passage that he had her version before him. If indeed he and Miss Horniman planned to revise the whole body of rituals, they apparently failed to complete the task. It should be noted that this revision was being done during the period of activity on the Celtic Mysteries.

15. See Appendix P. Since there is a copy in the Yeats papers, I assume that it was sent to many, perhaps all, of the members of the Second Order. Of course, Yeats's copy might have come from Miss Horniman.

16. The letter speaks of 'matters committed to the three Chiefs by the vote of the 3rd of May', suggesting that they had been elected, or the Bye-Laws had been ratified, or both on that day.

17. See Appendix Q.

18. See Appendix I.

19. See Appendix R. I am uncertain about the date of Q, which may also have been 26 June.

20. Unfortunately, her letters to Yeats during this time are lost or were returned before she migrated to India to become head of Rama-nathan College in Ceylon. From that time until her death on 29 April 1917 she and Yeats corresponded sporadically. Her letters of this period are preserved in the Yeats papers. Prof Josephine Johnson, of the University of Miami, is making a full-scale study of Mrs Emery which will no doubt help to trace her activities and explain her motives.

21. *Letters*, pp. 366-7, 370, 375-6.

CHAPTER 8

1. *The Speckled Bird*, ed. William H. O'Donnell (Dublin: Cuala Press, 1974). I am greatly indebted to Prof O'Donnell in the brief discussion of *The Speckled Bird* contained in this chapter. His essay 'Yeats as Adept and Artist: *The Speckled Bird*, *The Secret Rose*, and *The Wind among the Reeds*', to appear in a forthcoming issue of *Yeats Studies*, explores and extends the dichotomy suggested in the title of my chapter. Although Prof O'Donnell is not responsible for my conclusions, he kindly consented to read what I had written and to check my transcriptions while his edition was still in galley proofs. At this writing page numbers are not available for material cited in this note and notes 57, 59, and 78.

2. *Essays and Introductions*, p. 28.

3. Ibid.

4. The first paragraph of the 'Postscript' refers to the kind of experiences recorded in 'Magic' and makes clear not only that Yeats had been

collecting them but also that he intended to write about them: '... but I know from the experience[s] of a number of people – experiences which *I have carefully recorded* – that it soon produces a nearly perfect communion of mood and a somewhat less, though very marked, communion of thought and purpose' (my italics). See Appendix L.

5. See *Letters*, p. 262n. See also James W. Flannery, *Miss Annie F. Horniman and the Abbey Theatre* (Dublin: Dolmen Press, 1970). F. J. Horniman, Annie's father, was a wealthy tea merchant who gathered 'curiosities', to use Yeats's word.

6. *Essays and Introductions*, p. 33. This is the famous Enochian Tablet about which all Golden Dawn members received instruction.

7. Ibid., pp. 35-6. Blake was describing the composition of one of his Prophetic Books, probably *Milton*: 'I may praise it, since I dare not pretend to be any other than the Secretary; the Authors are in Eternity' (Blake, p. 825; see Chapter 6, note 32).

8. Ibid., pp. 37-8. The 'experiences some years afterwards' in Paris surely occurred during that momentous visit of late April and early May 1898. The experience recorded in 'Magic' is retold in *Autobiographies* (p. 338) and can be dated by the reference to the Spanish-American War. See also *Letters* (pp. 297-8) for allusions to the same visit. Although it is clear from unpublished letters from the Matherses that the primary object of Yeats's visit was 'to see visions' and consult about his Celtic Mysteries, he obviously participated in other visionary experiences. Considering the advance preparation for his visit and the recollections of it in later years, I can only assume that Yeats's experiences, both recorded and unrecorded, were greatly significant to him; and I wish the accounts were more complete, especially those on the Celtic rituals which Maud was to show so little interest in. (See Chapter 2, note 19, for details.)

9. Ibid., p. 40. As time went by, Yeats felt it important to record the dates of significant events in his life. Since he did not record dates systematically, he frequently jotted them down in notebooks or on scraps of paper, often relating the dates to astrological signs. One page of a notebook records five events in 1898, 1899, and 1901. Two of the entries are directly concerned with Maud (see Chapter 3, note 3). For further discussion of Yeats's concern for precise recording see my article in *Southern Review*, ' "Passion and Precision": Some Observations on Editing Yeats' (spring 1974).

10. Ibid., p. 44.

11. Ibid., p. 42.

12. Ibid., pp. 44-5.

13. Ibid., p. 46.

14. Ibid., p. 49. Although Yeats needed no authority for such beliefs, he found much support among the occult writers he read during these years. Compare, for example, the following from Éliphas Lévi: 'We have said that there is no religion without mysteries; let us add that there are no mysteries without symbols. The symbol, being the formula or the expression of the mystery, only expresses its unknown depth by para-

doxical images borrowed from the known' (*The Key of the Mysteries*, trans. Aleister Crowley [London: Rider, 1969] p. 16).

15. Ibid., pp. 50-1.

16. Ibid., p. 51.

17. Yeats was, in fact, frequently scornful of many experiments performed by his colleagues. See, for example, the postscript of a letter to Lady Gregory dated 20 January 1902. 'My alchemist', he writes, 'is very anxious to have a look at that magic book of Robert's.... He has just made what he hopes is the Elixir of Life. If the rabbits on whom he is trying it survive we are all to drink a noggin full – at least all of us whose longevity he feels he could honestly encourage' (*Letters*, p. 365). He was referring to the Rev William Alexander Ayton (see note 33).

A. E. Waite, in *Shadows of Life and Thought*, describes Ayton as 'a member of the G.D. almost *ab origine*, a sound Latin scholar and one who had been active for years in all the occult movements, that of H.P.B. included' (p. 134). In 1903 when Waite and a group of followers left Isis-Urania and formed a new Hermetic Society retaining the name of Golden Dawn, one of the Chiefs was Ayton, 'he being Senior Adept among us' (p. 228). See also King, who reports the story about the Elixir of Life and comments upon the alchemical interests of the Order (*Ritual Magic*, pp. 95, 169).

18. J. M. Hone, 'The Speckled Bird: William Butler Yeats', *The Bell* (March 1941) 23-30; Curtis Bradford, 'The Speckled Bird: a Novel by William Butler Yeats', *Irish Writing*, No. 31 (summer 1955) 9-18.

19. See Bradford, pp. 10-11, for a brief outline of the book. I am indebted to Prof O'Donnell, who plans an edition of the manuscript, for checking the observations and conclusions I make here.

20. Ibid.

21. *Letters*, p. 361.

22. Ibid., p. 370.

23. Bradford, p. 9.

24. *Letters*, p. 376.

25. Ibid., p. 350.

26. Ibid.

27. He refers to the violent controversy in May 1899 over the production of *The Countess*. A brief pamphlet entitled 'Souls for Gold! Pseudo-Celtic Drama in Ireland' accused him of blasphemy and heresy, and Cardinal Logue condemned the play in the newspapers. Yeats countered by asking two priests (Fr Finlay and Fr Barry) to pass judgement on the play's intention. It was produced on 8 May 1899 under rather tense conditions. For details, see Una Ellis-Fermor, *The Irish Dramatic Movement*, 2nd ed. (London: Methuen, 1954) pp. 35-6, 210, 218-19. Yeats's account appears in *Autobiographies*, pp. 413-18.

28. *Letters*, pp. 350-1.

29. Ibid., p. 361. The meeting probably took place on Monday, 23 December 1901.

30. *Autobiographies*, p. 376.

31. *The Speckled Bird*, II, 15. Ayton was a member of the Societas

Rosicruciana in Anglia. He and his wife were among the first members of the Golden Dawn and among the first to be promoted to the Second Order (Howe, pp. 20, 31).

32. *Letters*, p. 365. See note 17.

33. On the scrap of Coole Park stationery referred to earlier the list of dates headed 'Events for rectification' begins with '1890. June ♀ event. E. Little'. Since according to a letter from Ayton to F. L. Gardner (dated 21 June 1890) the Bergson-Mathers wedding had occurred 'last Monday', Yeats's note may refer to their marriage. He was, of course, already in love with Maud Gonne (whom he met on 30 January 1889) and may be referring to some '♀ event' connected with her. But there is some evidence (in the 'Dedication' to *A Vision* and elsewhere) that he had been extremely fond of the beautiful Moina Bergson, whom he probably knew before he met Maud.

Of course, the note may be connected with E. Little, whom I cannot identify. Robert Wentworth Little was a prominent member of the Societas Rosicruciana in Anglia, and Grace Little (one of two sisters) married Ernest Rhys, one of Yeats's good friends, in January 1891.

34. *The Speckled Bird*, II, 19-20.

35. See Appendix A for the full text of the letter.

36. See Howe, pp. 203-5 and 237-8, for details, including the full text of Mathers's letter.

37. King, *Ritual Magic*, p. 82. I am indebted to King's account in Chapter 9, 'A Bogus Golden Dawn', for other details.

38. King suggests that the 'Horos case' may have been the cause for the withdrawal of many members about this time (p. 93). But one of the notes to the 'Manifesto from the Three Chiefs' dated 26 June 1902 implies other reasons for their resignation as well as the name change: 'Kindly look most carefully through the list of present members so as to avoid any mistake in speaking to anyone who has resigned'. That suggests strife within the group rather than with outsiders like the Horoses, though both reasons were surely influential in the action of the Chiefs.

39. After joining the Theosophical Society in 1888, Yeats kept a Journal which records some of his interests as well as reservations. He notes that he had trouble with two of the pledges he was asked to take: 'promise to work for theosophy and promise of obedience to HPB' [Mme Blavatsky]. He insisted upon deciding for himself 'what theosophy is', considering his work on Blake 'a wholly adequate keeping of this clause'. Too heterodox for Mme Blavatsky, he was asked to resign in 1890, after he had joined the Golden Dawn. See Ellmann, pp. 65-7, for a transcription of the Journal and a discussion of Yeats's experiences in the Theosophical Society.

40. See especially Maitland, II, 116-71. Watkins, Maitland's publisher, was a member of the Golden Dawn and a friend of Yeats, who frequented his famous bookshop in London.

41. Ibid., II, 185-6.

42. Letter from George Russell to Mme Blavatsky, quoted in Ellmann, p. 64.

43. Donoghue, p. 281. His transcription varies slightly from Ellmann's.

44. So too did Mathers, according to his wife. In a Preface (dated July 1926) to a new edition of *The Kabbalah Unveiled*, she wrote: 'After some years of seclusion in the country, where my husband led a student's life in preparation for his future work, he met Anna Kingsford, who introduced him to Madame Blavatsky. Madame Blavatsky invited him to collaborate with her in the formation of her Society. After deliberation, notwithstanding his profound admiration for that remarkable woman, this invitation he was compelled to decline. Their ideals were not the same. At that time he was more in sympathy with Anna Kingsford's ideals of esoteric Christianity and of the advancement of woman' (pp. xii-xiii).

Just when Mathers met Mrs Kingsford and Maitland I have not discovered, but he apparently knew them well by 1886, when he lectured on 'The Kabala' (June 3) and 'The Lower or Physical Alchemy' (July 8) for a series of Hermetic lectures they conducted. Among other lecturers in this series were Westcott and Mohini M. Chatterji, whom Yeats had met at the Dublin Hermetic Society headquarters in 1885 (see Maitland, II, 257-8, and Ellmann, pp. 41-3). In 1887 Mathers dedicated *The Kabbalah Unveiled* to Mrs Kingsford and Maitland: 'I have much pleasure in dedicating this work to the authors of *The Perfect Way*, as they have in that excellent and wonderful book touched so much on the doctrines of the Kabala, and laid such value on its teachings. *The Perfect Way* is on of the most deeply occult works that has been written for centuries' (quoted in Maitland, II, 169).

45. Yeats apparently knew one of Maitland's books entitled *The New Gospel of Interpretation* (1891), perhaps also *The Story of Anna Kingsford and Edward Maitland and of The New Gospel of Interpretation* (1893).

46. *The Speckled Bird*, II, 23.

47. Maitland, I, 135. The relationship of this couple was strange indeed. On the very morning Mrs Kingsford received her new name, Maitland records that she was transformed 'into the complete likeness of my wife' (I, 135), who had died many years before. Although Maitland and Mrs Kingsford travelled and lived together (in the same quarters at least) for several years, she was never permanently separated from her clergyman husband and child, whom she visited occasionally, sometimes accompanied by Maitland. Needless to say, Maitland's biography says little of Rev Kingsford.

48. Ibid., II, 4. Maitland is quoting from *Clothed with the Sun* (1889), which Yeats may have read. See also I, 46 (where the difference between Mary Magdelen and Christ is discussed) and I, 15.

49. Ibid., II, 440. See also I, 173. A few months after Mrs Kingsford's death (on 22 February 1888) Yeats saw Maitland at Lady Wilde's. 'He talked much of Mrs. Kingsford', and told the company a 'spiritualistic story' of a correspondence between the dead woman and a young Scotch

girl who had known her only slightly. Sceptical but impressed, Yeats wrote to Katharine Tynan on 21 December: 'for the first time Mrs. Kingsford interested me. She must have been good to have inspired so many people with affection'. He appreciated Mme Blavatsky's observation that 'there were two Mrs. Kingsfords, "a good woman and a woman of the world who dyed her hair"' (*Letters*, p. 97). Eight years later Maitland recorded in much greater detail the 'spiritualistic story' Yeats heard (Maitland, II, 415-18).

50. Ibid., I, 229. See also I, 12, 13, 15; II, 244-5.

51. *The Story of Anna Kingsford and Edward Maitland and of The New Gospel of Interpretation*, 3rd ed. (Birmingham, 1905) p. 95. See note 45 above; also Maitland, I, 353-4.

52. *The Speckled Bird*, II, 23.

53. *Autobiographies*, p. 376.

54. See King, *Ritual Magic*, p. 28, for brief sketches of MacKenzie, Hockley, and Lévi; and Maitland, I, 269-75, for Harris. In the *Autobiographies*, immediately following two paragraphs devoted to Mathers, Yeats records an experience of taking 'hashish with some followers of the eighteenth-century mystic Saint-Martin. At one in the morning, while we are talking wildly, and some are dancing, there is a tap at the shuttered window ...' (p. 347). This is, I think, another of the experiences he recorded carefully, and may have occurred during the visit to Paris in April-May 1898. It is characteristic of his inquiring mind that he should want to know about the Martinists.

55. Many of his books are being reissued by Rider and Co. in the translations of A. E. Waite and Aleister Crowley.

56. For the text of this article see King, *Ritual Magic*, pp. 28-38. See also Howe, pp. 27-33.

57. See note 1. 'Fama' is a reference to the *Fama Fraternitatis*, which Yeats no doubt read in Waite's *The Real History of the Rosicrucians*, pp. 65-84. See Chapter 6, note 26.

58. Ibid.

59. Ibid. See note 1.

60. The letter is glued into the notebook at the appropriate place. Yeats wrote P I A L (Maud's motto initials) on the flap and dated it 26 June. The year was 1908. See Moore, *Unicorn*, pp. 197-204, for an account of the renewal of their spiritual marriage in 1908. See also Chapter 3, note 3, for a further account of the mystical marriage of 1899.

61. *The Variorum Edition of the Plays*, p. 340.

62. *The Shadowy Waters* (London, 1900) pp. 8-9. Unfortunately, since the *Variorum* and the *Collected Plays* print only the acting version of 1911, the dramatic-poem, as Yeats called the identical first and second editions, is not readily available.

63. Ibid., pp. 56-7.

64. *Essays and Introductions*, p. 10.

65. Ibid.

66. Ibid., p. 203.

67. Ibid.
68. See note 57.
69. Ibid., p. 204.
70. Ibid., pp. 206, 204.
71. Ibid., p. 206.
72. Ibid., p. 207.
73. Ibid., p. 210.
74. Ibid., p. 77.
75. *Letters*, p. 323.
76. *Bibliography*, p. 64.
77. *Essays and Introductions*, p. 78.
78. *The Speckled Bird.* See note 1.
79. *A Vision* (1925) pp. 9-10. See also p. xix: 'I found that though their Sacred Book had been lost they had a vast doctrine which was constantly explained to their growing boys and girls by the aid of diagrams drawn by old religious men upon the sands ...'.
80. *Essays and Introductions*, pp. 78-80.
81. Several of Taylor's books appeared in cheap reprints during the 1890s: *The Eleusinian and Bacchic Mysteries* (1891), Apuleius's *Metamorphosis; or, Golden Ass* (1893), *Sallust on the Gods and the World* (1893), Plato's *Republic* (1894), *Select Works of Plotinus* (1895), Plotinus's *Essay on the Beautiful* (1895), *Iamblichus on the Mysteries of the Egyptians, Chaldeans, and Assyrians* (1895), Porphyry's *Cave of the Nymphs* (1895), *Hymns of Orpheus* (1896), *Mystical Hymns of Orpheus ... Demonstrated to be the Invocations Which were Used in the Eleusinian Mysteries* (1896). Plotinus's *Essay*, Porphyry's *Cave* and Orpheus's *Hymns* were reprinted by Theosophical organisations. For details, see Kathleen Raine and George Mills Harper (eds), *Thomas Taylor the Platonist: Selected Writings* (Princeton: Princeton University Press, 1969) pp. 532-3. Sallust, Iamblichus, and Orpheus were in the Westcott Hermetic Library (founded in 1891), which Yeats certainly knew and probably used. Fred Leigh Gardner (De Profundis Ad Lucem) was the librarian of both the Westcott Hermetic Library and the Library of the Societas Rosicruciana in Anglia, and he probably prepared the copy for the publication of both catalogues in 1897. The scope and variety of books and periodicals listed under the 286 numbers in 'The Catalogue of the Westcott Hermetic Library' surely demonstrate that the members of the Golden Dawn were dedicated to learning. Though I do not mean to sugest that Yeats or any of his colleagues read all these books, it is surely not too much to say that the critic who seeks to comprehend the Yeats of the 1890s should examine this list with care. See Appendix S.
82. *Essays and Introductions*, pp. 94-5.
83. Ibid., pp. 53-4.
84. Ibid., p. 53.
85. Ibid., p. 54.
86. Ibid. By describing Morris with phrases from Blake, Yeats links the two, in contrast to Shelley and Rossetti, as he does several times in the

essay. He was himself torn between the two sides of life represented by the two pairs of poets.

87. Ibid., pp. 63-4.

CHAPTER 9

1. See Appendix Q.
2. See Appendix R.
3. *Letters*, p. 393.
4. See Appendix R.
5. *Shadows of Life and Thought*, p. 228.
6. Ibid.
7. *Ritual Magic*, p. 96.
8. *Shadows of Life and Thought*, p. 228.
9. Howe, p. 245.
10. *Shadows of Life and Thought*, pp. 228-9.
11. Ibid., p. 229.
12. Howe, pp. 253-4. Howe was unable to locate Waite's manifesto of 24 July.
13. Ibid., p. 254.
14. Ibid., pp. 255-6.
15. Ibid., p. 257. Howe does not know when the new temple was founded and the name adopted.
16. Pamela Coleman Smith, an American artist of some talent, came to London in 1899 and called on Yeats at Bedford Park (*Letters*, p. 383n). They became quite good friends, and he was probably instrumental in her joining the Golden Dawn. When the division of 1903 occurred, however, she chose to go with Waite. He describes her as 'a most imaginative and abnormally psychic artist ... who had drifted into the Golden Dawn and loved its Ceremonies – as transformed by myself – without pretending or indeed attempting to understand their sub-surface consequence'. In 1910 Waite chose her to illustrate under his supervision a set of the 22 Trumps Major cards of the Tarot because he thought she 'could produce a Tarot with an appeal in the world of art and a suggestion of significance behind the Symbols which would put on them another construction than had ever been dreamed of by those who, through many generations, had produced and used them for mere divinatory purposes' (*Shadows of Light and Thought*, p. 184; see also p. 195). Waite's well-known book, *The Pictorial Key to the Tarot* (London, 1910) included 78 plates 'illustrating the Greater and Lesser Arcana, from designs by Pamela Coleman Smith'. It has recently been reprinted by Rider and Co. (London, 1971).
17. Howe, p. 258.
18. 'Investigations into the Foundations of the Order and the Source of Its Teachings (Abridged)', dated June 1922 and signed Il Faut Chercher (that is, Miss Stoddart).
19. 'Inquire Within', *Light-Bearers of Darkness* (London, 1930), pp.

95-6. Hereafter cited by this pseudonym under which Miss Stoddart wrote a series of articles for *Patriot*.

20. See Appendix T.

21. Since Yeats also preserved a copy of the ritual for 'The Mystical Grade of 7=4', it may be that he advanced through that Degree. According to Miss Stoddart's 'Investigations', Felkin had the notes for this ritual as early as 1912. The ritual of the 7=4 (and presumably that of the 6=5) is much briefer and more poetic than the rituals of 0=0 through 5=6, which Mathers composed. Among the records Miss Stoddart preserved is a note (dated 25 December 1907) presumably from the Sun Masters to Felkin, which comments on both advanced degrees:

> To the G. H. Frater D.D.C.F. the former Chief of the Order the genuine Ritual of the 6=5 was given— He would have attained to the full Grade of 7=4 & possessed the Ritual & all its privileges had he continued the diligent & obedient student that he was at first – but as the Angels fall of pride so fell he & was cut off – when thou hast reached by labour & study the Grade of 6=5 the Ritual will be imparted to thee at once even as was that of 5=6.

22. *Shadows of Life and Thought*, p. 229.

23. Howe, p. 277. The Anthroposophical Society was founded by Rudolph Steiner, about whom more later.

24. Ibid., p. 276. Eighty-three were in the Outer Order, forty in the Second Order. The record was dated 11 November 1915.

25. The copy is in a brown folder with alphabetised pockets which she used for various Order materials. The printed form, which she signed G. Hyde-Lees, instructs the signer to return it to 'Dr. R. W. Felkin, 47 Bassett Road, North Kensington'. 'The Address on the Pillars' was written by Mathers and published as early as 4 June 1888.

26. 'Inquire Within', pp. 92-3. See also Howe, p. 273.

27. Ibid., p. 103. See also Howe, p. 269, who records the name of the temple as *Smaragdum* Thalasses.

28. I quote from the notes in 'Investigations'.

29. 'Inquire Within', p. 137.

30. Cf. Howe, pp. 277-8.

31. 'Inquire Within', p. 133.

32. See Howe, p. 279, and King, *Ritual Magic*, p. 127: 'Felkin was forced to close the Temple down'.

33. I am indebted to Senator Yeats for permission to read and reproduce these letters from Miss Stoddart. I have been unable to locate her heirs.

34. *Letters*, p. 660.

35. The reason for Miss Stoddart's concern was made clear in a letter of 3 June 1920 to Felkin: 'You must realise that unless we know the SOURCE of our INNER Teaching and the foundations of our Order, also may I add unless we get further teachings from a recognized source we are merely the blind leading the blind' (Howe, p. 279). For a number of years Felkin had informed the members of Stella Matutina

that he was receiving teaching from the Third Order, either directly or through Ara Ben Shemesh, a mythical Arab Adept about whom they could discover very little.

36. See Howe, p. 277, and 'Inquire Within', p. 101. Hammond was an original Chief of one of the branch temples (The Secret College) founded in 1916. Since another of its Chiefs, Dr Carnegie Dickson, was to figure prominently in affairs of Amoun, the Secret College may have closed and merged with Amoun by 1919.

37. Howe, p. 279.

38. See Joseph Hone, *W. B. Yeats* (New York: Macmillan, 1943) p. 342: 'The tour lasted well into May'.

39. For information about Mrs Macrae, see Howe, pp. 96, 99, 143, 251.

40. See Appendix R.

41. See Howe, pp. 262-6.

42. According to Howe, Dr George Dickson was among 'the first of the fourteen medical men, apart from Westcott and Woodman, who were in the G.D. before 1900' (p. 51). He refused to sign the petition for Miss Horniman (p. 144). If Howe is correct that Dr George Dickson's motto was Fortes Fortuna Juvat, he must have passed it on to his son.

43. See Howe, p. 277, and 'Inquire Within', p. 101. Miss Stoddart quotes at length from the 'New Constitution' which Felkin used as authority for founding the three new temples.

44. See note 35.

45. I am quoting from a rejected version of the Dedication 'To Vestigia' intended for *A Vision* (1925).

46. Ibid. Mrs Emery died in 1917, Mathers in 1918, and Horton in 1919.

47. In *A Vision* (1925) he changed 'different' to 'practical' (p. xi), and omitted 'intimate'.

48. 'All Souls' Night', line 13.

49. The Rev. J. C. Fitzgerald (Deus Meus Deus), of Falmouth, '... had formerly been connected with the Anglican House of the Resurrection at Mirfield, Yorkshire' (Howe, p. 274; see also 'Inquire Within', p. 102, and King, *Ritual Magic*, p. 129). I can find nothing about Bernard Hamerton, an Oxford man, and little about the Rev F. N. Heazell (Evocatus Paratus), though he appears frequently in Miss Stoddart's correspondence. L.O.E. (Lux Orta Est) was Miss C. E. Hughes, a prominent member of Stella Matutina as early as 1914 (Howe, p. 271).

50. See Howe, pp. 268, 281.

51. Ibid., p. 265n.

52. See Appendix U.

53. I can find nothing further about him. Howe assumes, incorrectly I think, that the Order included a Mr Sandrieux (p. 265n) and a Mr Landrieux (p. 281). He may be correct that the 'Messrs. S. and C.' in a letter quoted by King (*Ritual Magic*, p. 105) are Sandrieux and Collison. But Miss Stoddart's capital S before vowels is very similar to her capital L, and I am uncertain about the name.

54. Ex Oriente Lux, Neville Meakin, was chosen by Felkin to succeed him as Chief of Amoun Temple (King, *Ritual Magic*, p. 106). His unexpected death in 1912 may have been the reason for Felkin's return from New Zealand to make new arrangements for the government of the Temple (see Howe, pp. 264, 269). According to Miss Stoddart, 'Dr. Felkin was told that he must find someone to take E. O. L.'s place as etheric link!' ('Inquire Within', p. 132).

55. Howe says that the letter was written to 'an unidentified Frater' (p. 280). I am relatively certain that it went to Sandrieux.

56. Ibid., pp. 280-1.

57. See Appendix V.

58. See Appendix W.

59. Hone, pp. 357-9.

60. I cannot identify Miss Imrie and Mrs Jones.

61. In *Light-Bearers of Darkness* Miss Stoddart refers frequently to the notorious *Protocols of the Elders of Zion* and relies strongly on Mrs Nesta Webster's *Secret Societies and Subversive Movements* to prove that 'the Golden Dawn, Freemasonry, and many another body were in the hands of an international body of Jewish financiers seeking world domination' (Regardie, *My Rosicrucian Adventure* [St. Paul: Llewellyn Publications, 1971] p. 28). In fact, of course, the Golden Dawn was a remarkably tolerant society. Since its teachings, in the beginning at least, were based primarily on the Cabbala, the Order tended to be pro rather than anti Jewish. The first initiate of the Golden Dawn was, after all, a Jewess: Moina Bergson.

62. Miss Stoddart quotes frequently from Weishaupt in *Light-Bearers of Darkness* to document her thesis: 'that this present movement for World Revolution leading to World Domination is but an age-long and culminating, fanatical effort on the part of some Overshadowing Power working through many secret illuminised sects' (p. 1).

63. See 'Inquire Within', p. 140, for further development of her argument.

64. I am quoting from an unpublished letter from Q.L. (Mrs Felkin) to Yeats dated 15 November 1908.

65. Howe, p. 282.

66. See note 18.

67. Howe, p. 283. Unfortunately, if he had access to the list, Howe did not publish it.

68. Book 1 was published as *Four Years* (Dublin: Cuala Press, 1921). It was finished appropriately on All Hallows' Eve, 1921 (almost exactly one year after the composition of 'All Souls' Night') and published in December.

69. In the 'Autobiography' as first drafted Yeats wrote: 'I found him a gay, companionable man, very learned in his own subject, but [without] the standards of a scholar' (Donoghue, p. 74).

70. See King, *Ritual Magic*, Chapter 16, especially p. 141.

71. *A Vision* (1925), p. ix.

72. *Letters*, p. 703.

73. See Appendix A.

74. *A Vision* (1925), p. ix.

75. *Autobiographies* (London: Macmillan, 1926) pp. 471-2.

76. Ibid., p. 232. See *The Trembling of the Veil*, p. 73, for the early version.

77. Ibid., p. 227. Yeats noted in the added passage that he had been initiated 'in May or June 1887'.

78. Ibid., p. 472.

79. He was not in England very often after the purchase of the house at 82 Merrion Square, Dublin, in February 1922. Howe conjectures that 'Yeats probably left the Stella Matutina' by 25 March 1923, the date of a letter from Miss Stoddart to an unidentified Frater: 'At last I am free from No 56!' she wrote from her brother's home in Essex. 'Never again for me! It is very nice out here and it is a great relief to have got rid of that awful incubus-house and Order' (p. 283).

80. *Autobiographies* (1926), p. 471. The edition of 1956 quoted throughout most of this study has numerous changes in punctuation and spelling (see pp. 575-6).

81. *A Vision* (1925), pp. ix-xiii, 253-6.

82. The brass-founder may have been Thomas Henry Pattinson (Vota Vita Mea), a watch and clock maker. He was a member of the Societas Rosicruciana in Anglia, the Theosophical Society, and the Golden Dawn as early as 1888. A very active member over a long period, he became Imperator of the Horus Temple in Bradford (see Howe, pp. 45n, 54, 189). Allan Bennett (Iehi Aour), a close friend of Aleister Crowley (see *Confessions, passim*), founded the Buddhist Brotherhood of the West. (For an interesting account of Yeats's discovery that Bennett had become a Buddhist see *Letters*, p. 499.) Horton and Yeats had been intimate friends, having corresponded from 1896 to 1918, three months before his death. Yeats wrote an introduction for *A Book of Images* (1898), and probably induced him to join the Golden Dawn. Although Wade (*Letters*, p. 260n) and others have said that Horton did not join the Order, numerous letters from him and a typescript copy of the Dedication to *A Vision* make clear that he did. Yeats referred to him as follows but crossed out the italicised words when he sent the copy to press: 'A third *who remained our fellow student but a short time for some dream or vision warned him that our meat could not be his* lived through that strange, perhaps strangest of all adventures – Platonic love'. A devout Christian, he explained in several letters to Yeats his reason for leaving the Order.

83. *A Vision*, p. ix. Yeats's acknowledgement is stated more strongly in a rejected version of the Dedication which pays tribute to MacGregor as well as Moina: 'In all probability this "Vision" of mine would never have been written but for those discussions in some London or Paris studio, when you and one other – with whom I quarrelled years ago – were accepted by all [marked through by Yeats] governed the discussions. I seemed alone to know, to have seen.'

The careful wording of one passage in the final draft is important

in the context of my discussion of Yeats's relationship to the Matherses :
'. . . when the first draft of this dedication was written I had not seen
you for more than thirty years, nor knew where you were nor what
you were doing . . .'. (In an early draft he is certain that 'you follow
the old study'.) Between the first draft and the final, he had apparently
received her recriminatory letters about the sketch of Mathers in
The Trembling of the Veil. Her accusations obviously disturbed Yeats
and probably were responsible for the conciliatory tone of the Dedication.

84. Ibid., p. xi. In the typescript of the Dedication Yeats wrote, 'I
look back to it as a time when we were full of a folk-lore that has perhaps been handed down for generations'. In revision he changed 'folk-
lore' first to 'reverie' then to 'phantasy' and marked through 'perhaps'.
He also changed 'folk-lore' to 'phantasy' in the sentence I have quoted
in the text.

85. This is the first of many significant alterations in the galley
proofs. I am preparing, with the permission of Senator Yeats and the
collaboration of Walter K. Hood, a critical edition of *A Vision* (1925).

86. *A Vision*, p. xi.

87. *Autobiographies*, p. 576.

88. *A Vision*, p. xii. In the typescript of the Dedication Yeats marked
through the opening paragraph of Part III, which contains a reference
to 'All Souls' Night', perhaps because he intended to replace the poem
with a prose Epilogue he was composing 'To Vestigia'. The rejected
paragraph, somewhat different from the published version, illustrates
Yeats's dilemma with admirable clarity : 'As I most fear to disappoint
those that come to this book through some interest in my poetry, I
have printed what they would greatly dislike in italics, that they may
dip here and there in the verse or into my comments upon life or
history undisturbed. Upon the other hand my old fellow students
or their pupils can confine themselves to the italicized, explanatory
and technical part.'

89. Ibid., pp. xii-xiii.

90. *Autobiographies*, p. 576.

97. 'All Souls' Night', *A Vision*, p. 255.

92. Ibid., p. xiii.

EPILOGUE

1. *Letters*, p. 712.

2. Ibid. See Richard Taylor, *Frank Pearce Sturm: His Life, Letters, and
Collected Work* (Urbana : University of Illinois Press, 1969). Sturm
was interested in a wide variety of esoteric lore. He visited Yeats at
Oxford in February 1921, and they corresponded sporadically for more
than twenty years. Several of the letters are about *A Vision*. Taylor has
published all the letters he could find (pp. 73-110).

3. *Letters*, pp. 728, 733.

4. Ibid., p. 739.

5. *Bibliography*, p. 191. By this time so much of the first version 'has been omitted and so much new material added, that this is almost a new book' (p. 192).

6. Having joined the Golden Dawn in 1894, Rosher advanced to 5=6 as early as 1896. He was one of those who signed the petition for the reinstatement of Miss Horniman (Howe, pp. 143, 154n). In the reorganisation of 1900, after the expulsion of Mathers, Rosher was made a member of the Adepti Litterati to instruct in Symbolism.

7. *Confessions*, p. 179. Rosher lived briefly with Crowley in 1899 but 'found the strain intolerable' (p. 188). Crowley described him as 'a widely travelled Jack-of-all-trades. He had invented a patent water-closet and been court painter to the Sultan of Morocco' (p. 179). In the letter to Yeats, Rosher mentions having written 'a Series of Stories & pieces about Morocco'.

8. Yeats's interest in 'The Vision of an Archer' dates from 1896, according to *Autobiographies* (pp. 372-5, 576-9). Over the years he must have discussed the meaning of this vision with many people, including William Wynn Westcott, who informed him: 'You have hit upon things that you can never have read of in any book; these symbols belong to as part of the Christian Cabbala' (*Autobiographies*, p. 374). For an excellent account of the utilisation of Yeats's vision by Fiona Macleod (William Sharp) see William F. Halloran, 'W. B. Yeats and William Sharp: the Archer Vision', *English Language Notes*, VI, no. 4, (June 1969) pp. 273-80.

9. I cannot identify Soror F.E.T.

10. I am indebted to Halloran for the information that Jones did the coloured plates for Peter C. Mitchell's *The Childhood of Animals* (London, 1912).

11. *Letters*, p. 770. I cannot identify the Cabbalistic Hegelian professor.

12. Ibid., pp. 770-1.

13. The reference to Masonic brethren raises the question of whether or not Yeats may have belonged to some branch of Masonry. During the residence at Oxford Georgie Yeats signed a Declaration of intent to join 'The Honourable Fraternity of Antient Masonry', having been proposed by Marion L. Halsey, G[rand] M[aster]. The brief 'Instructions for Candidates' emphasise that 'Antient Masonry aims at filling the traditional forms of Masonry with a spiritual content'. The admonition to the candidate that 'he should be prepared to *know*, to *will*, to *dare*, and to be *silent*' looks as though it might have come directly from 'The Historic Lecture to Neophytes of the Golden Dawn' which urged the students to '*Will, Dare, Learn*, and *be Silent*'. Although I do not know whether or not Yeats was also proposed for membership in Antient Masonry, it seems likely that he would have been proposed at the same time as Mrs Yeats. If so, however, I have not discovered

a copy of his Declaration, and he was usually careful to preserve the records. I cannot identify Marion Halsey.

14. This account may not be quite right. There is evidence that Waite's group kept the properties when they broke away from Felkin's group in 1903 (Howe, p. 254). I rather imagine that the properties were never stored in the name of Mrs Mary Felkin (Felkin's first wife). I do not know why they would have been stored or why they would have passed to Waite's group if they had been.

15. *Shadows of Life and Thought*, p. 228.

16. See King, *Ritual Magic*, pp. 154-5, for a brief account of the Stella Matutina and the Alpha and Omega in the 1930s.

17. Alfred Tennyson, 'Morte D'Arthur', lines 241-2.

18. *A Vision*, pp. xix, xii.

19. *Letters*, p. 773.

Appendixes

APPENDIX A

WITHOUT PREJUDICE.

LIST OF DOCUMENTS*

ATTESTING THE ACCOMPANYING STATEMENT.

DOCUMENT.

I. *February 16th*, 1900. Letter from D.D.C.F. to S.S.D.D. accusing S.A. of forgery.

II. *March 18th.* Letter from L.O. to D.D.C.F., explaining how the position of the Order was affected by Doc. I.

III. *March 18th.* Letter from D.D.C.F. to S.S.D.D. refusing to recognize the Committee or to go into the question of Doc. I.

IV. *March 23rd.* Letter from D.D.C.F. to S.S.D.D. purporting to remove her from her post in Second Order.

V. *March 23rd.* Letter from D.D.C.F. to L.O. of similar purport.

VI. *March 24th.* Resolutions passed by the Second Order, empowering the Committee to act for them.

VII. *March 24th.* Letter from L.O. to D.D.C.F. showing that the suppression of Doc. I would amount to compounding a felony.

VIII. *March 25th.* Letter from S.S.D.D. to D.D.C.F. explaining the reason of the formation of the Committee.

IX. *March 29th.* Report of Committee on an interview between L.O. and S.A. with regard to his correspondence with S.D.A.

* I have occasionally changed confusing errors in capitalisation and punctuation throughout these Appendixes.—G.M.H.

X. *April 2nd.* Letter from D.D.C.F. to L.O. refusing to acknowledge right of Second Order to elect Committee, and threatening members with the Punitive Current.

XI. (a) *April 17th.* Account by H.E.S. of the forcing of the rooms by Crowley and Miss Simpson.

(b) Printed Summons from Crowley.

(c) *April 19th.* Account of Crowley's arrival to interview members.

(d) Printed document from Crowley.

XII. (a) *April 26th,* 1900. Letter from D.D.C.F. to M.W.Th. proving identity of Crowley and the "Envoy."

(b) Telegram from Crowley to M.W.Th.

XIII. *April.* Resolutions passed suspending D.D.C.F. and his Council.

XIV. Speech by D.E.D.I. on D.D.C.F.'s position.

XV. *April 21st.* Regulations passed by Second Order framing the New Constitution.

WITHOUT PREJUDICE.

DOCUMENT I.

N.B.—*Read this letter carefully before showing any part of it to anyone!*

87, Rue Mozart,
Auteuil, Paris,
16th February, 1900.

C. et V. H. Soror, S.S.D.D.,

My time is just now so enormously occupied with the arrangements for the Buildings and Decorations of the Egyptian Temple of Isis in Paris, as well as other matters, that I *must* write as briefly as possible.

(a) I have never wished to interfere in your private affairs, but if you choose to bring mine into a discussion in a Second Order Meeting, the matter concerns me as well as yourself.

(b) As you did not date your letter to me, and as I received it on the 13th January, 1900, it was difficult for me to conceive that it had been written *after* instead of *before* the meeting on the twelfth. I possess a copy of the minutes of that meeting.

(c) I *refuse definitely* to close Isis-Urania Temple, and am prepared to receive the Resignations from their offices of those chiefs who no longer wish to serve as such. I can understand in your case, that in addition to your somewhat heavy work in the Second Order, holding office in Isis has been an additional load.

(d) Now, with regard to the Second Order, it would be with the *very greatest regret* both from my personal regard for you, as well as from the occult standpoint that I should receive your Resignation as my Representative in the Second Order in London; but I cannot let you form a combination to make a schism therein with the idea of working secretly or avowedly under "Sapere Aude," under the mistaken impression that he received an Epitome of the Second Order work from G. H. Soror, "Sapiens dominabitur astris." For this forces me to tell you plainly (and, understand me well, I can prove to the hilt every word which I here say and more, and were I confronted with S.A., I should say the same), though for the sake of the Order, and for the circumstance that it would mean so deadly a blow to S.A.'s reputation, I entreat you to keep this secret from the *Order*, for the present, at least, though you are at perfect liberty to show *him* this if you think fit, *after mature consideration.*

(e) He has NEVER been *at any time* either in personal or in written communication with the Secret Chiefs of the Order, he having *either himself forged or procured to be forged* the professed correspondence between him and them, and my tongue having been tied all these years by a previous Oath of Secrecy to him, demanded by him, from me, before showing me what he had either done or caused to be done or both.—You must comprehend from what little I say here, the *extreme gravity* of such a matter, and again I ask you, both for his sake and that of the Order, not to force me to go farther into the subject.

I again reiterate that *every atom* of the knowledge of the Order has come *through me alone* from o—o to 5—6 inclusive, and that it is I alone who have been and am in communication with the Secret Chiefs of the Order.

I may further incidentally remark that "Sapiens dominabitur astris" is now in Paris, and aiding me with the Isis movement.

Lastly, I again ask you to consider well this letter, and not to put me in such a position that I shall be compelled to act publicly.

Yours in fraternity and sincerity,

DEO DUCE COMITE FERRO,

7—4,

Chief of the Second Order.

DOCUMENT II.

69, THORNTON AVENUE,
BEDFORD PARK, W.,
March 18th, 1900.

CARE EST V. H. FRA, D.D.C.F.

I enclose you copy of a letter which I addressed to you on the 4th inst., in case by any chance it has miscarried.

On the other hand, it may be that, for reasons which you are doubtless better able to judge of than ourselves, you have hitherto refrained from making a reply. It has therefore seemed desirable to my Committee that I should state more clearly the views which have actuated them.

I am accordingly requested to say that your statements respecting forgeries by G. H. FRA, N.O.M., appearing likely to shake the confidence of the whole Second Order in some of its fundamental traditions, it appeared best in the first instance to confine the consideration of the matter exclusively to the seven members whose names I have indicated.

We find ourselves in the position of having lent ourselves— and such influence as our long connection with the Order may constitute—to the dissemination of ideas, traditions or actual teaching to others who have come into the Order after us, and it is consequently with deep concern that we now gather reflection is cast on some of them—a state of mind which is contributed to by the uncertainty at present surrounding the matter.

If therefore you can see your way to accede to our suggestion (made in response to your offer to prove the matter completely) we shall all feel at least assured and be able to deliberate, if need be, in conjunction with yourself as to the desirability of taking further action, in order to place the Order on its true basis.

Yours fraternally,
LEVAVI OCULOS.

DOCUMENT III.

87, RUE MOZART,
AUTEUIL, PARIS,
18th *March*, 1900.

C. ET V. H. SOR, S.S.D.D.

I approve your choice of officers for the ensuing 6 months for Isis-Urania, Temple No. 3, viz. (here follow names of officers, password, name of candidate for admittance to o—o.)

I in no way recognise any Committee formed by you to consider my *private* letter to you concerning the matter upon which I wrote; and I shall not discuss the matter further for the present unless I deem it advisable so to do.

All those complications could have been avoided had you written me an open straightforward letter at the beginning of the year, saying you wished to retire *from office*.

I duly received Mrs. ——— and her daughter's resignations, which are just as well.

All good wishes from yours fraternally and in haste,

DEO DUCE COMITE FERRO.

DOCUMENT IV.

87, Rue Mozart,
Auteuil, Paris,
March 23rd, 1900.

C. et V. H. Sor. "Sapientia Sapienti Dono Data."

My letter was a personal one to you, I did not empower you to form any Committee for its consideration, and I refuse to recognise such Committee. I forbid the meeting of the Second Order called for to-morrow; and I charge you on your pledge of obedience to me as a Theoricus Adept to abstain from further action in the matter.

I, furthermore, remove you from your position as my Representative in the Second Order in London, for I can no longer feel confidence in you as such.

Yours fraternally,
DEO DUCE COMITE FERRO.

Chief of the Second Order. 7—4

DOCUMENT V.

87, Rue Mozart,
Paris,
March 23rd, 1900.

C. et V. H. Fra. "L.O."

I thank you for your courteous letters. I in no sense acknowledge the Committee you mention; neither do I intend to go into the matter with you at present.

My letter was a private letter to my then representative, "S.S.D.D."

By this post I write to relieve her of that office. I forbid the meeting of the Second Order called for to-morrow, and I charge you on your pledge of obedience to me as a Theoricus Adept to abstain from further action in the matter.

Yours fraternally,
DEO DUCE COMITE FERRO.

Chief of the Second Order. 7—4

To V. H. Fra. Levavi Oculos, Th. Ad. Mi. 5—6

DOCUMENT VI.

RESOLUTIONS PASSED AT A MEETING OF THE SECOND ORDER, DULY CONVENED AND HELD ON MARCH 24*th*, 1900.

1. That V. H. SORORES, S.S.D.D., Deo Date, and V. H. FRATRES, D.E.D.I., Hora et Semper, M.W.Th., Volo Noscere and Levavi Oculos, are hereby appointed by this representative Meeting of Members of the Second Order to act as a Committee and to investigate the questions which have been placed before this Meeting concerning the circumstances surrounding the foundation of this Order, and to report thereon in due course.
2. That all official work or actions of the Order, apart from the special work of the Committee and such part of the routine work of the Order as they may think desirable, be suspended until the Committee report.

———

DOCUMENT VII.

69, THORNTON AVENUE,
BEDFORD PARK, N.
24*th March*, 1900.

CARE ET G. H. FRATER, D.D.C.F.

I am in receipt of your letter, contents of which I note. I regret, however, that it did not arrive before my departure this morning, one consequence of which has been that members of the Second Order met together this afternoon in ignorance of your wishes.

At that meeting, Resolutions were passed, copies of which I enclose you.

It is unfortunate that you did not mark your letter to S.S.D.D. "private" in the first instance; now, however, that it has been freely disclosed within the Second Order, members feel—and I am bound to say I concur in the view—that the constitutive warrant upon which the Order was originally founded is im-pugned, because the correspondence which now turns out to be forged (and which I and others remember quite clearly) led up to the warrant, granting it in fact to the three original chiefs.

Abstention on our part to follow the matter up, would clearly be the equivalent of compounding a felony, and the universal feeling is—and here again I cannot refuse my concurrence—that no obligation subversive of morality can be binding either by natural law or the law of the Land.

That this, too, is your own view is clear from the action which you have recently elected to take in somewhat similar circumstances, and the necessity for which no one deplores more than myself.

One more thing I wish to point out as regards myself and that is that the correspondence in question, shown to me as it was, years ago, was not without its influence upon my mind, assuring me (as I considered) in some positive measure of the existence of the secret Chiefs of the Order; indeed, as I analyse these impressions, I find they were almost exclusively derived from that source. Certainly this was so in the earlier stages. While, therefore, I do not say that had these notions been lacking, I should not have progressed further, it is clearly open to others to take that position. As a piece of historical evidence, I know I have often mentioned the matter of these letters and their contents to others in the Second Order both before and since their withdrawal, and to that extent at least, have un-wittingly assisted in the perpetration of the deception. To such, in justice to myself, I owe the duty of making a correc-tion.

Yours fraternally,
LEVAVI OCULOS.

DOCUMENT VIII.

Bromley,
25th March.

Care et G. H. Frater.

Your letter to me was marked "consider this letter well before showing any part of it to anyone." I did so—I went into the country and spent days of thought on the whole subject. I saw that if I kept silence I should become a party to a fraud, and therefore took the advice of some Members of the Order who have always been friendly to your interests. We sent you repeated messages, couched in most respectful terms, pointing out as delicately as possible the impressions conveyed by your letter. You refused to recognise this friendly Committee, so the only thing to be done was to get the Committee appointed by the 2nd Order Council of Adepts. This has been done, and neither I nor any one else have power to prevent the matter being carried to its legal conclusion.

I did not receive your letter of 23rd of March until I returned to my private address at 12 o'clock on Saturday evening, where it had been forwarded as usual from 36,————. Our oaths are covered by the written assurance that nothing contrary to our civil, moral or religious welfare is demanded from us.

Yours fraternally,
S.S.D.D.

DOCUMENT IX.

March 29th.

Fra. L.O. reports having seen V. H. Fra. S.A., who gave his honourable assurance that for anything he knew to the contrary the German lady, Fräulein Sprengel, the author of the letters alleged to be forged by him (S.A.) was the person she purported to be; his communications with her had only been by letter, and he had bona fide posted letters to her in Germany and received letters in reply.

————

DOCUMENT X.

87, RUE MOZART,
AUTEUIL, PARIS,
2nd April, 1900.

C. ET V. H. FRA. "LEVAVI OCULOS."

I do *not* recognise the right of the Second Order either to elect a Committee without my authorization and consent, or to take upon themselves the responsibility arresting of the work of the Order, save and only by my direct commands. I *annul* the Committee and I *annul* the Resolutions passed at the meeting of the 24th March, 1900. I cannot therefore accept your report of that meeting, and I return you herewith the typewritten copy of its proceedings which you sent me.

I stand by my manifesto issued to the Theorici Adepti on Thursday, October 29th, 1896, after the comprehension of which each Theoricus Adept sent me a written Declaration of allegiance which I have kept as a pleasing momento of fidelity to their engagements, that of "De Profundis ad Lucem" (Gardner) is especially of value in the view of the line of action he has recently taken.

I have always acknowledged and shall always maintain the authority of the Secret Chiefs of the Order, to whom and the Eternal Gods I bow, but to *none* beside!

I know to a nicety the capacities of my human brain and intelligence and what these can of themselves grasp, and I therefore know also when the Forces of the Beyond, and the Presences of the Infinite manifest, and when the Great Adepts of this Planet still in the body of flesh, the Secret Chiefs of our Order are with me.

Do you imagine that where such men as Count de Gébelin, Eteilla, Christian and Levi failed in their endeavour to discover the Tarot attributions that I would be able of my own power and intelligence *alone* to lift the veil which has baffled *them?**

You have seen the development of the Theosophical Society, and that since the death of Madame Blavatsky nothing but

---

* These attributions are given in the Cypher MSS., and were not found through D.D.C.F.'s lifting the veil, whether alone or otherwise.—S.S.D.D.

turmoil and strife have arisen, and that that association is tottering to its fall. And I tell you plainly that were it *possible* to remove me from my place as the Visible Head of our Order (the which *cannot* be without my own consent, because of certain magical links) you would find nothing but disruption and trouble fall upon you all until you had expiated so severe a Karma as that of opposing a current sent at the end of a century to regenerate a Planet.

And for the first time since I have been connected with the Order, I shall formulate my request to Highest Chiefs for the Punitive Current to be prepared, to be directed against those who rebel; should they consider it (after examination of the Status of the London Order) advisable.

Some of you have been pleased to remark that I have condoned a felony. I would sooner condone any number of offences against the Law of Man, than I would fail in the first duty of an Occulist, which is Fraternity and Fidelity, and it is the want of these in the English Order which has been the root of all mischief.

It is a very easy thing for you to ask "Sapere Aude" for the address of "Sapiens dominabitur astris," and find out if she lived there, Fraulein Sprengel I think he said her name was, and I believe the address he gave was Ulm, Heidelburg or Nuremburg, also it should be easy to get from him the copy of the correspondence which he retired. But I have nothing to do with all this, and "S.S.D.D." has acted injudiciously in making my letter to her as my representative a lever for increasing dissension in the Order.

I thank you, as always, for your courteous manner of writing, and you have my best wishes.

I have been and am so occupied that I could not answer your letter before. Athor Temple alone takes much of my time and it is increasing rapidly in numbers.

Yours in haste and with best wishes,

DEO DUCE COMITE FERRO.

DOCUMENT XIA.

Statement by Fra, H.E.S.

On Tuesday, 17th instant, I received telegram from Miss Cracknell to come at once to Blythe Road. On arriving, I found that the rooms which had been closed by Order of Mrs. Emery had been broken into. On entering, after a certain resistance, I found there Aleister Crowley and Miss Elaine Simpson, who declared that they had taken possession by the authority of MacGregor Mathers, and showing me documents to that effect. I said the authority of that gentleman had been suspended by a practically unanimous vote at a duly convened meeting of the Members of the Society. Crowley said that Miss Cracknell, who had entered with me, must leave the room, as she had been suspended from membership, which, of course, I refused to allow, except with that lady's consent.

In the meantime, Mrs. Emery arrived, and, seeing the state of affairs, fetched a constable.

Unfortunately, Mr. Wilkinson, the landlord, was absent, and we could not then satisfactorily prove to whom legally the rooms belonged.

They had forced open the doors, put on fresh locks, and so for the time being were practically in possession.

If I had known the character of the man who goes under the name of E. A. Crowley, Aleister MacGregor, Count Svareff, I should not have allowed him to remain longer than I could have helped in the rooms of the Society. I did not then realise that he had no right there, having been absolutely refused admission to the London Society of the R.R. et A.C. Nevertheless, as subsequent events proved, it was well that MacGregor Mathers was enabled to further carry out his contemptible, theatrical farce as far as he did.

DOCUMENT XIb.

17th April, 1900.

You are cited to appear at Headquarters at 11.45 a.m. on the 20th inst.

Should you be unable to attend, an appointment at the earliest possible moment must be made by telegraphing to "MacGregor," at Headquarters.

There will be no meeting on the 21st inst.

By order of DEO DUCE COMITE FERRO,
Chief of the S ∴ O ∴

DOCUMENT XIc.

STATEMENT BY FRA, H.E.S.

Early Thursday morning, Mr. Yeats and I called on Mr. Wilkinson (the landlord), and asked him how it was that he had allowed anyone to break into the rooms. It seems that Mrs. Emery's injunction as to the closing of the rooms had not been reported to him by his clerk, and that Mrs. Emery had not given written instructions to that effect; he knew, of course, that members came and went as they liked. We, therefore, felt that we could not hold him responsible for the intrusion. Mr. Wilkinson said Mrs. Emery was his tenant; she always paid him the rent for the rooms, and he held her responsible for the same.

Mrs. Emery had given us a letter to the landlord authorising us to have the locks changed, which we had done forthwith.

About 11.30, Aleister Crowley arrived in Highland dress, a black mask over his face, and a plaid thrown over his head and shoulders, an enormous gold or gilt cross on his breast, and a dagger at his side. He swiftly passed the clerk in the shop below, which he had no right to do, but was stopped by Mr. Wilkinson in the back hall, who sent us word upstairs. Mr. Yeats and I went downstairs and told him he had no right whatever to enter the premises. By his request the landlord sent for a constable, who, on learning the situation, told him to go, which he at once did, saying he should place the matter in the hands of a lawyer. A man arrived about 1 o'clock, who showed a letter from Mr. Crowley, asking him to attend at 36, Blythe Road, at 11 o'clock, but he had been all over London searching for Blythe Road. He did not quite know what he had come for, he thought there was some sort of entertainment on. Mr. C. had engaged him, he said, outside the Alhambra, evidently in the official capacity of chucker-out. I took the man's name and address. Mr. Wilkinson was interested in the matter of Mr. Crowley's intrusion from the fact that his name was on the black list of the journal of the Trades' Protection Association, to which Mr. Wilkinson belonged. Mr. Crowley gave as his authority for entering the rooms, the Earl of Glenstrae, otherwise Count MacGregor. There were numerous telegrams that day for MacGregor, 36, Blythe Road, and late in the evening a foreign telegram. These were all refused, name being unknown. A parcel early in the morning arrived from Clarkson, wigmaker, for Miss Simpson, which was handed to her on her departure.

DOCUMENT XID.

15, RANDOLPH ROAD,
MAIDA VALE, W.,
Monday, April 23rd.

The Envoy of G. H. Frater Deo Duce Comite Ferro, 7°–4°, Chief of the S.O., unto all members of the London Branch of the S.O.

GREETING.

It is first fitting that I express my sincere regret that members of the S.O. should have been put to unnecessary trouble.

In defiance of a promise* given by Mrs. Emery, Miss Cracknell, and Mr. Hunter, to V.H. Soror Fidelis and V.H. Frater Perdurabo, the rooms were forced open and various property of

* Inaccurate.—S.S.D.D.

mine detained, while the projected interviews were made impossible.

The Courts of Law will shortly decide further concerning this action.

It should be mentioned that the story of the masked man is altogether untrue.

I hereby suspend V.H. Sorores S.S.D.D., and Tempus Omnia Revelat, and V.H. Fratres Hora et Semper, Levavi Oculos, and Demon est Deus Inversus, from both orders.

I must now request that an appointment be made with me by each individual member of the S.O., and at the above address.

Letters may be addressed to Miss Elaine Simpson.

Failing this, or a serious and reasonable excuse, suspension from both orders will operate automatically at noon on Tuesday.

My authority for this action will be shown to each member on arriving at the interview.

Witness my Seal.

DOCUMENT XIIA.

This is NOT a private letter!

87, RUE MOZART,
AUTEUIL, PARIS,
April 26th, 1900.

C. ET V. H. FRATER "Ma Wahanu Thesi,"

I have received your letters and recognise that both in them and in your recent action there has been much more precipitation than discretion, and while admitting from what I know of you that your intent has been to act rightly, I none the less condemn the manner of such action and the liberty of speech in which you have dared to indulge regarding what I have thought fit to do and to command to be done. The only excuse I see in your favour beyond what I have already admitted is that in the midst of a current of absolute mania which appears to be acting in the London Second Order, you would seem to have somewhat of sanity left.

To that quality in you therefore, I address the rest of this letter. And I am not writing thus with the purpose of insulting you, but rather of endeavouring to aid you to arouse yourself to a clearer comprehension of your environment.

(a) Your remarks *re* the matter of "Sapere Aude" not being desired to lead by certain members of the Second Order are difficult to reconcile with the FACT† of "Demon est Deus Inversus" having asked him to lead them should they succeed in shaking off my authority; as well as with S.S.D.D's having implied or expressed such an idea as she believed S.A. to have received an Epitome of the Second Order working from "Sapiens dominabitur astris." I would advise you on another occasion to be more certain of your premiss major before risking an enthymeme to me.

(b) You appear to discern no perfidy in "S.S.D.D's" making public a letter of mine to her of which every line bore the meaning of a privileged communication, neither do you seem to see any error in the malignant hurry with which she endeavoured to place either "Sapere Aude" or myself, or both, in a position of public humiliation, notwithstanding the many kindnesses she has received in the past from us both and especially from "S.A."

(c) As regards mistakes in the Order Knowledge it does not appear to have struck these would-be critics that the subject was beyond their criticism. But I admit that I *have* committed one great though unavoidable fault, which is this: in giving these persons so great a knowledge I have not also been able to give them brains and intelligence to comprehend it, for this miracle the Gods have not granted me the power to perform. You had better address your reproaches to the Gods rather than to me, unless some spark of returning wisdom can make you recognise in such "critics" the swine who trample the Divine teachings underfoot.

You say "am I to understand that there is never to be any truth and light let in upon our order?" I tell you there has been too much truth and too much light let in upon these rebellious children of clay, and it has blinded them!

† This "fact" is fiction.—D.E.D.I.

(*d*) For my Envoy—I sent him as my *impersonal* representative, wherefore I selected a man in whose fidelity I could trust (a very rare factor in the London Second Order), who, being the latest admitted, was without influence gained therein by seniority or grade; and still further to mark his impersonality in this matter, I distinguished him by a symbol, and not by a name, and advised him further to wear a mask of Osiris as laid down in Z, should the same be necessary; so as completely to separate and distinguish between his individuality and the office with which I had invested him.

And I may remark that to term the Highland Dress a "masquerade" is hardly even *English good taste* when the blood of the Highland Regiments is reddening South African earth; though in my opinion shed in a mistaken quarrel and in the wrong cause.

How difficult it seems for many of the London Second Order to comprehend that I am neither to be bought, bribed, persuaded, tricked, bullied, frightened nor ridiculed into any line of action that I do not see fit to take! Could they only have understood this, the present difficult position in which they have voluntarily placed themselves would not have arisen.

Yours still fraternally,
DEO DUCE COMITE FERRO.

Chief of the Second Order.   7—4

DOCUMENT XIIB.

Inland Telegram.

329, VAUXHALL BRIDGE ROAD, S.W.,
27th April, 1900.

To BLACKDEN,   Handed in 3.23 p.m.
    6, Topsfield Parade, Crouch End.
MacGregor's admission identify envoy made in error, please keep it secret for everybody's sake.

PERDURABO.

DOCUMENT XIII.

April 19th.

RESOLUTION PASSED AT COMMITTEE MEETING.

That Messrs. MacGregor Mathers and Dr. Berridge, Mrs. and Miss Simpson, are hereby suspended from membership in R.R. et A.C. in London, pending the decision of the College of Adepti. And furthermore that no person shall be deemed to belong to the London Branch who has not been initiated by that body in London.

DOCUMENT XIV.

A meeting of the Society of the R.R. et A.C. in London was held on Saturday, the 21st of April, 1900. The chair was taken at 3.45 p.m. After V.H. FRATER, L.O. had read the minutes of the previous meetings, V.H. SOROR Vigilate proposed, and V.H. FRATER Causa Scientiæ seconded, the adoption of the report.

Thereon, V.H. FRATER, D.E.D.I. gave an address on the history of the Order, and explained the illegalities which had crept in, in recent years. At the commencement of the Order there were three Chiefs, the G.H. FRATRES, M.E.V., N.O.M., and D.D.C.F., but at the G.H. FRATER, M.E.V.'s death, no Chief was appointed in his place, and again upon the G.H. FRATER, S.A.'s resignation some four years ago, no one was appointed in his place. Therefore, instead of the three Chiefs required by the constitution there came to be only one Chief—the G.H. FRATER, D.D.C.F. The speaker spoke of the personal sorrow that it gave him to describe the actions which the G.H. FRATER, D.D.C.F. had taken. The G.H. FRATER, D.D.C.F. had gradually become entirely autocratic, and furthermore, moved as it seems by jealousy, he had made a charge against the V.H. FRATER, S.A., of forging, or causing to be forged, the documents on which the warrant was based and the Order established. This charge, when requested to do so, the G.H. FRATER, D.D.C.F. absolutely refused to substantiate or to withdraw. He then referred to the not less lamentable, though altogether ludicrous, proceedings of the past week, which were referred to in the Committee's report, and went on to say, that although he was sure we should all agree in our gratitude for what the G.H. FRATER, D.D.C.F. had done for us, yet his amazing actions showed that a change must be made in our constitution. He then referred to the legal aspects of the matter and to the property of the Order, and explained the pecuniary transactions which had taken place between 1892 and 1896. He then went on to refer to the resolutions which the Committee proposed for the reconstruction of the Order.

DOCUMENT XV.

April 21*st.*

RESOLUTIONS PASSED BY 22 MEMBERS OF R.R. et A.C. ON THE 21*st* OF *April.*

1. That the past Constitution of the Order of R.R. et A.C. in London is hereby declared at an end.
2. That the Order R.R. et A.C. in London consists of those who are here present, and of such among the old Members who are unable to be present but who shall hereafter assent to the resolutions of this meeting, and of such members of the Society known as the G.D. in the Outer, as shall be invited by the Executive Body.
3. That the Executive Body of the R.R. et A.C. shall consist of 3 Chiefs, and of 7 Members who may or may not be amongst those most advanced but who shall as far as possible be specialists in the various studies of the Order.
4. That the aforesaid 3 Chiefs and 7 Members shall be first nominated by the 12 most advanced members of the Order; then elected by the members of the R.R. et A.C. in London, and they shall stand annually for re-election.
5. If at any time there be more than 12 members in the

highest degree, they shall choose 12 from among themselves, either by election or according to seniority in progress, who shall act as nominators of the Executive.

6. The Committee of 7 which was appointed on March 12th shall administer the affairs of the Order until the new Executive has been fully constituted.

7. Soror Vigilate to take the place of M.W.Th. on the Committee.

8. Frater Æquo Animo to take that of Volo Noscere.

9. That the Executive acting in conjunction with the most advanced members of the Order enquire into the question of how far the system of teaching and the rituals of the Order should be altered, with a view to separating what may be genuine from what may have been added by the personal fantasy of any member of this Order.

10. Expulsion only to take place when the Executive and the 12 advanced members sitting together agree by a three-fourths majority, at least three-quarters being present.

11. That this change in the Constitution of the Order in no way affects its connection with the Rosicrucian Order.

APPENDIX B

Copy of a letter sent to Sub Spe 17th Jan 1901

87 the Grove Hammersmith.W.

Care V H Fra Sub Spe.

It seems necessary for me to make a semi-official statement to the Theorici regarding my work in the Order during the last 3 years in order to account for the present state of feeling of which naturally you became aware on your visit to London.

You may remember at the end of the year 1895 I came across an Egyptian Adept in the British Museum and freely told other members of the possibilities opened out. On Jan 27th 1896 I received a long letter from DDCF. in reply to a letter of mine sending a charged drawing of the Egyptian and asking him if I were not grossly deceived by her claiming to be equal in rank to an 8–3 of our Order at the same time giving me numbers which I afterwards calculated to be correct for that grade. I still possess his letter approving altogether of my working with her, and saying it was necessary to make offerings & then all would be well – &c &c. I soon found there was a considerable prejudice against Egyptian Symbolism amongst the members of the Order and I began to hold my tongue after having recommended the various clearly marked groups of thinkers (such as Indian, Christian and so on) to work steadily and regularly by themselves each under some more advanced person. To you and to those who were not antipathetic I spoke more freely. When the splits in the Order itself became more and more pronounced my work with 3 others having become extremely interesting we resolved to carry out a plan suggested by an Egyptian for the holding together of a strong nucleus on purely Order lines. This was done by using the symbol of the globular sephiroth : formulating it regularly once a week, each of us formulating the whole symbol, so that the strong should counterbalance the weak, placing it over the Order, the planet, then gradually increasing in size and imagining the symbols disposed as in the star maps on the visible universe. Here we invoked the light from the true Kether that the spirit of life and growth might be evoked by that light and that the great guardian wall of the sephiroth might shed its influence upon the planet and the Order. This being done the Light was carefully concentrated upon the earth and upon the Sphere of the Order and upon our own spheres. This was done regularly once a week, and members were warned it was to be used for no purposes of personal desire, but for all. If we invoked the light upon the evil that was as yet unfitted for transmutation it was to be prevented from operating by the Great Guardian of the formula and not one of us has been allowed to work for our own selfish aims by means of the formula. It is quite true that in my experience of the working of the Order I have found several very capable persons who cannot interest themselves in many of the Order formulas of clairvoyance and divination yet who were intensely interested in the end I had in view and which is expressed above, the late soror Volo being one of them. Others were interested in the study of the Egyptian religion but did not take interest in mediaeval symbolism. The Order passed into an apparently more and more hopeless state. There appeared no possible way in which it could emerge from the dishonesties which desecrated its symbols. Endless divisions, bickerings, and scandals choked its activity. In the mean time the group I had founded and the groups you and others founded continued their work and at last in 1899 the time came. In the early months of 1900 matters were so arranged by the eternal powers that we were freed from the load of dishonesty under which we had been struggling.

All went well until September 1900 when I found everything I proposed was objected to. After a few weeks I discovered that my group which had been working quietly for 3 years was being violently attacked. First on the ground that we used the Order Rooms. It was then arranged that on Mondays and Wednesdays Members should by giving a weeks notice have the right to engage the rooms for 2 hours at a time. I was very glad of this as I had frequently been unable to go into the rooms myself when other Members were using them and it was a convenience all round to know when this was likely to be the case.

I was then accused of keeping valuable information to myself. You will understand I think that with the anti-Egyptian Feeling about I shall still refuse to discuss Egyptian formulae with anyone not specially in sympathy with the ancient Egyptians. As for the working of my group we each sit at home and go through the stages of the invocation, we each simply invoke light upon the perfectly balanced symbol of the tree of life projected on a sphere, we do not work at clairvoyance or divination in any special way and I do not admit that we are concealing knowledge from anyone seeing that the whole of the symbol is explained in the Star maps lecture. I have written to you at great length because you are in the country and I have no opportunity of speaking to you. Would you kindly send this letter to soror Veritas Vincit. I have recently put up the following notice at 36 B.R.

SSDD wishes to say that any Member of the Order who feels sympathy either for the study of the Egyptian Book of the Dead or for the symbolism of the Tree of Life projected on a Sphere will be very welcome to join her group on their attainment of the grade of Theoricus.

Yours under the wings of the eternal O
Sapientia Sapienti Dono Date 5–6 T.A.M.

APPENDIX C

Letter from Miss A. E. F. Horniman to F. L. Gardner
23 Nov 96

Care 'Daffodil'

I was so really sorry about the misfortune with the papers. You never spare yourself, I know, and always try so hard that it is a real pity that they are lost. But on no account be discouraged – do them over again at once – it will seem easier this time and this six months' added experience ought to make you do even better. Time is not really lost when one is studying even on other subjects. I will look out for the book you mention in the little accompanying paper. Naturally I am glad that I am 'missed' – it shows that I was useful – but I must assure you for the 100th time that you now know far more than I did when I began to teach.

For Tarot Cards, etc. I can only tell you what I have found out for myself by experience and practice. I take the High Priestess the Moon in my hand and look at the figure and imagine it as a stately woman in golden mitre in red gold-bordered robes on a throne with a book in her hand. I make the Lunar Hexagram saying Shaddai El Chai, Gabriel, Malka, Chasmodai, Gimel and pass through the figure I have made, as we do through a Tatwa symbol (I do this as I write). I seem to stand before a solid figure, similar to what I have built up but large and brilliant against a pale bluish atmosphere – her face is pale and rather round and very peaceful and calm with blue eyes. I repeat Hexagram and Names and make LVX signs and she bows gravely and asks what I want. I ask if this be the right way to pass into the domain of the High Priestess? She bows, raises her right hand and uplifts a small silver rod or sceptre with a crescent on top. I test it and it becomes the source of white brilliancy and she points upwards with it. I thank her and salute and return. – Of course that is only just the starting point of a 'journey'.

For the Altar take water for instance. Build over the 'He' circle a blue round in a white circle with the Eagle in orange and the 'H' in White Light. Make the Pentagram of water, say the Names and make the Grade Sign. Pass through and explore the watery region if you like. Then rise straight up until you find the Eagle which I have generally found floating up in the sky and so large as to almost stretch from horizon to horizon. Make LVX and Water signs. Pass up higher and higher into a more rarified atmosphere until you reach (generally coming up through the floor) into a great circular temple. The walls decorated with orange coloured symbolical eagles and in the centre there will be a very tall circular pedestal (also surrounded by orange eagles or eagle-heads). Rise so as to see the Figure thereon.

It is rather a severe strain for quite beginners. I have found this Water Figure to be that of a very large solidly built woman with a scroll on her lap, she sits meditating on what she has read and I was told it was the reflective and spiritually reviving (?) power which she symbolises.

I hope that Cavendo Tutus wont become less interested in his work – he may at first but it will be a great pity if he does not go on. Give him my good wishes please. I hope he will be happy in the change of his outer life. Vigilate tells me that a group of men are to take their Portals this week so there will be plenty of beginners soon for you to teach. As soon as you are Theoricus mind you learn up the Ch(ief) Ad(ept)'s part in the Pastos so as not to upset a candidate. I am glad that I was not present on the occasion when C R had to be prompted!

What a time of it you must give S.S.D.D. (Florence Farr Emery). She wants me to study Egyptian too, but I find one new language enough at a time and am hard at work at Italian. I am very comfortable and happy in this charming city – I know it quite well. I shall be here at least two months longer and have plenty of time in the evening to answer letters.

How to go to the planes of the Paths on the Tree of Life is familiar to you – to visit Gimel and the High Priestess you might stop after leaving Tiphereth and there invoke with the Hexagram and Names as I told you in the beginning of this letter and show the guardians of the barrier the Tarot Card astrally with the LVX signs if they wish to stop you. I hope

that I have been able to give you the explanations required –
if I am not quite clear, please let me know which are
[remainder of letter missing]

APPENDIX D

THE SCRIBE'S ACCOUNT OF THE EXECUTIVE DIFFICULTY.

For the Council Meeting on Feb. 1st, 1901, I had drawn up a long and important agenda paper which contained a careful scheme for the coming elections besides much Order business. On Jan. 25th I received a letter from Ma Wahanu Thesi proposing four motions, one of which he called "a slight amendment" for my election scheme. This I placed on the Agenda with the election affairs and the others, of which more anon, at the end; as likely to cause contention. My Agenda was accepted by the Moderator.

After the Minutes had been read the Moderator said that we would take Ma Wahanu Thesi's resolutions first, I asked her to let the Bruce Pledge Form take precedence as it had been long in hand. But she over-ruled me and said we would begin with my election scheme.

I read it out with some small interruptions, asking them to hear it through first and then to discuss it step by step. The first portion was violently contested until I explained that my proposal that the Twelve Seniors should nominate such Adepti as they thought fit and then send their motions direct to me would save time; and that I should ask those who had not already notified their willingness to sit on the Council, would be a saving of useless labour and a little more trouble to me. This part was then accepted. The extremely simple proposal that I should send out a list of candidates to each member and to tell him to put a cross after the mottoes of the ten he thought most suitable brought forth an extraordinary proposal from Ma Wahanu Thesi. He at first said that it was to save future scribes from embarrassment, but when he launched forth and his words were neither hushed down nor disapproved of, I saw that it was an organised attack. He proposed that two more Scribes should be appointed and that there should be a

triple election to avoid errors! Each member would receive
three papers, would fill up his ten votes on each one, and send
them back separately to the three Scribes. I spoke of the extra
liability to errors, and took no notice of his idea that three postage stamps should be enclosed, one with each voting-paper, for
the use of the electors! My first impulse was to shut my Minute
Book and leave the room, but then I remembered that my duty
is to the Order, not to the Council; so I sat quietly and reasoned
with him until the proposal to confuse the electors was
dropped. All the time the "group" members were encouraging
in their attitude towards their companion, but the Demon
got very excited and when I had gained my way, he burst
out with something like this, – "You let that proposal drop
when you found that Fortiter could not burn the ballot-papers
she objected to." That made a great scene of excitement, the
"group" all calling for "order" as soon as a voice was raised in
defence of the Scribe. The next point was the fuss made about
the examination of the voting-papers, until I explained for the
second time that I should not know who the letters were from
as I should provide printed envelopes and that the voting-paper
would be in a second envelope. Suddenly Lucem Spero who was
on the other side of Sapientia began to cross-examine me, and
whenever the Demon made any objection there was always a
cry to "let Fortiter speak." None of the "group" showed that
they minded the following scene. Sapientia lent back and I sat
forward. Lucem Spero asked me where I intended to open the
ballot papers; I was confused and puzzled, the various rooms in
my flat came into my mind. He then said, raising his finger in
front of my face, "Now mind – think – where did you intend
to open the papers?" I answered that the idea had never struck
me but that they should be opened in my own house by the
Scruteneers. I was not in the least angry at his impertinence,
and as by this time I had made up my mind not to take charge
of the elections under the circumstances, I determined to see
how far he would go. I looked round and asked if anyone would
suggest another address; someone, I don't remember who, said
"36"! That was obviously to my mind a suggestion to put the
latest member of the "group" into my place of responsibility,
but I could not refer to her with decency, as though present at
the Council meetings, she does not sit nor speak on it. I made

all the obvious objections as to the letters at "36" being comparatively unguarded and free to be trodden on by the other inhabitants of the house, and I firmly refused to allow the voting-papers of the members to be sent to any house but mine. I rather sarcastically asked "And how would they be addressed here?" A voice said "Scribe care of etc.," evidently a little shame-facedness appearing for the moment in the speaker. Then Lucem Spero, dropping that point, began to ask me where I got my ideas from. I explained that I had thought much about the scheme and had got the idea from the voting of the Fabian Society a year ago. The Demon said that it was like that of the Irish Literary Society. Lucem Spero was most scornful in the way he put these Societies' procedure aside; he was not checked at all by the Moderator and she did not show any displeasure at his behaviour. He talked a great deal of City Companies and Masonry and ballot balls and wanted all our elections to be personal. I objected strongly on behalf of the country members (who are not "group" as it happens) and he said they ought to be willing to come to London for the purpose. The Demon said that that would be fining them heavily and I put such stress on this point that at last the disenfranchisement of the country members was dropped. Then there was a scene about the ballot papers until I forced the "group" to observe the specimens of envelopes I had brought which showed that perfect secrecy would be ensured and the "group" appeared satisfied with that part of the scheme, but they were not any more polite. Lucem Spero insisted on a Balloting Meeting for London Members and again I held out for the sake of busy and delicate people. He insisted on dictating these words to me; I wrote them to humour him, on the back of the card of directions, they were not put to the Council. The "group" were all evidently pleased at the grace and style and politeness of the following, – "To be brought to the Ballot Meeting if possible. If you cannot possibly attend send this by post before the"   . I was told by the "group" that instead of the two scruteneers I had asked for (the mottoes of Causa Scientiae and Nobis est Victoria are written in my paper, fortunately their names were not read out) I must bring the envelopes complete to Blythe Road and put them in the box and that all the members present would remain to watch the counting. I let that go, as too bad to be worth making any objection to on my part.

The "group" all seemed quite pleased at the way they had insulted the whole Order in my person and that they could count the votes themselves. Then Sapientia took Ma Wahanu Thesi's famous three motions. His letter of the 25th mentions them as "four in number" and then gives 1 – 2 – 3 and at the end 1 and 2. To explain their order and to fit them into what went on at the Council is beyond my mental capacity. As far as I can write out such a scene, this is what happened. (I need hardly say that a copy of these motions has not been given to the Scribe as I believe is the usual custom.)

First he wanted the omissions from the Hod Clause of the Obligation to be replaced, but when I explained that the alterations in the $5=6$ Ceremony were now in consideration by the Twelve Seniors, and we really could do nothing in the matter at present and that if the Council objected to the eventual decisions of the Twelve they must appeal to them again, he dropped that motion. He made no fuss as he had plenty more to bring forward. Then he read a letter from me, quite in harmony with the compromise between Sapientia and the Demon. In it I declared that although I disapprove of "a group" I would show my fraternal feeling by helping to hush up the scandal. As I consider that their doings are harmful to the Order and certain to bring suspicion and curiosity of an unpleasant kind and every sort of ill-feeling amongst us, I wrote this phrase seriously and with good intention. The "group" instead of showing gratitude for my forbearance indulged in further insults towards the Scribe. Lucem Spero resumed his cross-examination, the Moderator again sitting back for his convenience and calling "order" whenever the Demon showed signs of his non-group mental attitude. I explained how I had fought the mutilation of the $5=6$ Ceremony diagram and how I had also protected the Order and also a proposed Candidate by arranging properly a proposed irregular initiation. Then I dropped details and spoke of the way I had returned from exile, and how painfully suspicions as to the "group" had grown up in my mind from various irregularities done on their behalf, and then I asked "Where did these suspicions come from?" Amongst many confused ejaculations and remarks Deo Date's statement "They came from your own mind

Fortiter," was very clear. When I declared that the "group," not I, had made the situation they took no notice. Then the cross-examination was resumed. I spoke slowly as my words were written down or notes taken of what I said. I drew their attention to this, but again my politeness was not appreciated. Although I had denied both in writing and words over and over again, that I had ever accused them of *evil* Lucem Spero brought the charge against me in a most impertinent manner. I stretched out my hands and said words like these "I solemnly declare on my word of Honour that I have never accused you of Evil, that I have never thought that you were working for Evil, and I have never even been tempted to think that your work was evil but I cannot judge of your working except by its fruits such as I know them, they are Ignorance, Selfishness and Discourtesy." I might have added "an absence of a sense of humour", for as soon as I stopped they all began to ask me for evidence! I then noticed that my out-stretched left hand had been pointing to the Cross of the Obligation, my right at Lucem Spero. I explained how more than three years ago when many of the "group" were still beginners in the Order, that I had been shown their first Diagram by one of themselves, a Soror of the highest honour, who had never thought that she, a Zelator, was not free to show to a Theoricus, a G.D. paper which she did not understand; how I had found one trivial error and one most serious omission, – that their sphere left a larger portion open to the Lower forces below them than to the Higher above. A few days later, Sapientia had written to me that the matter was to be a secret, that I was to be silent on the subject and if I though about it at all, that I was to consider myself in the centre. I wrote back to her that as I did not like it at all I should try to forget it. Much later when in the British Museum I had by chance felt a force which was not harmonious to my nature coming from a small statue which I found to be that of their Adept. At that time it gave me a sense of ruthless destruction and a sweeping away of obstacles and a disregard of the weak and helpless. Things now grew very confused for there were many advocates of the "group" and only one besides myself who spoke for the general good of the Order. The Demon made a speech which by its beauty enforced silence but it fell on the ears of an audience who were on a different plane of thought. Lucem Spero called it "a pretty sermon but not to the point" or words to that effect. At about this stage of the proceedings Sapientia made her only speech. She energetically enquired from the Demon "who and what are <u>you</u> in the Order" or words to that effect. Motives of delicacy to the "group" might have urged her to be silent as to Order progress as he is one of those who are next to the Seniors in the Order. I spoke most earnestly as to the horrible dangers for all of us in the future when the Order having legally bound itself by "group" legislation would be helpless to even object to the most pernicious practices in our Tomb. Ma Wahanu Thesi pointed to the Cross and talked of the Obligation, I answered that Crowley had taken it in Paris. That he seemed to think irrelevant and the "group" took no notice when I reminded them of Berridge. By this time it had got very late, Dum Spiro and Vigilate had gone. Silentio made a little speech telling us how <u>she</u> had not been offended when she had heard of the beauties of the "group" studies; she had evidently forgotten how, when in exile I had been asked to stand in the centre. This proposal I refused because I was sufficiently grounded in our studies to comprehend the defect of the symbol and to object with reason to Sapientia's choice of members for carrying out the scheme. During the excitement a person (Ma Wahanu Thesi, I think) had let out that there were more "groups" than one and Silentio did not deny her membership of one or other of them, though I have two denials that Silentio belongs to <u>the</u> "group" in Sapientia's handwriting. Evidently she may have a little one all to herself with some beginners. At some time during the turmoil the Demon proposed arbitration; but he was told that there was nothing to arbitrate about and the idea was scouted. I must also add that most kindly Lucem Spero (who has not even done A and B) told me how sorry he was for me and how he hoped that my ignorance would protect me from the terrible consequences of resistance against or objection to their workings. His enthusiasm did not give me the slightest desire to exercise my right as a Theoricus to ask for admittance. He told us how he had aided the rebellion against one tyranny, and would never allow another tyrant to arise. This must have meant the Demon as several weeks earlier

I had arranged to leave the Twelve Seniors and not to stand for office again.

The motion was now put; – "groups" were to be legalised, no one of any seniority or grade is to be allowed to make any enquiries or to see after the working of members in any way. "Groups" are to be encouraged and the Order merely used as a screen. Per Aspera ad Astra, who did not vote at all, showed good feeling by insisting that "and prying" should be removed from the motion. Six voted for it and the Demon and I against it. We were beaten and the "group" triumphed on the Council.

I then requested that such ordinary business as was absolutely necessary to give me directions for my work should be transacted. Sapientia now proposed that we should now take the Bruce Pledge Form, but she consented at my request to hold it over to the next Council Meeting, as naturally we were all tired. I made a strong appeal that a meeting should be held for business for the sake of all the members and it was appointed for to-day. L. O. was to be invited to take the Chair at the General Meeting and various small items were arranged.

After all was over and I could speak to some of the members as Fortiter, I was very decided in the expression of my opinions as to their treatment of such an old member. I explained my position in the Order and I drew their attention to the fact that non-"group" members might object to my responsibilities being put on to the shoulders of their latest "group" Soror. I told Ma Wahanu Thesi that he was like the cat in the story of the chestnuts in the fire and the monkey; and drew his attention to the fact that matters had now been left so that a little hot water and neatness of hand would make it easy for me to open all the country envelopes and to place therein ballot-papers marked in any way I chose, then to close them and bring them to Blythe Road! He showed a sense of good behaviour by trying to assure me that he had meant no insult. I quite believe him as meaning this, but I cannot fit it in with the Moderator's determination to bring on the Election Scheme before his motions and the fact that he wrote to me the words at the beginning of this statement. It would indeed require a high Adept of piercing intellect and great knowledge of human nature as well as the skill of an able lawyer to gather together the "group" information I have received into a coherent whole.

As it is, maybe the common sense of the Adepti will show them what they may expect if they legalise "groups."

Written on February 6th by

Fortiter et Recte. T.A.M.

APPENDIX E

Feb. 2nd 1901.

To the Twelve Seniors.

Care et V H Fratres & Sorores

I do not know whether it would be your wish to nominate me as a member of the Executive Council. But I think that it may save you trouble if I asked you not to do so, you will have no difficulty in understanding my decision when I have brought to your attention a very remarkable scene which took place yesterday at a meeting of the Executive Council.

Two resolutions were brought forward, one proposing that two extra Scribes be appointed by the Council to ensure that the Scribe appointed by the whole body of the Adepti should not juggle with the election papers; and one proposing for still greater security that the balloting papers of country members should be sent to 36, Blythe Road, and not to the Scribe, who alone is responsible for their safe keeping.

These resolutions were withdrawn as soon as the proposers discovered that her scheme, read to them at the opening of the meeting, gave her no opportunity of discovering which papers she might possibly disapprove of, but on the contrary insured the secrecy of the ballot. I need hardly point out that this made matters no better, but only made these amazing suspicions the plainer. It is my duty to add that only one of the Adepti and he not the most guilty has apologized. I feel that it would ill become my dignity to continue longer than my duty towards the Order requires, an elected member of a Council where party feeling has run to such extravagance. I am ready to teach anything I may know of magical philosophy to any fratres and sorores who may desire; but I shall take no other part in the business of the Second Order until its moral health has been restored. I have sat on many committees in my own country and elsewhere, but I am proud to say that I have never met among the mechanics, farmers and shop-assistants with whom I have worked in Ireland, a stress of feeling so ignoble or resolutions so astonishing as those I had to listen to yesterday. I desire to keep my reverence for the august symbols of our Order, but I could not do so if I had to sit through more scenes of the kind before the very door of the <u>Tomb of Christian Rosenkreuz</u> in the very presence of the <u>Cross of the Obligation</u>.

Vale Sub Umbram Alarum Tuarum.

יהוה

D E D I

18, Woburn Buildings,
Euston Road.

APPENDIX F

A First Letter to the Adepti of R.R. et A.C. upon the Present Crisis.

Care et V. H. Fratres & Sorores,

I was among those who invited you some months ago to throw off an unendurable burden and to make this Order worthy of its high purpose. The complicated reorganisation made necessary by this change came about swiftly and quietly, and there is now more ardour of study and of labour among us, than at any time I can remember. One anomaly was however forgotten, and it is now causing the only trouble that has arisen among us. We have cast out the tyrannical rule of Frater S.R.M.D., and we must see to it, that a "group" which originated from that tyranny does not bring the Order into a new subjection, which would be none the less evil because purely instinctive and unconscious, and because the mutual distrust and suspicion, it would spread among us, would have their foundation in good intentions.

About 1897 when through distrust of Frater S.R.M.D., the Order had lost much of its central fire, Soror S.S.D.D. in London and Frater Sub Spe in Edinburgh formed private groups and bound them with some kind of understanding or promise of secrecy. When the change came the Edinburgh group abandoned its secrecy, but the London groups continued as before. Those of us who did not belong to them had forgotten their existence or had never heard of them, or we would have urged their immediate dissolution.

The scribe you appointed at the last General Meeting, was the first to give them serious thought, and she became convinced rightly or wrongly, that they were the cause of various irregularities in the working of the Order, that they led to unconcious favoritism and neglect of fratres and sorores who do not belong to them. She urged their dissolution in private, and drew attention to the irregularities before the Council. It was her duty to do both, but she found (as everybody has found, who has had to do with secret societies, that busy themselves even unconsciously with matters outside their own borders) that if she complained of one member, all the members were indignant, that everything she said had as many echoes, and often very distorting echoes, as there were members in the group. She discovered, too, that of the 11 members of the Council, 7 certainly belong to a group of twelve, which tries to keep its membership and its doctrine secret, one almost certainly to a smaller group, working under the same leadership and under the same conditions, and that one of the three remaining was married to a member of the larger group.

She was powerless, and face to face with an ever-growing suspicion and ever-deepening irritation. She resolved not to seek re-election, and to leave the matter to mend itself, as the Order grew more interesting, and slowly gathered the fire into its own heart again. – Meanwhile I thought I had arranged a compromise, Soror S.S.D.D., the organiser of the groups, was to invite members of the Theorici degree, who were sympathetic, to join the larger group, and to make a statement of formulae to all Theorici, and as I thought to admit no more Zelators. I hoped by this means that the "Group" would gradually be absorbed by the Theorici degree, where it would be a strength and not a weakness to the Order. The invitation was given, and the statement made though somewhat meagrely,* but suddenly the "Group" resolved to force itself upon the Order. The Council was to invite you to declare it not only legal but admirable. – A Council meeting was summoned. It began with a strange event, which I can but describe to you by quoting a letter that I wrote to the Twelve Seniors in the first heat of my indignation. [At this point Yeats quoted the entire letter "To the Twelve Seniors", Appendix E.]

To such a wonderful state of suspicion† has a number of well bred and friendly people been reduced by a secret society, in itself quite harmless, but moving within our Order, using its rooms and its formulae, or a modification of its formulae, but not responsible to our Order, and seeking ends that are not

---

* Your Scribe has only received it through the courtesy of Frater Sub Spe.

† Their suspicion was an outburst that they doubtless remember with astonishment. It was perhaps irritation masquerading as suspicion. They all knew in their hearts that our Scribe's sense of law is almost too great. Party feeling is a wonderful thing.

entirely its ends. The Frater who so insulted your Scribe, and you, in the person of your Scribe, is Frater Lucem Spero, who has never past an examination in the Second Order, who has not even consecrated his implements. A Hierarchy which is not ours has given him courage to flout our traditions of courtesy, and to deny the respect that we owe to the Heads of our Order. I have requested him to resign his position as Sub-Imperator of Isis-Urania till he has apologised to your Scribe, but no apology can make amends for such a scene.

After this scene, whose object is obscure, if indeed it had any object which I doubt, a resolution was past, pledging the Council to invite you to declare all "Groups" of whatsoever kind legal and admirable. A General Meeting is to be summoned for the purpose. The Majority consisted of members of the "Groups," and the Minority of the Scribe and of one Frater, who like the Scribe does not belong to any. A Soror, who is only married to a member of a "Group", did not vote, but got an offensive word removed from the Resolution. – I cannot quote the Resolution, for no copy was given to the Scribe, an irregularity she is accustomed to, but I have given its sense with accuracy. Its oratory, which was all about freedom, if I remember rightly, I cannot give.

When this resolution is brought before you at the General Meeting, I shall propose the following amendment – "That this Order, while anxious to encourage among its members, friendly associations which are informal and without artificial mystery, cannot encourage associations or "Groups" that have a formal constitution, a formal obligation, a distinct magical personality which are not of the Constitution, the Obligation, or the Personality of this Order." Furthermore I shall ask you to call upon S.S.D.D. to invite two members of the larger "Group" to add their signatures to the statement of formulae issued to the Theorici. This is necessary, because we are making a precedent and because we are told that the formulae of this "Group" varies among its members. One person must be liable to give undue importance to his or her own practice. I shall ask you also, and this is the most important point of all, to call upon Soror S.S.D.D. to admit no more Zelators into any formal Group.

Should you desire to go further, and to call upon her to dissolve her "Groups," I shall sympathise with you, but shall think that you are asking, it may be, too much of human nature.

Vale Sub Umbram Alarum Tuarum

Demon est Deus Inversus, —

Imperator of Isis-Urania Temple.

APPENDIX G

A Second Letter to the Adepti of R.R. et A.C. on the Present Crisis.

Care et V. H. Fratres & Sorores

I have delayed this letter day after day in the hope that the fratres and sorores who were anxious to have "groups" declared not only legal but admirable would make a reply to my letter which would be as public as my letter. I am sorry to say they have confined themselves to private letters which I cannot answer fully as only faint rumours of their contents have come to me. I am sure that had they considered the matter they would have seen that it would have been fairer to have answered my letter openly. Even the most careful of us do not always remember these things in controversy. The chief of the faint rumours is that they re-affirm the harmlessness of their "groups" and blame your Scribe for suspiciousness and for a passion for red tape. I must therefore go into certain details, which I would prefer to pass over in silence and make certain criticisms upon the business capacity of the organiser of the "groups," which I hope you will receive in the spirit in which I make them. Were I to speak of her in any other capacity than that of an official of this Order I would have no occasion for anything but praise.

During the proceedings that led to the disposition and expulsion of Frater S.R.M.D. I found that her inexperience in the procedure of Societies was so great that she could not hope to carry this Order safely through the necessarily unsettled period that would elapse before the new Constitution had become a habit. Though I would sooner not do so I must give a couple of examples for the decision you will have to make on Feb. 26th is too important to be made in ignorance. On one occasion during the crisis she told me that a certain decision had been come to by a certain committee of seven. I knew that the committee, of which I was a member, had not met and asked for an explanation. She told me that she had consulted three of the members, who accepted her proposal, and that this was legal as three members constituted a quorum. A little later this committee was empowered to draw up a constitution for the Order. Two meetings, at which the Moderator was present, discussed a certain clause, which was perhaps the most important of all, and at the second meeting the clause was written out by the Moderator in the form that had been unanimously decided upon. I need hardly point out to you that it is usual for the members of a committee to sustain before a General Meeting the decisions they have come to in committee. This custom is necessary to prevent a General Meeting from pushing too far its right to upset after a few moments of careless discussion, decisions, which have been come to after long and anxious thought. At the General Meeting the Moderator proposed that all the clauses of the constitution be taken "en bloc." I objected as I thought that the Meeting should have full opportunity for discussion. When I moved the adoption of the clause, which I held in the hand-writing of the Moderator, she rose and moved its rejection on the ground that she had never given it any consideration or understood it before. Her influence, which depended largely, though I did not know this at the time, upon the existence of secret "groups" was sufficient to secure the rejection of the clause with very little discussion. If I had not known that Soror Fortiter et Recte was ready to return to the Order I would have despaired of the future of an Order where the only person who had the leisure to devote herself to its affairs and the influence to make her devotion effective, was so unfitted by nature to consider the little wearisome details on which its stability depended. With the unanimous consent of all the working members, though with much regret, as I knew that it would look like bad taste to invite the return of a member he had expelled, almost in the hour of S.R.M.D.'s own expulsion, I invited Soror Fortiter et Recte to return to the Order and to become its Scribe. We had all perfect confidence in her business capacity. Before I went to Ireland I remember saying to her something like this. "You will have a hard task, you will have to see that laws and precedents are observed, that everything is recorded." And I remember adding that in every society or movement that succeeds there is some person that is built into it, as in old times a sacrificial victim was built alive into the foundations of a bridge. I knew that for most of us the Order was one of several things we cared for, but that for the new Scribe it would be the chief thing in life and that she had the leisure to devote herself to its welfare. When I returned I found that she no longer considered it possible to carry out her duties successfully. I heard that attempts had been made to evade laws and precedents and that the effort to get everything recorded had been wearisome in the extreme, and that she laid the blame upon the action, the doubtless unconscious action of certain secret "groups." On her first coming into office she noticed great irregularities in the list of members and in the book of Admissions and Examinations, the most important record that we possess; and only after considerable difficulty got the information necessary to put this right, but her chief complaint was that the Moderator tried continually, not I think because of any deliberate desire, but because of unusual inexperience, and a constitutional carelessness in all such matters, to act without consulting the Council. I will summarise certain of these irregularities but only summarise as full details will be placed in the hands of the Chairman of the General Meeting. I am very sorry that it is necessary to go into the matter at all. The Scribe prevented an addition being made to the Corpus Christi Ceremony without the consent of the Council and the Twelve Seniors, she remade the diagram of the Minutum Mundum, the central diagram of our system, on finding that it had been altered avowedly for the greater convenience of the "groups." She prevented the set of lectures which are known as the Portal Lectures being withdrawn without consulting the Council and the Twelve Seniors. She was unable to prevent an altered form of the Portal Ceremony being performed without the consent of the Council and the Twelve Seniors, and most important of all she had to oppose vigorously a perfectly serious and decided proposal to admit a candidate "privately" with "a modified $0=0$" ceremony without the consent of the Council. I need not remind you that the admission of a candidate is among the most important business that can come before an Order such as ours. These irregularities are little worse than I have heard of in connection with Catholic Religious Houses, which have begun to occupy themselves with business affairs, but none the less they would have made a series of precedents, that would have established an autocracy like that we have thrown off with so much difficulty. Under ordinary circumstances they could have been quietly pointed out and quietly corrected and no discomfort would have followed, but the existence of "groups" bound to the Moderator by a bond formed in the super-conscious life, the closest of all bonds in the nature of things, made every correction, no matter how quietly made, raise a general irritation. The Scribe found herself alone on a hostile or indifferent Council fighting for the Order against a carelessness that threatened its constitution. The Council voted always honourably, when their attention was drawn to irregularities, but only the Scribe felt free as it seems to point them out. She was soon in a very invidious position and I confess that when I returned from Ireland I thought that one who had raised so much irritation against herself could hardly be in the right. It is only now when I have gone through all her papers carefully that I understand the difficulties of her position; a position that became impossible instead of merely difficult when the irritation against her broke out into the strange scene of February 1st. But for her the inexperience and carelessness of the Moderator, supported artificially by her secret "groups", would have modified beyond recognition the Constitution, that we formed with so much difficulty.

In addition to the faint rumours of the replies made by the "group" to my first letter, I have been sent one whole sentence. "Our group is bound by no oaths nor ruled by any Constitution." I never said that the "groups" were bound by oaths, though they certainly have an understanding or an obligation to keep secret their membership and their doctrines; but I have said or implied that they have a formal constitution. The members of the chief "group" have certainly formed themselves into a magical personality made by a very formal meditation and a very formal numerical system. Unless magic is an illusion, this magical personality could not help, the moment it came into contact with the larger personality of the Order, from creating precisely the situation it has created. It was a formal evocation of disruption, a formal evocation of a barrier between its own members and the other members of the Order, a formal intrusion of an alien being into the conscious and what is of greater importance into the super-conscious being of our Order, an obsession of the magical sphere that has descended to us, as most of us believe, from the <u>Frater Christian Rosencreuz</u> by a sphere created at a time of weariness and disappointment. Such a peronality, such a sphere, such an evocation, such an obsession even if it had not supported the real disorders I have described, would have created, so perfectly do the barriers of the conscious life copy the barriers of the super-conscious, illusionary suspicion, illusionary distrust more irremediable than if they had real cause. We who are seeking to sustain this great Order must never forget that whatever we build in the imagination will accomplish itself in the circumstance of our lives.

Nobody proposes to pass a law condemning even the most formal "groups" and I would oppose any such law, for all such matters must be left to the individual conscience, but I have a right to believe that you will not pass a law giving your sanction, and the sanction of this Order to this "group" or to any "group" of the kind. I shall therefore propose the amend-ment, which I again repeat. "That this Order whilst anxious to encourage among its members friendly associations, which are informal and without artificial mystery, cannot encourage associations or "groups" that have a formal constitution, a formal obligation, a distinct magical personality, which are not the constitution, the obligation or the personality of this Order.'

Vale, s.u.a.t.

ירה

D.E.D.I.

P.S.   As I have not received Frater Lucem Spero's resignation I have suspended him from his office as Sub-Imperator of I.U.T. till he has made such apology as may be acceptable to the Scribe and to the General Meeting for his principal share in the scene of February 1st.

APPENDIX H

Care Fratres et Sorores,

I have just received from the Chairman of the General Meeting a copy of the Resolution that is to declare all "groups" of whatsoever kind not only legal but admirable. It is long, the longest Resolution I have ever seen made out of such light material, and yet it contains but a single sentence. This sentence winds hither and thither with so much luxuriance, that I am convinced it requires a closer study than you could give it at the General Meeting. I therefore send it to you – it is as follows:

"If the liberty and progress of individual members – and of this Order as a whole – is to be maintained – for progress without liberty is impossible – it is absolutely necessary that all members of the 2nd Order shall have the undisputed right to study and work at their mystical progress in whatsoever manner seems to them right according to their individual needs and conscience – and further it is absolutely necessary that they shall be at perfect liberty to combine, like minded with like minded, in groups or circles formed for the purpose of that study and progress, in such manner as seems to them right and fitting and according to their consciences, and that – without the risk of suffering from interference by any member of any grade whatever, or of any seniority whatever, – and furthermore that this is in perfect accord with the spirit and tradition of our Order which is always to allow the largest liberty for the expansion of the individual, and has always discountenanced the interference of any and every member with private affairs, whether mystical or otherwise of any other member."

After some difficulty I have discovered amid this luxurience certain distinct ideas (1) that all fratres and sorores shall be free to do anything they like so long as it is something mystical, (2) that they shall be free to form any kind of groups they like so long as they are mystical, (3) that to do so is true not only to the spirit but to the letter of the <u>Father Christian Rosencreuz</u>, (4) that nobody, no not the highest or the oldest of our Adepti, shall "interfere" with them in any way.

That is to say, that this Order is to surrender the right it has always possessed to "interfere" with fratres and sorores who flagrantly misuse their <u>magical</u> knowledge, and that these fratres and sorores have only to organize themselves into secret groups to be free to misuse that knowledge in the Rooms of the Order itself. They may even <u>evoke the genius</u> of another, a forbidden thing even when done without evil intention; they may cast about that <u>genius</u> an enchantment of sensual passion; they may <u>evoke the spirits</u> of disease to destroy some enemy – and a member of this Order who is now expelled once boasted that he had done no less – they may hold any kind of Witches Sabbath they like before the door of the Tomb, and thereby send out among the fratres and sorores from that symbolic Tiphereth, that symbolic Heart, a current of evil <u>magic</u> and merely because they call themselves a group, no officer of this Order, "of any grade whatever, or of any seniority whatever" shall have even the poor right of knowing what they do. They may be the youngest members of the Second Order, and he the oldest, but he cannot even be present, much less object.

You, the Adepti of R.R. et A.C. are responsible before the Laws of this Land, and before far subtler Laws, for all that happens in the rooms of your Order, but you must not "interfere" and you have no right even to be curious. You have recently expelled certain fratres whose "consciences" and whose expression of what "seems to them right" were not to your minds, and I have heard even members of the "groups," and in Open Temple too, accuse some of these expelled fratres of the worst of evil <u>magic</u> but from next Tuesday onward for ever you are to trust everybody. You are to believe no longer in the ancient <u>magical</u> tradition that bids even the highest look lest he fall, and you are to trust to your clairvoyants and introducers so profoundly that you are to believe no unfit person shall ever again enter this Order. The medium, the mesmerist, the harmless blunderer or the man who seeks a forbidden pleasure by symbols that are now better known than they were, may form his secret "group" from the moment he has passed the ceremony of $5=6$, and gather his secret "group" about him in the rooms of your Order.

I ask you to examine this Resolution carefully, and to ask yourselves whether it has come from the Powers who represent the Personality of this Order, its Constitution, its Tradition and its future, or whether it has come from powers that could see, with indifference, the dissolution of this Order, its Constitution, its Tradition and its future. All that we do with intensity has an origin in the hidden world, and is the symbol, the expression of its powers, and even the smallest detail, in a profoundly magical dispute may have significance. This Resolution is not a small detail. It is the chosen weapon of the members of the Council who belong to the secret "groups." I do not say that it has come from evil powers, but it seems to me that it has come from powers that seek ends that are not the ends of this Order, and that say to their followers as the Evil Powers once said to theirs "Your eyes shall be opened and ye shall be as Gods knowing Good and Evil."

Sometimes the sphere of an individual man is broken, and a form comes into the broken place and offers him knowledge and power if he will but give it of his life. If he give it of his life it will form a swirl there and draw other forms about it, and his sphere will be broken more and more, and his will subdued by alien wills. It seems to me that such a swirl has been formed in the sphere of this Order, by powers, that though not evil in themselves are evil in relation to this Order.

Vale s.u.a.t.

יהוה

D.E.D.I.

February 21.

P.S. I gather from a letter received this morning, that the private replies to my first open letter say that only a "group" can decide whether it has a "formal constitution" or not, and that therefore no group must be condemned. This is an example of the confusion of mind that hangs over this dispute. It is the members of "groups" and not we who have proposed legislation. We know from the statements of its founder and of others that the largest of the existing groups has what we consider a "formal constitution," but in most cases nobody could know; and this is one of the reasons why I have stated that I would oppose any legislation against groups, as such. At the same time this must not be understood as surrendering the right that the Order already possesses to "interfere" with any collective or individual practice of a distinctly mystical kind, which is a dangerous breach of our obligation or its right to any supervision over its rooms it may think necessary.

D.E.D.I.

February 22.

APPENDIX I

Statement Issued to Adepti by the Majority of the Council Feb 1901

Cari V H Fratres et Sorores.

It is necessary that you should have further information with regard to the subject for the consideration of which the General meeting on the 26th Feb has been called – i.e. the advisability of working in private groups.

In the Minute Book entries to the following effect will be found under date April 1st 1897.

That V H SOR SSDD (hereafter called Sapientia) was appointed head of the London branch of the Order. The formation of secret groups was advised and legalised on the same occasion with the consent of DDCF. Sapere Aude also approved and formed a group himself as Silentio can bear witness. Any experienced occultist will tell you that it is impossible for a large number of persons to perform practical magic with effect; and in all ages secresy has been an indispensible adjunct to such work. Thus small, secret groups are supported by magical tradition and by both the original chiefs of the Order. As there is no prospect of further official Knowledge we consider it necessary to the life of the Order that members shoud be encouraged to investigate freely and to use the knowledge already received as much as possible as a basis for further development. And we consider that the Oath of fraternity should protect members from the suspicion and criticism of those with whom they do not happen to be working at the time. Those of us who belong to the Sphere group hereby deny that we have taken any oath or formal obligation of any kind apart from our obligation to the Order, or that we work on Formulae opposed to the Order teaching and method.

The case of Very Hon. Sor. F.E.R. (hereafter called Fortiter). This Soror was out of the Order from 1896 to 1900 when we were all very glad to welcome her back from what we considered an unjust exile. She had left us when many members were her juniors to whom 3 years of hard work had naturally made a considerable difference. They gladly yielded to her her old seniority as a matter of courtesy. Unfortunately she considered her position gave her the right to find fault with their methods and override their teaching. This no doubt caused great friction, as different occultists have widely different views as to the relative importance of different details in teaching.

One of Fortiter's first actions was to try and reestablish the supreme right to honour and authority in the Order of those who had passed examinations. D.D.C.F., our late chief, neglected examinations because he came to see the practical imperfections of the system in dividing the fit from the unfit. Sapientia agreeing with him did not enforce examinations during her term of office, 1897 to 1900, though members were free to go through this curriculum if they found it helpful. Though we, the undersigned, do not desire to discontinue the examination system, we do not consider that the occult work of a member should be gauged solely by the examinations that he has passed, we think due recognition should be given to those whose interest is centred in one branch of occultism, and who as specialists in that branch may be of great service to the Order.

Fortiter next turned her attention to groups and in a letter in Sapientia's possession says that she asked various members to make formal complaints that the rooms at Blythe Road were occasionally closed while members were working. Several meetings of students for various purposes have been identified erroneously with Sapientia's Sphere group, that group has hitherto used the rooms once or at most twice a year. The right of engaging the rooms has been duly legalised by the council for the benefit of all Second Order members.

Since last November Fortiter has literally persecuted persons she suspected of belonging to the Sphere Group by word of mouth and in written letters and lectures, endeavouring to prove that it is a disintegrating force. As it has worked for three years and its members are those active members who before and since the Revolution have spent and been spent in the service of the Order this accusation is on the face of it absurd. Nearly all of you have the lecture on the star maps and know the desirability of turning the Kether of the earth to the true

Kether. That is the object of the Sphere group work. There is no secresy or heresy about its formulae.

Fortiter has said that the Group is responsible for the scandal she has made and for her suspicions. A would-be homicide might just as well plead that if his victim had not been born he would not have attempted to kill him.

A colour scheme of the 4 scales was given by the late chief in Paris to Jeh Aur to Volo Noscere and to Crowley (all juniors). Sapientia had known it and had kept it secret for many years. Jeh Aur told her he had been told it was received in vision by Vestigia. Sapientia showed it last spring to a few seniors who agreed in thinking it incorrect and took no further interest in it. V.H. Fra. M.W.T. (hereafter called Mawahanu) was present at the time when Crowley was freely discussing these scales, and he came to the conclusion that a correct version could be constructed with some perseverance from the materials given, and we are working it out on scientific lines, when it is completed you will all in due course be informed of the result. Fortiter prefers not to have the benefit of Mawahanu's training as an expert because he has "not passed his D". This ommission is principally due to the fact that much of his time has been spent working on sub-committees, as vice-Praem : and as Officer in Isis Urania. Among other things he has made a careful translation of 2 chapters of the Book of the Dead for the Lecture on the Pillars.

For some time past it has been impossible to ignore the fact that in the mind of Fortiter there has been a growing and groundless suspicion and distrust of Sapientia; which has led to constant distortion of her words and acts. Harmless remarks from Sapientia have been exaggerated to her detriment, unworthy motives sought for in the most trivial occurrences, unjustifiable attacks made on her in Council and elsewhere, malice of the most petty description attributed to her. The most serious charge that Fortiter has brought against Sapientia is that she has conducted examinations unfairly.

Sapientia's reply is – That she has no time even if she had the inclination to indulge in futile acts of spite or favoritism. Fortiter's further accusations are – That Sapientia had when Chief altered the Minutum Mundum diagram to suit the group. This was done to suit the more esoteric teaching given in the

Microcosm lecture and to enable the student to identify himself with the symbol more easily.

Fortiter says she had difficulty in getting dates and information from Sapientia. This was entirely her own fault for instead of sending the Examination book to Sapientia when it was resolved to continue the examination system for a time, she wrote to Sapientia a separate letter for every item of information required. Last December Sapientia had to look up the books on four separate occasions for information which anyone could have got from the Roll and an address book in one sitting. Sapientia did this patiently because she knew Fortiter's nerves were upset at the time, but she cannot admit that she created the difficulties.

Deo Date made an obvious joke at a meeting on the 12th Jan. which has been taken very seriously by Fortiter, and throughout the Autumn the lightest remark made in casual conversation by a member suspected of belonging to the group has been carefully put in the archives by Fortiter as an example of a serious offence against rectitude.

The case of V H Fra DEDI.

This frater did you all great service during the Revolution as you know from your printed documents. Since then he has attended the Council meetings at intervals and we all bear him witness that he has talked at greater length than all the other members put together. His position among us is due to his long connection with the Order, the originality of his views on Occult subjects and the ability with which he expresses them rather than the thoroughness of his knowledge of Order work and methods which is somewhat scant. He is however a shining example of the help we may get from Members who have no special talent for passing Examinations. Unfortunately he has put himself forever beyond our sympathy by a recent flagrant piece of audacity before which the little tyrannies of our late Parisian Chief pale. As Imperator he has, without attempting to consult the Praemonstratrix or Cancellaria, demanded the retirement of a Vice Chief of Isis Urania Temple because they had had a difference of opinion on Council. The matter rose from the following circumstances. Anyone who is familiar with the methods adopted at elections knows that it is an unheard of thing that a person interested in the result should come for one instant in contact with the balloting apparatus. Frater Mawahanu brought forward a proposal to have the election arrangements on more usual lines than those proposed by Fortiter. When this attempt to make the mode of election as unexceptional as possible under the circumstances was mentioned on council DEDI lost his temper completely, pretending that our desire to act in accordance with custom was a personal attack on the integrity of the Scribe.

Frater Lucem Spero, a freemason and a member of many occult bodies who seconded the above resolution, wishes to make the following statement.

"Mawahanu & I distinctly stated that the motion was impersonal and was simply an effort to secure a ballot to which less exception could be taken, in view of the fact that the council was creating a precedent. This however was of no avail, V.H. DEDI insisting on the idea of suspicion which was introduced on the Council by him and by him alone. As a compromise the motion was subsequently modified accepting Fortiter's & DEDI's scheme as far as country members were concerned, on condition that those able to attend the general meeting in March should be allowed to ballot in the ordinary way.

The following statements regarding myself have been made by V.H.DEDI.

A   That I was solely responsible for Mawahanu's ballot proposal. This is incorrect.

B   That my action caused V.H.FER to decide on resignation. This is also incorrect as I understand the Soror in question expressed this determination previously.

C   That I have not consecrated my implements. It is somewhat difficult to see what this has to do with the case, or how the information was obtained. It is equally incorrect.

D   That I relied for courage on some Hierarchy.

I am really at a loss to understand what is meant by this, but in seconding Mawahanu's resolution, I am not aware that I relied on anything but the common sense of the majority of the Council. As to the illegal attempt to deprive me of my position as Vice Imperator I will only commend it to your consideration as a specimen of the kind of tyranny that we are endeavouring to render impossible in our Order. Personally I have no ambition whatever for either office or influence though it has naturally been a great pleasure to me to find that the confidence of many of my Fratres and Sorores in me has been so great that offices have been conferred on me."

signed, "Lucem Spero."

To sum up.

We wish to state that we do not allow that the Theoricus rank warrants those who hold it in taking upon themselves the responsibility of acting as the conscience of other members of the 5=6 grade. The whole spirit of the Revolution was to exalt the expert at the expense of the seniors, if a senior happens to be an expert so much the better, but we refuse to be controlled in any way by seniors simply because they have passed examinations.

We believe that in countenancing a system of carefully organised groups we are advocating a policy which will give the Order the status it abandoned when it abandoned the authority of D.D.C.F. And we do not believe that any occult work can be benefitted by the criticism or supervision of those not actually engaged in it. We have now to state that if the General meeting decide to take away the right we at present enjoy to form groups in which we are at liberty to work with any members who have special knowledge or qualities whether they have passed examinations or not, the following members will withdraw, taking no further active part in an Order in which such stultifying regulations are approved.

Sapientia. Vigilate. Deo Date. Silentio. Dum Spiro Spero. Hora et Semper. Mawahanu Thesi. Lucem Spero.

APPENDIX J

London,
Feb. 27th 1901.

Care et V.H.Fratres et Sorores,

At the meeting to consider Ma Wahanu Thesi's Resolution which was held last night Frater Sub Spe proposed the following amendment –

"That before any other matter can be considered it is necessary that the Constitution and Rules of the Order shall be revised and formally adopted and that a small Committee be forthwith appointed to draft and submit to the Order a scheme for this purpose. And that in the meantime there shall be no interference with any group which does not transgress the laws of the Order, and that no group shall interfere with or alter the working of the Order." A state of things which Sub Spe speaking to his amendment described in the language of Mediaeval politics as a "Truce of God."

This amendment was negatived apparently by a mechanical majority, who failed to comprehend its effect, for the same proposals were afterwards affirmed by the same majority. Frater D.E.D.I. then proposed his amendment in the following modified form –

"That this Order while anxious to encourage among its members associations which are informal and without artificial mystery neither desires to encourage nor condemn associations, or "groups" that have a formal constitution, a formal obligation, a distinct magical personality which are not the Constitution, the Obligation or the Personality of this Order. That the resolution proposed by Frater Ma Wahanu Thesi and this amendment be submitted in writing to all the Adepti of the Second Order and that this Meeting adjourn until the votes have been received, those who cannot attend personally to be permitted to vote through the post." This amendment was negatived.

The principle of non-interference of "groups" who did not

transgress the laws of the Order was the substratum of Ma Wahanu Thesi's vague resolution as he explained it to the Meeting. And on his explaining that he did not ask for a vote of confidence in any "group" or for any positive action being taken, Frater Sub Spe said that this was identical with the last sentence of his amendment and he accordingly voted for the motion. Soror Fortiter et Recte and Frater D.E.D.I. did not vote with him in this.

Frater Sub Spe affirms that –

The Meeting not only did not express its confidence in any "group" but that it did not and could not give them any legal status. Nothing that has happened has any force either to reduce the primary authority of the Obligation nor the right and responsibility of the Order which it derives from the Obligation itself to enforce it.

The expediency of a revision of the Rules was unanimously acknowledged, but we must also state that this revision is a legal necessity. Two of the signatories were unaware of the legal aspect of the matter until the last few days. There are at present no rules that are binding on the Order except the Obligation. The body of Adepti should understand that at present the power heretofore possessed by D.D.C.F. resides in them as a whole. There is no power to take any single step even by a majority of the Adepti until a unanimous vote of the whole body has given such power, either to a majority of the whole or to a committee, when this is done a committee can draft a constitution and revise rules. These must then have the assent of the whole body or of such majority as the whole body shall determine. The necessity for such rules was abundantly proved and acknowledged at the Meeting and only as above pointed out can they be made binding on the whole Order. The long experience of Fortiter et Recte in the business of the Order has taught her that fixed rules and a just enforcement of them would give the members that peace which is necessary for occult study.

After the discussion on the Rules, the case of Lucem Spero came up for consideration; he was voted back into his place by a large majority. Frater D.E.D.I.'s action was declared illegal and unjust. (A certain number of members did not vote at all considering that there can be neither legality nor illegality where there are as yet no laws.) Frater D.E.D.I. has resigned his position as Imperator of Isis-Urania Temple, but not because of this vote; having considered the legal aspects he cannot acknowledge the tribunal which considered the matter. He resigns because he does not wish to be a cause of dissension in the Order; he hopes that the Order when the new Rules have been formed will return to its normal state.

Vale s.u.a.t.

Fortiter et Recte T.A.M. Late Scribe.

Sub Spe T.A.M. Late Imperator of Amen Raa.

Demon est Deus Inversus. Late Imperator of Isis-Urania.

P.S. In the statement of the majority of the Council various accusations have been made against me, all of which I hereby categorically deny. F.E.R.

P.S. I do not think the latter of 'the majority of the Council' calls for any comment from me. Nobody untroubled by party feeling will believe that I removed Frater *Lucem Spero* from his office because of a difference of opinion at a meeting of the Council, and the other statements in so far as they concern myself are unimportant. D.E.D.I.

APPENDIX K

Is the Order of R.R. & A.C. to remain a Magical Order?
Written in March, 1901, and given to the Adepti of the Order
of R.R. & A.C. in April, 1901.

I.

We are about to make a legal constitution by the vote of all
the Adepti. We must, therefore, go to first principles, and decide what we mean to do with the Order – whether we intend
to keep it as it has come down to us, or to change it into some
new shape. We have even to decide whether we intend it to
remain a Magical Order at all, in the true sense of the word.

"The majority of the Council" have described themselves as
advocating "a system of carefully organized groups." The
committee which is about to be appointed to draw up laws and
bye-laws will have to consider this proposal or proposals aris-
ing out of it; and as whatever the committee decides upon
must come before you, that it may be legal, you yourselves
will have to decide between system and system. I regret that
differences have arisen among us, but none the less I must
submit to you a system which is not, so far as I can judge
from a recent open letter, the system of "the majority of the
Council."

II.

I propose that we neither encourage nor discourage "groups"
officially, while retaining our right to do either in our personal
capacity, but that we endeavour to restore the Order to that
state of discipline, in which many of us found it on our initiation into the second Order some eight or nine years ago. This
can be done:

(1) By insisting on a strict obedience to the laws and by-laws.

(2) By making the giving out of the knowledge lectures dependent on the passing of examinations.

(3) By giving the highest Degree (or Grade) weight in the

government of the Order, and by retaining the old respect for the Degrees and seniority.

(4) By restoring the oath taken upon the Cross on Corpus Christi Day, until recent years, by one of the seniors as a representative of the Third Order.

The passing from among us of Frater S.R.M.D. has thrown the whole burden of the unity and continuity of the Order upon the Order itself. They have no longer the artificial support of his vigorous and imaginative personality, and must be supported alone by the laws and by-laws and symbols, by the symbolic personality of the Order, a personality which has, we believe, an extreme antiquity, though it would still be alive and active, had it arisen out of the evocations of these last years. The next few years, perhaps the next few months, will decide whether it has been sufficiently embodied "in London" to bear this sudden burden, and of a certainty if it bear it, it will do so because we have strengthened and not weakened a discipline that is essentially symbolic and evocative, and because we have strengthened and not weakened a system of Degrees that is a chief element in this magical personality. Everything that can be said against the magical examinations can be said, and has been said, against every kind of examinations, whether of the Civil Service or of the Army or the Universities, while the magical examinations can be defended by an argument that can defend them alone. They are more than a test of efficiency, they are more even than an Ordeal, which selects those who are most devoted to the Order. The passing by their means from one Degree to another is an evocation of the Supreme Life, a treading of a symbolic path, a passage through a symbolic gate, a climbing towards the light which it is the essence of our system to believe, flows continually from the lowest of the invisible Degrees to the highest of the Degrees that are known to us. It matters nothing whether the Degrees above us are in the body or out of the body, for none the less must we tread this path and open this gate, and seek this light, and none the less must we believe the light flows downward continually.

It is indeed of special, perhaps of supreme, moment to give the Degree of Theoricus, the highest Degree known to us, enough of importance to make the Fratres and Sorores look towards it with respect and attention, for the Degree of Theoricus is our link with the invisible Degrees. If the Degree has too little knowledge or too little authority, we must give it knowledge from our intuitions and our intellect and authority from the laws and by-laws of the Order. If we despise it or forget it, we despise and forget the link which unites the Degree of Zelatores, and through that the Degree of the Portal and the four Degrees of the G.D. in the Outer, to the Third Order, to the Supreme Life. When I say increase its knowledge, I do not merely mean increase its erudition, or even its understanding of its traditional knowledge. I think we might readily discover for its Adepti some simple form of meditation to be used at stated periods, some symbolic vigil in the mystic tomb of which ours is but the image, to bind them together in a strong indissoluble bond, and to call among them, and through them into the whole Order, some new descent of the Supreme Life, or may be the presence, whether in the body or out of the body I know not, of some great Adept, some great teacher. The link that unites us to that Supreme Life, to those Adepti and teachers, is a double link. It is not merely an ascent, that has for symbols the climbing of the Serpent through the Tree of life and of the Adepti through the Degrees that we know of, but a descent that is symbolised by the Lightning Flash among the sacred leaves, and that should be symbolised, if the Order has not abandoned an essential part of its ritual, by the obligation spoken on the day of Corpus Christi by some senior in the name of the Third Order, which thereby takes upon itself the sins of all the Fratres and Sorores, as wisdom takes upon itself the sins of the world.

The obligation is indeed necessary, for by it the stream of the lightning is awakened in the Order, and the Adepti of the Third Order and of the Higher Degrees of the Second Order summoned to our help.

Because a Magical Order differs from a society for experiment and research in that it is an Actual Being, an organic life holding within itself the highest life of its members now and in past times, to weaken its Degrees is to loosen the structure, to dislimn, to disembody, to dematerialize an Actual Being; and to sever the link between one Degree and another, above all between the Degrees that are in the Heart, in the Tiphereth, in the $5=6$, is to cut this being in two, and to confine the magical life of its visible Adepti to the lower substances of this being. To do this last thing is to create an evil symbol, to make the most evil of all symbols, to awake the energy of an evil sorcery. On the other hand, to create within this Order, within this Actual Being formal "groups," centres of astral activity, which are not the Degrees of this Order, the organs of this Being, is to create centres of life, which are centres of death, to this greater life; astral diseases sapping up, as it were, its vital fluids.

III.

The proposal to substitute for the old discipline, the old tradition, "a carefully organized system of groups," is not only to produce this magical evil, and the complex and obscure practical evils, which will be its shadow, but to produce certain practical evils and anomalies which are so obvious that anyone accustomed to the work of societies can foresee them.

These "carefully organized groups" are not to be organized by any committee or Council of the Order, or by any authority recognized by the Order, but apparently by a single member, who will be responsible to nobody. No member, no matter how great his faith in the official teachings of the Order, or in its official government, if he have not perfect faith in this member, will be able to introduce students to the Order lest they come under what he thinks an undesirable secret teaching, at once irresponsible and semi-official.

It may be, indeed, that other members are to be encouraged to form "groups," that the magical teaching of this Order is to pass, as its influence and extent increases, into the hands of a number of Fratres and Sorores, who will hide their perhaps ill-balanced ideas from one another and from the Order as a whole, and thereby escape from that criticism which is the essence of all collective life, and of nearly all sane life, in a kind of rabbit-warren of secret "groups." These "groups" will hide not only their doctrines but their membership from one another, and our Fratres and Sorores will exchange that mutual help and understanding, that fruitful discussion, which a common knowledge and a common practice make possible, for distrust and misunderstanding, or at best for the indifference that must arise among people who live in separate rooms with perpetually locked doors. The Council of the Order will be the first part of the Order to suffer, for a "group," the moment one of its doctrines or one of its more influential members is criticized, can hardly avoid passing from the quiescence of a clique to the activity of a caucus. Sooner or later too, even though these "groups" have but one organizer, they will come to have different personalities, and the Council will become a place of battle between people who vote upon a prearranged plan, uninfluenced by the arguments used in the Council itself. I cannot, indeed, imagine any system so well devised as this "system of carefully organized groups" to bring our Order, or any order or society, to an ignominious end.

Every one of these "groups," if they follow the plan of those already founded, will have a separate numerical arrangement* on which it will meditate at stated times, every member representing one of the sephiroth; and will have in its midst what professes to be an Egyptian or other spirit seeking to come into relation with our life. The numerical arrangement and recurrent meditation alone are enough to create a magical personality, having its distinct horoscope, and to call into activity a spirit without any formal evocation; and this personality, if it has any continued life at all, is bound to grow stronger, to grow more individual, and to grow more complex, and to grow at the expense of the life about it, for there is but one life. Incarnate life, just in so far as it is incarnate, is an open or veiled struggle of life against life, of number against number, and of all numbers against unity. The fact that the numerical arrangement, which is the foundation of these personalities, is the same as that of the Order will not identify their interests with that of the Order, any more than the foundation upon the one numerical arrangement of the personalities of men and women, stocks and stones, creatures of air and water, keeps them from warring upon one another and upon the great life they come from. It is but a necessary foundation for their separated lives, for were they not established in the sephiroth they could not exist for a moment. The Powers of Disruption

---

* I would not mention these details of organization, which the founders of "groups" have tried to keep secret, had not these founders invited the support of the Order through "the majority of the Council," and thereby given the Order a right to information.

may indeed have discovered that the Order could overcome any attack of a mere Frater or Soror, and have so resolved to create these personalities, that will have each one the strength of many. The more vigorously they evoke the White Light in their recurrent meditation, the more active will their personal life become, the more decisively will it diverge from the general life, the more perfectly will it realize its isolated destiny. The White Light is in itself an undifferentiated energy, and receives its differentiated impulse from the symbol that collects it.

If indeed we must make this change, this transference of influence from Degrees, which are like wheels turning upon a single pivot, to "groups" which will be like wheels turning upon different pivots, like toothed wheels working one against the other, this surrender of ancient unity to anarchic diversity, let us make it as complete as possible. Let us re-shape the Order, Inner and Outer alike, destroying that symbolic Organization which, so long as it exists, must evoke a Being into a continuous strife with these alien bodies within its spiritual substance. For even if it came about at last that every member of the Second Order was a member of some "group," that no one, however despised, stood for the Order only, this Being would be for ever present in dreams and visions, or in that deeper life that is beyond even dreams and visions, seeking to answer the but half-forgotten evocation of the Degrees and symbols, and throwing all into disorder and disquiet. We have no choice but to remain a Magical Order, whose organization is a Talisman, or to become wholly a mere society for experiment and research, with an organization empty of magical significance though sheltering smaller organizations that have a magical significance. If the doctrine of talismans and symbols is true – and if it is not, "groups" and Order are alike folly – there is no position between these extremes that is not dangerous to our spiritual and material welfare.

It must not be supposed that these "groups" will have only such effects in the astral and in the material life as the intellect can foresee, or understand. It is a recognized tradition of Magic that talismans – and every "group" is a talisman reconsecrated at regularly recurring periods – act less often immediately upon the souls of them that use them, than indirectly by an unforeseeable and mysterious action upon the circumstances of life. A group whose astral personality had become active would in all probability bring its separated life to a complete fruition of self-consciousness through circumstances that would arise suddenly and without any apparent relation to itself. It would come to this fruition like a man who, let us say, makes a talisman for courage and grows courageous through being suddenly thrown into some unforeseen danger, which he does not understand has been called up by the talisman. The central principle of all the Magic of power is that everything we formulate in the imagination, if we formulate it strongly enough, realises itself in the circumstances of life, acting either through our own souls, or through the spirits of nature.

IV.

It is said that these "groups" which keep, or try to keep, their doctrines and their membership secret, are necessary for magical progress, that the mere circulation of their formulae among Fratres and Sorores would interrupt Adepti upon their paths. If this idea has been put into the mouths that speak it by beings that seek to grow at the expense of the general life, I understand it; but if it has not, it is unintelligible. Does the circulation of the "Microcosm Ritual" among us make its formulae powerless, or has our Magic been struck by palsy because the Fratres and Sorores of the Outer know our names? It is said, too, that these alien personalities, each one made up of many, are necessary to Adeptship. This argument seems to me sheer dillettanteism, mere trifling! Was Plotinus one of a "group" organized on "the globular sephiroth" when he was thrice united with God while still in the body? It is by sorrow and labour, by love of all living things, and by a heart that humbles itself before the Ancestral Light, and by a mind its power and beauty and quiet flow through without end, that men come to Adeptship, and not by the multiplication of petty formulae. What is this formula of the "groups," the utmost of their present practice as they say, that is to be a ladder into heaven? Now that the secresy is a little faded we know enough of it to know that it is nothing new or wonderful. They use a simple meditation that has for one effect the welding those who use it into one, a little at the expense of their individual souls, which, instead of remaining each a distinct circle, become, as it were, segments of a circle that has no very great or rich life to give them in payment; and for another effect, the awakening of a sympathy, which is limited to those who use this meditation at the same hour and as part of the same sphere. A partly similar meditation is sometimes used by lovers or friends to make their union the closer, to make more intense that love which somebody has called "an egotism of two," and sometimes, and I know one rather terrible case, it makes the union so close that those who use it share not only emotions, but sicknesses and follies. Because of this sharing of all by all, I doubt very much if these meditations should ever be used without certain ceremonial precautions of a rather elaborate kind. In an Order like ours there is, or there should be, the ceremonial sacrifice of one through whom the Third Order takes upon itself and gathers up into its strength, which we believe to be the creation of centuries, the frailties of all. But in a "group" frailty must bear the burdens of frailty, and as it seems without the joy of a conscious sacrifice and with none to lighten the burden but some wandering spirit, itself, it may be, seeking help. Surely Adeptship must come more easily in an order that "reaches up to the throne of God himself, and has among its members angels and archangels," than in a "group" governed by an Egyptian spirit found, it may be, by accident in a statue.

If any were to become great among us, he would do so, not by shutting himself up from us in any "group," but by bringing himself so near to that continual sacrifice, that continual miracle, whose symbol is the obligation taken by the Senior, that he would share alike in its joy and in its sorrow. We receive power from those who are above us by permitting the Lightning of the Supreme to descend through our souls and our bodies. The power is forever seeking the world, and it comes to a soul and consumes its mortality because the soul has arisen into the path of the Lightning, among the sacred leaves. The soul that separates itself from others, that says "I will seek power and knowledge for my own sake, and not for the world's sake," separates itself from that path and becomes dark and empty.

The great Adept may indeed have to hide much of his deepest life, lest he tell it to the careless and the indifferent, but he will sorrow and not rejoice over this silence, for he will be always seeking ways of giving the purest substance of his soul to fill the emptiness of other souls. It will seem to him better that his soul be weakened, that it be kept wandering on the earth even, than that other souls should lack anything of strength and quiet. He will think that he has been sent among them to break down the walls that divide them from one another and from the fountain of their life, and not to build new walls. He will remember, while he is with them, the old magical image of the Pelican feeding its young with its own blood; and when, his sacrifice over, he goes his way to supreme Adeptship, he will go absolutely alone, for men attain to the supreme wisdom in a loneliness that is like the loneliness of death. No "group," no, not even a "group" "very carefully organized," has ever broken through that ancient gate.

V.

If we preserve the unity of the Order, if we make that unity efficient among us, the Order will become a single very powerful talisman, creating in us, and in the world about us, such moods and circumstances as may best serve the magical life, and best awaken the magical wisdom. Its personality will be powerful, active, visible afar, in that all powerful world that casts downward for its shadows, dreams, and visions. The right pupils will be drawn to us from the corners of the world by dreams and visions and by strange accidents; and the Order itself will send out Adepts and teachers, as well as hidden influences that may shape the life of these islands nearer to the magical life.

Those who would break this unity would do so, it seems, if I am to judge by what I read and hear, in the name of freedom. I too might talk of freedom, for I do not recognise as its supporters those who claim the right to do and teach in secret whatever pleases them, but deny me the right to oppose them with the only means I have used or desired to use, criticism; but I have preferred to talk of greater things than freedom. In our day every idler, every trifler, every bungler, cries out for his freedom; but the busy, and weighty minded, and skilful handed, meditate more upon the bonds that they gladly accept, than upon the freedom that has never meant more in their eyes than right to choose the bonds that have made them faithful servants of law. It was the surrender of freedom that taught Dante Alighieri to say "Thy will is our peace"; and has not every man who ever stooped to lift a stone out of the way, or raised his hand to gather a fruit from the branch, given up his freedom to do something else? We have set before us a certain work that may be of incalculable importance in the change of thought that is coming upon the world. Let us see that we do not leave it undone because the creed of the triflers is being cried into our ears.

D.E.D.I.
In the Mountain of Abiegnos.

APPENDIX L

A Postscript to Essay called "Is the Order of R.R. & A.C. to
remain a Magical Order?"
Written on May 4th, 1901.

Soror S.S.D.D., the founder of the "groups," has written asking
me to tell all to whom I have given my essay, that "she strongly
disapproves of the kind of magic alluded to on page 24" of my
essay, "and has never suggested or still less encouraged any
practice of the kind." Soror S.S.D.D. is one of my oldest friends,
but even if she were not I would gladly do as she has asked me.
I understand her words to mean that she never intended to
create any kind of astral union among the members of the
"groups." I never said that she did, for I knew, what I have
always considered her over-watchful individualism, too well to
be certain that it did not blind her to the obvious effect of the
formula, she has given her disciples. I must add, however, that
nothing is more certain in my eyes than the powerlessness of
her intention to alter the effect of a formula, which must seek
continually to perfect a spiritual and astral union that I am
not alone in believing already to exist. It is a first principle of
our illumination that symbols and formulae are powers, which
act in their own right and with little consideration for our
intentions, however excellent. Most of us have seen some
ceremony produce an altogether unintended result because of
the accidental use of some wrong formula or symbol. I can see
nothing to limit the intensity of the union evoked by the
meditation of the Globular Sepheroth, except the degree of
power of those that use it and the lack or plentifulness of
other occupation. Such a formula is seldom able to produce
the full effect I have spoken of, but I know from the experience[s] of a number of people – experiences which I have
carefully recorded – that it soon produces a nearly perfect
communion of mood and a somewhat less, though very marked,
communion of thought and purpose. This communion, which

pre-supposes the creation of a powerful collective personality, is not an evil in itself, for individuality is not as important as our age has imagined. It becomes an evil when it conflicts with some larger communion, some more powerful or more wise personality, or when its relation to the supernatural life is imperfect, or when its constituents have been unwisely chosen.

I find that there is a misunderstanding about the oath that should be spoken by a senior upon Corpus Christi Day. Certain Fratres and Sorores think that the senior takes upon himself the sins of the Order, as the legendary Sin Eater takes a dead man's sins upon himself. This is an error, whose origin I cannot understand. The senior who speaks the oath is the Chief Adept, whose office is now so purely ceremonial, that it can be taken, if necessary, by any senior who happens to be present; and the Chief Adept is the symbolical representative of the Third Order, and takes the oath for the Third Order. He lays the sins of the Fratres and Sorores, and his own sins among them, in the hands of the Third Order, and instead of laying a burden on himself, lightens his own burden and the burdens of others.

D.E.D.I.

APPENDIX M

Concerning the Revisal of the Constitution and Rules of the
Order R.R. & A.C.

Very Honoured Fratres and Sorores.

As the original proposer of a revisal of our Constitution and
Laws, may I address to you a few words on the present logical
position of our Order, and the questions which must ultimately
rest with you for decision.

You are aware that, originally, the Second Order in this
Country was governed absolutely by three Chiefs. Ultimately
their authority all devolved on one; our late Chief, the G. H.
Frater, D.D.C.F., who was practically recognized as Autocrat.
When, for reasons I need not enter into, the Order deposed and
expelled him, the authority devolved on the whole body of
Adepti who chose to remain connected with this branch of the
Order; *i.e.*, all who signed the form of adherence, and whom I
now address.

By this form you declared that the authority heretofore
possessed by the G. H. Frater, D.D.C.F., should be vested in an
"Elective Council," thereby delegating the authority that vested
in yourselves to a Council to be chosen by you, but only delegating it when such Council had been chosen. At the time when
this form was signed a Council was in existence, which assumed
provisional authority and responsibility, it was, however, not
an elective or elected Council; you, as a body, had no voice
in its constitution. It is for you now to consider whether or no
you will confirm the acts of that provisional Council; these acts
are at present not binding on you.

You have decided, by signing that form, that you will be
governed by an elective Council, but you have not decided how
the election shall be conducted, by what majority members
shall be elected, or even the number of the Council. These
points must be settled before any Council can bind the Order.

Up to this time, therefore, no elective Council exists. The

present so-called Council is not elective in any sense, for (1) it consists of six members in whose election you have no voice – viz., the Officers of I. U. T. – and of ten members who are said to be elected. (2) Moreover, by the process adopted of nominating a candidate for a particular post as teacher of Divination, or Chess, or the like, if only one candidate is nominated, or only one accepts nomination for a particular office, that one must be elected, there being no contest. Thus, if only three offices have a single nomination each, it is obvious that out of the sixteen members of Council there are nine (a clear majority) in whose election you have no voice. Plainly the authority devolving on you is not delegated to this Council, and their whole acts are invalid until confirmed by you by unanimous vote. This Council being, therefore, provisional until confirmed by you, it follows that no legal act can be done by any of its officers, not even a legal receipt or discharge for money, or any other property, can be given by any officer, which is binding on any but the individual members of the Council who appointed him.

It rests with you, therefore, now to decide whether you wish to retain any voice in the affairs and government of the Order; or, assuming that, having deposed and expelled one autocrat, you desire to come under the sway of another, it rests with you to decide whether you wish to exercise any choice as to who that autocrat shall be, or to leave it to chance for the first strong hand to seize the reins.

Secondly, if you wish to retain any control over the Order, it rests with you to decide whether you will be governed by three Chiefs, as was the original form; by one Chief, which was the form you repudiated; or by an elective Council, which was the form you consented to; or by any other as yet untried form; and, whatever is your decision, to take measures to carry it out.

I need hardly point out the method of nominating candidates to special teaching posts, and electing them by general vote, has little to recommend it. How, for example, can those Adepti who as yet know nothing of Chess decide whether A or B is the better teacher thereof? Yet these Adepti, whether they know Chess or not, have an equal right to elect to the Council. Again, an Adept may as a good man of business be extremely valuable on the Council, yet be unable or unwilling to teach any specific subject. Such a one would be ineligible at present.

It rests with you, then, to decide whether you wish your elective Council to consist merely of teachers of the Second Order and Office-bearers of I. U. T. (in the choice of the latter of whom, at all events, you have no voice), or of persons chosen by yourselves as capable of ruling the Order wisely and well. A possible and not unusual arrangement would be that you should elect ten members of Council, leaving it to them to appoint their own Warden, Moderator, and Scribe (if such are the office-bearers you decide on), also leaving it to them to name teachers of different subjects (these to be either members of their own body or not as they choose, but if not members thereof, of course to have no voice on the Council), and similarly to appoint office bearers of I. U. T. (who also would have no voice on the Council unless duly elected thereon). Your duly elected representatives would then absolutely control the Order, being responsible to you only, and the system would have the merit of simplicity and practicability.

If you decide that the Order should be ruled by an elective Council, headed by three Chiefs, one might be responsible for the general administration of the Order, one for teaching and the conduct of ceremonies, and the third for the correspondence and finances. This is merely a suggestion of a logical division of duties.

When the Constitution has been thus settled according to the general wish of the Adepti, it will be necessary to pass rules and bye laws. For example, the rooms at headquarters and all the furniture and properties therein are yours, and every one of you has equal rights to the use of them; they vested in you when you signed the form under which you now exist as a body, and are maintained by your subscriptions. Careful regulations are necessary to ensure the use of the rooms to all of you for all lawful purposes of the Order, and to prevent your property from being monopolised by a few.

Again, the rights, privileges, and obligations both of the office-bearers of I.U.T. and their sub-officers, how and by whom they are appointed, and their tenure of office, and also of the officers of your Council, need to be definitely settled, and some form of suspension or degradation provided in case any members persistently break the rules and defy the authority of the Order.

Many other subjects readily occur which need to be provided for by rules and bye-laws, but such might well be left to the elective Council when formed, only observing that every rule, to have any binding force, must have the assent of the whole body of Adepti.

It is obvious to any one who has watched the progress of the Order in the last few years, that with us, as with every other institution that has any vitality, there are two parties – the one desiring to preserve all our old customs and rules, even where notoriously faulty, the other desiring to make a clean sweep of all that we have, and make an entirely fresh start. It is well, and a sign of the health of the Order, that these should both exist. I say not which I think is right. Probably neither are absolutely right; but I do strenuously assert that the party in power should be the one which commands the general assent and confidence of the whole body on a free and unfettered expression of opinion.

This expression of opinion you have never had an opportunity of pronouncing, and until such opinion is pronounced, there is no Council, no Government, no rule or order that is of any more than provisional validity, waiting for your confirmation.

In saying this I have taken simply the legal and material view of the question, as of a purely human institution; I seek not to bias your judgment in any way, but merely to point out the questions on which, if you were dealing with a purely human institution, you would have to pronounce a decided opinion. I do not forget that ours is an occult and magical Order, and I for one firmly believe in the guidance and supervision of higher powers (whether you call them the Third Order or by any other title), and I believe that such higher powers will take care that all that is worth preserving in the Order as we know it will be preserved. But I also believe that whether our particular Branch is worth preserving depends entirely on whether we do our duty – whether, having accepted the responsibility that devolves upon us, and taken upon our shoulders all the authority formerly exercised by Frater D.D.C.F., we each and all of us do our best to maintain the Order by forming the best judgment we can on the questions coming up for decision, taking a vital interest and actual share in the concerns of the Order, and, if defeated, agreeing willingly to the desire of the majority and loyally insisting upon that desire being carried into effect.

If we do this faithfully, I believe the Order will flourish and go on from strength to strength and from knowledge to knowledge, and that the Masters of Wisdom will guide our counsels. But if we fail herein, and supinely allow the affairs of the Order to drift, and say to ourselves that "others will manage them," I believe that our Branch will perish as no longer worth preserving.

Personally, I can only say that my best services are, as they have always been, at the command of the Order, and therewith I remain,

Yours always fraternally,
Sub Spe, Th. A. M.
Former Imperator of Amen Ra.

APPENDIX N

May, 1900.

R. R. A. C. in London.

Second Order Bye-Laws.

Membership.

1. The members shall be those Adepti whose names are now upon the roll, and those Lords and Ladies of the Portal or Adepti of other Temples who shall be added by the permission of the Executive Council.

2. Candidates for the Outer must be introduced by a Philosophus, or a Lord or Lady of the Portal, but preferably by an Adept, who will state his conviction as to the suitability of the person.

The candidate will be interviewed by a Frater and a Soror separately. Another Frater and Soror shall then make separate clairvoyant investigations. These five reports shall be laid before the Executive Council for their final decision.

3. The Executive Council consists of : – the Moderator, the Scribe, and the Warden; the seven Adepti Litterati; and the Three Chiefs of I. U. T. and the Hierophant, Hiereus, and Hegemon of I. U. T. These officers shall be first nominated by the 12 most advanced members of the Second Order, then chosen by the Adepti at an annual election.

4. The annual subscription to the Second Order is 10s. 6d., in addition, voluntary donations are accepted from members.

It must be clearly stated at the time of presentation whether gifts of books, furniture, &c., are to be the permanent property of the Order, or merely temporary loans.

Members requiring the return of their loans must formally make request to the Moderator.

The Property of the Second Order is vested in two members appointed by the Executive.

The accounts shall be audited annually by two Adepti appointed by the College of Adepts.

5. Resignations are accepted by the Executive. Expulsions can only take place at an Assembly of the College of Adepti by a three-fourths majority, notice having been sent seven days before the meeting to every member.

6. Each Chief of I. U. T. shall have two Subordinates; who shall be responsible to him for the performances of their duties, with the right of appeal to the Executive Council. One Chief or Sub-Chief must be present to legalise an Outer Order meeting. It is the duty of the Cancellarius to ensure the presence of at least one Chief or Sub-Chief.

7. If ten members wish to hold a special meeting, on receiving their signed petition stating the purpose, the Executive Council shall instruct the Scribe to summon the meeting at a convenient date.

8. All Order intimations must be sent to each member in a separate envelope.

Verbal notices are sufficient when given formally.

9. All Rituals, Lectures, Knowledge Lectures, Side Lectures, Extra Lectures, Ordinances, Bye-Laws and communications from the Cancellarius and other members, must be kept together and preserved in a box, case, or cover, duly labelled and protected from the view and investigation of all outsiders. The label must specifically state that the contents are not personal, and that they are to be sent in case of illness or decease to a certain person, at a certain place; this nominee should preferably be the Cancellarius.

Each member of the Order undertakes to return to the Cancellarius, on demand, all Rituals, Lectures and other MSS. relating to the Order, in case either of his suspension, demission, resignation or expulsion from membership.

10. The meeting of R. R. A. C. in London for the election of the Executive Council shall take place not later than the Vernal Equinox of each year.

Financial report to be made on the same occasion.

APPENDIX O

June, 1902.
Isis-Urania Temple of the M. R. in the Outer.
(Der Scheine des Lichtes.)

BYE-LAWS.

Membership.

1. The members shall be :– first, those whose names are on the Roll of the Temple; second, persons who have been initiated by permission of the Second Order; third, those who have been affiliated after initiation in other Temples.

Membership may cease :– from demission, following abstention from attendance, want of progress, or omission to render dues; from resignation or from removal by decree of the Second Order.

2. The admission fee is Two Guineas, the annual subscription half-a-guinea. The grade fees, viz :– half-a-crown for each grade, are payable on passing the Ceremony.

No person who is deemed able to profit by the teachings of the Order shall be excluded therefrom on account of poverty : the Chiefs of the Temple will privately remit or reduce any fee in cases they deem appropriate.

3. The annual subscription shall be paid in January of each year. Grades of advancement are not conferred upon members who are in abeyance.

4. If any person who has ceased to be a member desires readmission, this can only be granted by the Second Order, who will require a recommendation from the Chiefs of the Temple.

Members of other Temples who desire to join this Temple must furnish a clearance certificate from the Chiefs of the Temple to which they belong.

The Funds and Property of the Temple.

5. The funds are vested in the Cancellarius, and the property

of the Temple is vested in the three Chiefs of the Temple in trust for the subscribing members.

The Three Chiefs and Subordinate Chiefs.

6. The three Chiefs are the Imperator, who rules; the Praemonstrator, who instructs; and the Cancellarius, who records. The choice of these Chiefs is in the absolute discretion of the Second Order.

The officers of the Temple are appointed by these Chiefs, subject to the Veto of the Second Order.

In case of absence of any of the Chiefs, their Subordinates shall take their place and render an account of the duties they have performed.

The three Chiefs shall together hear and decide all matters which members refer to them or remit any question to the Second Order for final decision.

Any member who does not accept the decision of the three Chiefs may directly appeal through any Chief or Subordinate Chief to the Second Order.

The Cancellarius and his Subordinates shall keep the Roll of the Temple, collect the dues, circulate lectures and rituals, supervise examinations, and issue all notices. They shall furnish all members with their official addresses and give them immediate notice of change of address.

The Cancellarius shall once in each year, at the Vernal Equinox, report in Open Temple on the financial state of the First Order, the number of members, and the progress made by them; this report shall be forwarded to the Second Order for preservation in the Archives.

The Cancellarius himself shall notify, when necessary, those members who have not made satisfactory progress.

The Three Chiefs and Subordinate Chiefs must see that the Bye-Laws are strictly enforced.

Assemblies.

7. Regular assemblies shall be held as nearly as possible once in every month (on days convenient to the Chiefs and the Hierophant) for the admission of candidates, the advancement of members, and for purposes of instruction

There shall be an Assembly at the Vernal and at the Autumnal Equinox; these, every member must attend or explain cause of absence.

Emergency Assemblies may be called by the Three Chiefs, or, on the petition of any member for advancement, on payment of expenses.

8. Members should receive notices of all Regular Assemblies, according to grade; but only such members as the Cancellarius deems able to attend shall be notified of Emergency Assemblies.

9. Members living out of England and such as cannot be directly communicated with, will not receive notices of Assemblies, except by special arrangement wih the Cancellarius.

10. All officers of the Temple must attend each Assembly or send to the Cancellarius a reasonable excuse two days before the date of the Assembly, so that other members may be ready to carry out their duties.

Insignia.

11. Every member must wear at each Assembly the sash of his grade. The Cancellarius will supply the Neophyte sash and the signs of subsequent grades can be added as required. Any member may make his own insignia, if he desire to avoid this expenditure.

12. The Grade Rituals and the Side Lectures may only be possessed by Philosophi; they must bear the official label, and the fact of their possession must be registered with the Cancellarius. They must not be lent, and must not be copied by anyone without the written permission of the Praemonstrator. Knowledge Lectures may be possessed by the members of the appropriate grades under the same conditions. Extra Lectures, such as are delivered from time to time by the Praemonstrator or other Adepti may be, by the permission of the Cancellarius, copied and possessed without registration, but are to be considered as private documents.

13. All Rituals, Lectures, Knowledge Lectures, Side Lectures, Extra Lectures, Bye-Laws and communications from the Cancellarius and other members must be kept together and preserved in a box, case, or cover, duly labelled and protected from the view and investigation of all outsiders. The label must

specifically state that the contents are not personal, and that they are to be sent in case of illness or decease to a certain person, at a certain place: this nominee should preferably be the Cancellarius. In any case the Cancellarius must know who the nominee is.

Each member of the Order undertakes to return to the Cancellarius, on demand, having signed a Stamped Agreement, all Rituals, Lectures, and other MSS. relating to the Order, in case either of his suspension, demission, resignation or expulsion, from membership.

14. Any member desiring to borrow or be supplied with any MSS. to which he is entitled, must apply to the Cancellarius; and all MSS. on loan must be returned to him, or to such address as he directs by post, and must be properly closed against inspection. If any time for the loan is expressed, this period must be adhered to strictly.

Admission and Advancement.

15. Candidates for admission have to receive the approval of the Second Order. Any member desiring to propose a candidate must apply to the Cancellarius, and inform him of the name, age, address, and occupation; and should say also whether he belongs to any other Society or Order which teaches any form of mystical or occult knowledge.

Advancement to the several grades which this Temple is authorized to confer is obtained by passing an examination in the requisite knowledge, and by the permission of the Second Order.

MS. Lectures on the requisite knowledge for the several grades may be obtained on loan from the Cancellarius, and should be copied by the candidate, who is permitted to keep his copy during his membership when duly labelled and registered by the Cancellarius.

16. When a candidate is prepared for an examination he shall inform the Cancellarius, who will arrange the time and place for it to take place.

17. If a candidate fail in his examination for a higher grade, one month shall elapse before his reexamination. But the

Chiefs of the Temple shall be at liberty to exercise their discretion in the full application of this rule.

18. An examination may take place on the authority of the Cancellarius in the presence of any Adept; by special permission, in presence of a lower grade member; and by dispensation, in presence of an uninitiate, provided that such person be discreet and reliable.

19. Answers may be considered and passed by an Adept named by the Cancellarius, provided that unless the answers be complete and correct one signature shall not suffice to authorize the Cancellarius to register the passing, in which case a second Adept shall report upon the answers. If the two examiners differ in opinion, a third Adept, if possible senior to both, shall decide the result.

20. No Practicus shall be advanced to the grade of Philosophus at less than a clear three months' interval, except under the most exceptional circumstances, and then only by the written direction of the Scribe of the Second Order.

21. No candidate can be admitted to a grade ceremony until the Cancellarius has registered the fact that the examination in the requisite knowledge has been duly passed.

Conduct.

22. Members must preserve inviolable secresy concerning the Order, its name, the names of its members, and the proceedings which take place at its assemblies. Members are forbidden to permit themselves to be mesmerized, hypnotized, or to lose the control of their thoughts, words, or actions. Infraction of the pledge in any of these points shall render a member liable to removal from the Temple by the decree of the Second Order, or to any lesser penalty they may inflict.

23. Members must preserve absolute silence in the Temple during the performance of the Ceremonies.

APPENDIX P

69 Thornton Avenue,
Bedford Park. W.
21.5.02.

Care et V.H. Soror Fortiter et Recte,

As the recently appointed Chiefs of the Second Order, you are aware that our commission comprises a return to the original constitution as far as practicable, and we have consequently taken upon ourselves the active government of the Order and incidentally of every matter pertaining thereto including all questions of symbols used and of the form which teaching should take.

Having this responsibility, it is essential that we assert and uphold our absolute authority and require the loyal cooperation of all members of the Order in securing and preserving the fraternal and benevolent relationship required by our obligation.

We have fully in view the recent "group" disturbances and other differences which have caused disharmony, and we are now considering a scheme for fully and finally dealing therewith. Meantime we must most earnestly request all the members of the Order who have thus placed their interests in our hands not to enter into any controversy, verbally or by letter, with any individual member who may appear to him or her to have been acting improperly, but in all cases to address such complaint formally to the three Chiefs.

We address you personally and formally in this matter as one of the senior members of the Order and as having taken a prominent part in the recent "group" disturbances, being convinced that as your object is identical with our commission to restore the original constitution and strict adherence to the Obligation, you will loyally support our authority and both refrain yourself and, so far as you can, restrain others from all further action in matters committed to the three Chiefs by the vote of the 3rd of May. In return we can assure you that any serious breach of the obligation or improper conduct by any member of the Order, duly and properly reported to the Chiefs, will at once be enquired into and if necessary dealt with.

We shall be glad to receive your acknowledgement of this letter and your assurance that you will loyally comply, because it is necessary for us to satisfy ourselves, prior to the Ceremony of C.C. that true harmony prevails.

In replying, please address yourself to L.O.

L.O.

F.R.

S.S.

APPENDIX Q

From the Chiefs of the Second Order to the Members of the Outer

Care Fratres et Sorores,

Greeting –

We have, with some reluctance, decided to change the Name of the Outer, and in future it will be known as – The Hermetic Society of the M.R. These letters convey the same meaning as the letters G.D., indicating as they do the German word Morgenröthe. We have taken this step owing to matters which happened at the end of last year and which rendered the retention of the letters G.D. inadvisable.

We wish to take this opportunity of reminding each member of the pledge of secresy which they have each given, and we point out that, under no circumstances whatsoever must the name of this Society or the names of its members or its place of meeting, or its objects, be mentioned to any, nor must its affairs be discussed even with any member known to you who cannot give you the current password. It has come to our knowledge that a certain slackness has obtained recently, but, after this notice, the Chiefs will take very serious steps in regard to anyone who breaks his or her pledge.

We wish it also to be distinctly understood that you have each promised to be earnest students and therefore we would urge you to take your degrees of advance at as early a date as possible, or, failing the wish to proceed, to send in your resignation, as it is neither for individual nor for collective good that any should remain members who are not working and do not intend to work, or who are in any way out of sympathy with the Order. We would further add that members are required to maintain a benevolent and fraternal attitude towards each other, and the Chiefs will not tolerate disregard of this most essential condition.

Finally, it is important that all who can possibly do so should attend the ceremonies, of which due notice is sent to all members, and that subscriptions or dues should be regularly transmitted to the Treasurer*.

A response to this communication is requested, to be sent in the enclosed envelope, as the list of members is now undergoing revision.

(Signed)
The Chiefs of the Second Order.

June 20, 1902
N.B. Full list of members, Bye-laws & new labels enclosed

* Address as enclosed.

APPENDIX R

Manifesto from the Three Chiefs

The Chiefs of the Second Order desire to consolidate & establish the fraternal link binding every member to each other & the Order; they ask of you your earnest cooperation in the resolution to permit no discord to mar our harmony. Absolute unanimity of purpose must pervade our Association, and absolute secresy as to our aims & methods is an essential condition of success. To this end members are required to maintain a benevolent & fraternal relationship towards each other and a strict silence towards all the outer world, and the Chiefs will not tolerate disregard of these most essential conditions.

Unity of will is the occult condition precedent to a realisation of our aspirations, unswerving fidelity on your part both to the ideals of the Higher Life & to the Chiefs of the Order will constitute the most practical evidence you can give of your desire to assist your brethren. To know, to do and to be silent is the triad of Occult Obligation.

(Signed)'

L. O.

F. R. ——— S. S.

June 26, 1902

N.B. Kindly look most carefully through the list of present members, so as to avoid any mistake in speaking to anyone who has resigned. Carefully destroy all labels & with the letters "G D", & note that you now belong to the Hermetic Society of the M.R. (not GD).

This is of vital importance, because there are some persons in London who have no connection with us whatever who have taken the name "G. D." & you must be careful not to identify yourself with them.

The change of name must be kept absolutely secret from everyone not upon the enclosed list, nor must persons who have resigned be told of it under any circumstances.

Lords & Ladies of the Portal $5=6$*
Virtute Orta. A Posse ad Esse.
Fortiter et Recte. Igitur Ergo Semper.
Shemeber. Levavi Oculos.
Causa Scientiae. Ma Wahanu Thesi.
Volo Aspirare. Tempus Omnia Revelat.
Veritas Vincit. Fortes Fortuna Juvat.
Migrabo. Nobis est Victoria. Prospice.
Sequor Ubi Signo Crux. Audeo.
Per Aspera ad Astra. Finem Respice.
Silentio. In Cornu Salutem Spero.
Per Augusta ad Augusta. Sub Spe.
Gnothi Seaton. Sub hoc Signo Vinces.
Che Sara Sara. Vive ut Vivas.
Servio Liberaliter. Quaeramus Astra.
Festina Lente. Deo Juvante.
Vigilate. Via Crucis via Lucis.
Persevera. Sursum Corda.
Non Sine Numine. Mens Conscia Recti.
Demon est Deus Inversus.
Adveniat Regnum Tuum.
Sacramentum Regis.

List of Outer Members
$4=7$. Umbram fugat Veritas. Bene Tenax.
A Cruce Salus. Ad Astra per Asper.
Magna est Veritas et Prevalebit.
Ultra Aspicio. Polemonium Ceruleum.
Deo Volente. Quaero Lucem.
Laborare est Orare. Aliis Nutrior.
Veritas sine Timero. Coelestria Sequor.
Sic Justus hec Timeus. Mehr Licht.

---

*I have taken these mottoes from a list in longhand which is some-times difficult to read. Although there are obvious errors, I have tried to copy the mottoes exactly as they appear. Among the many interesting ones is that of Maud Gonne – Per Ignem ad Lucem, under the Degree of $3=8$. Although she was inactive in 1902, she apparently had not resigned. See Appendix X for further information.

3=8. Lux e Tenebris. Fortes in Re.
Per Ignem ad Lucem. Constantia.
Labor Omnia Vincit. Neschamah.
Durchdacht.
2=9. Mantiyar Nun.
1 = 10. Per Crucem ad Lucem.
Sibi Imperiosus. Sic Ita ad Astra.
0=0. Hora Fugit Ora.

The following Fratres & Sorores have died or resigned during
the past 18 months: −
Luci. Audi Aude. Equanimiter.
Semper Virtute Verbis. Tenax Propositi.
Sapientia Sapienti Dono Data. Deo Date.
Cogito Ergo Sum. Hora et Semper.
Genethelo Phos. Dum Spiro Spero.
In Limine. Alta Peto. Aktis Heliou.
Oilexi Veritatem. Veritatem Peto.
Veritas in Deo est. Lucem Spiro.

APPENDIX S

THE WESTCOTT
HERMETIC LIBRARY.
Founded 1891. Revised Rules, 1897.*

1. This Library was founded by Dr. WILLIAM WYNN WESTCOTT, the Supreme Magus of the Rosicrucians of England. Fratres who are subscribing Members of any College of the Rosicrucian Society are invited to use this Library. The Founder reserves the right to permit other persons, who are desirous of studying works on Egyptology, Magic, Alchemy and the Occult Sciences, to have access to the Library.

2. The Library is now placed at West Kensington, London, W., in a room suitable for study, which has been provided by the courtesy of F. LEIGH GARDNER, Esq., the Librarian. All communications should be addressed to him at 14 Marlborough Road, Gunnersbury, London, W.

3. Donations of printed books and MSS will be accepted, and valuable books may be lent to the Library, on the understanding that the Founder will take all ordinary and reasonable care of the books, will insure the collection against fire, but he shall not be held liable for injury to, nor for the loss of, any volume.

4. Persons to whom access to the library is granted *may* be permitted to borrow *some* of the volumes for use at their own homes, on conditions to be obtained from the Librarian.

5. The founder will print a catalogue of the books, and this will be supplied by the Librarian on application.

6. If a volume be injured or lost by any reader or borrower, he shall at once make good the damage, replace the book, or pay to the Librarian the value of the volume,

---

* With few exceptions, I have followed the punctuation and spelling of the original.

such value to be assessed by the Librarian, whose decision shall be final.

7. Every reader shall sign a copy of these Rules, with his name, and the words "I agree to be bound by the terms of these Rules."

THE CATALOGUE
OF THE
WESCOTT HERMETIC LIBRARY.

A.

1. ABRAHAM ELEAZAR—An ancient Alchymic Work, Anon. Translated into English by W. S. Hunter, from a German MSS.; Frankfort, 1774. Now in the possession of Fk. Leigh Gardner.
2. ADAMS (W. D.)—Curiosities of Superstition; 8vo, cloth, London, 1882.
3. AESCH-METZAREPH, or "Purifying Fire," from the Kabalah of Rosenroth translated by A Lover of Philalethes, 1714, etc., vol. IV., of Coll. Herm; 8vo, cloth, Lond., 1894.
4. AGRIPPA, H. C.—De Incertitudine et Vanitate omnium Scientiarum; 12mo, calf, 1609.
5. AINSLIE (Herbert)—The Pilgrim and the Shrine; (The author was Edward Maitland); 8vo cloth, 1869.
6. ALBERTUS MAGNUS—De Secretis Mulierum; 12mo, calf, Argent., 1625.
7. ALCHEMY—Twenty-five Alchemic Tracts in Latin, no title page, place, or date; 8vo, half calf.
8. ALCHEMY—An account of some Experiments on Mercury, Silver, and Gold in 1782, by J. Price, etc.; 8vo, cloth, Oxford, 1782. (The last known account of an actual Transmutation.)
9. ALCHEMY—The Science of Spiritual and Material, by S.A.; 8vo, wrappers, Lond., 1893.
10. ALLGEMEINE und General Reformation, beneben der Fama Fraternitatis des loblichen ordens des Rosencreutzes, and other tracts. Regenspurg. 1681.

11. ALLEN (E. H.)—A Manual of Cheirosophy; 8vo, vellum, Lond., 1885.

12. ARATOS—The Phainomena, or Heavenly Display, translated into English verse by Robert Brown; 4to boards, 1895.

13. ASHMOLE (E.)—Mr. Wm. Lilly's History of his Life and Times, from 1602 to 1681; 8vo, calf, Lond., 1715.

14. ASTROLOGY—Lectures on the Science of Celestial Philosophy by Zuriel; 8vo, cloth, Lond., 1835.

15. ASTROLOGY—Urania, 1880; Fate and Fortune, 1890 in one vol.; 8vo, cloth, all published.

16. ASTROLOGERS—Vade Mecum or a Complete System of Prognostication from the Influence of the Stars by Hermes (Pseud.); 8vo, wrappers, Leeds, 1851.

17. AVATARS OF VISHNU—A volume of Photographic Designs by T. H. Pattinson; oblong folio, N.D.

B.

18. BACON (F.)—Novum organum scientiarum; 12mo, calf, Amst., 1660.

19. BAILLY (M.)—Histoire de l'Astronomie Ancienne depuis son origine jusqu'a l'etablissement de l'ecole d'Alexandrie; 4to, calf, Paris, 1775.

20. BAILLY (M.)—Traite de l'Astronomie Indienne et Orientale, etc.; 4to, calf, Paris, 1787.

21. BANGI (T.)—Caelum Orientis et Prisci Mundi, etc., Illustrated; 4to, calf, Hauniae, 1657.

22 to 29. BANIER (L'Abbé)—La Mythologie et les Fables expliquées par l'histoire, eight vols.; 8vo, calf, 1764.

30 to 33. BARRUEL (Abbé)—The History of Jacobinism, four vols.; half calf, Lond., 1798.

34 and 35. BEAUSOBRE (M. de)—Histoire Critique de Manichée et du Manicheisme, two vols.; 4to, calf, Amst., 1734.

36. BECHER (J. J.)—Tripus Hermeticus Fatidicus (three tracts on Alchemy), illustrated; 8vo, morocco, Franco, 1689.

37. BECKIUS (M. F.)—Ephemerides Persarum, etc.; folio, half calf, Augsburg, 1696.

38. BEITRAGE—Zur Philosophischen Geschichte, etc.; 8vo, N.P., 1786.

39. BELL's—New Pantheon, etc., two vols, in one; 4to, calf, London, 1790.

40. BERKELEY (Bishop)—Principles of Human Knowledge; 8vo, London.

41. BERKELEY (Bishop)—Treatise on the Nature of the Material Substance (and its relation to the absolute); 8vo, cloth, Lond., 1878.

32. BERTRAND (A.)—Du Magnetisme Animal en France, etc.; 8vo, cloth, Paris, 1826.

43 and 44. BETHAM (Sir W.)—Etruscan Literature and Antiquities, etc., illustrated, two vols.; 8vo, 1862.

45. [BLACKWELL (T.)]—Letters concerning Mythology; 8vo, calf, Lond., 1748.

46. BONWICK (James)—Irish Druids; 8vo, cloth, 1894.

47. BONWICK (James)—Pyramid Facts and Fancies; 8vo, cloth, 1877.

48. BORRI (G. F.)—La Chiave del Gabinetto—una Relazione esatta della sua Vita; 8vo, calf, Colon, 1681.

49. BORRICHIUS (J.)—Hermetis Ægyptiorum et chemicorum sapientia, etc.; 4to, vellum, Hafniae, 1674.

50. BOULENGER (S.)—La Geometrie, etc., illustrated; 8vo, half calf, Paris, 1627.

51. BOURGUET (M.)—Lettres Philosophiques sur la formation des sels et des crystaux, etc.; 8vo, calf, Amsterdam, 1729.

52 to 56. BOYLE (Hon. R.)—The Works of; five vols, folio, illustrated, calf, London, 1744.

57. BOYLE (P.)—Museum Brittanicum; folio, boards, London, 1791.

58. BRUCE's Travels to Discover the Source of the Nile; 8vo, cloth, illustrated, London, 1866.

59. BUNSEN (C. J.)—Egypt's Place in Universal History, vol I.; 8vo, cloth, Lond., 1867.

60. BURGOYNE (T. H.)—Celestial Dynamics, a Course of Astro Metaphysical Study (one of the MSS. lectures issued by the H. B., of L., privately); 4to, cloth, MSS.

C.

61. CAGLIOSTRO—Nachricht von des beruchtigten, etc.; 8vo, boards, Berlin, 1787.

62 and 63. CALMET (A.)—The Phantom World, translated by

H. Christmas, two vols; 8vo, half calf, Lond., 1850.

64. CARPENTER (E.)—Love's Coming of Age; 8vo, cloth, Manchester, 1896.

65. CATALOGUES—Occult, a volume of Booksellers' Catalogues of Mystical Subjects; 8vo, cloth, V.D.

66. CEBES, Tabula Cebetis, 1640; 4to, vellum.

67. CHAMBON (M.)—Traité des Metaux et des Mineraux; 8vo, calf, Paris, 1714.

68 and 69. CHRISTMAS (H.)—The Cradle of the Twin Giants Science and History, two vols; 8vo, cloth, Lond., 1849. (Contains one of the best Mystic Bibliographies we have.)

. COLLECTANEA HERMETICA, edited by Wm. Wynn Westcott.

91. I.—Hermetic Arcanum, by Jean d'Espagnet.

148. II.—The Divine Pymander of Hermes.

250. III.—Hermetic Art, by Philalethes.

3. IV.—Aesch-Metzareph.

252. V.—Somnium Scipionis of Cicero.

221. VI.—Chaldean Oracles.

227. VII.—Euphrates, by Eugenius Philalethes.

115. VIII.—Egyptian Magic, by S.S.D.D.

70. COLOUR-HEALING—Chromopathy or the science of healing diseases by colours by J. P. Jha; 8vo, wrappers, Madras, 1897.

71. COMBACHIUS (L.)—Sal Lumen et Spiritus Mundi Philosophici, or the dawning of the day discovered; 8vo, morocco, Lond., 1657.

72. COMENIUS (J. A.)—The Rosicrucians Divine Light; 8vo, half calf, Lond., 1651.

73 and 74. CONJURORS MAGAZINE, The; vols. I. and II., 1791-1793 (title misnamed, contains valuable articles on all mystical subjects).

75. COPTIC, *i.e.*, Egyptian Dictionary, by T. Young; Lond., 1831. TATTAM (H.)—Grammar of the Egyptian Language; Lond., 1830. MACDONALD (W. B.)—Sketch of a Coptic Grammar, all in one vol.; 8vo, half calf, Edinburgh, 1856.

121. COPTIC—A New Guide to the Study of, by R. C. Fisher; 8vo, calf, N.D.

76. CRATA REPOA—Oder Einweihungen in der alten geheimen Gesellschaft der Egyptischen Priester; 4to, wrappers, 1785.

77. CROSSET DE LA HAUMERIE (M.)—Les secrets les plus cachés de la Philosophie des Anciens découverts et expliqués; 8vo, calf, Paris, 1762.

D.

78. DALE (A. van)—De Oraculis, etc., illustrated; 4to, calf, Amst., 1700.

79. DEE (Dr. J.)—A true relation of what passed between Dr. Dee and some spirits, etc.; folio, calf, Lond., 1659.

80. DEE (Dr. John)—The Private Diary of; 4to, calf, London, 1842.

81 and 82. DE FREVAL (J. B.)—The History of the Heavens, etc., illustrated, two vols.; 8vo, Lond., 1740.

83. DELEUZE (J. P. F.)—Practical Instruction in Animal Magnetism or Mesmerism; 8vo, cloth, Lond., 1843.

84. DEMONOLOGIA, or Natural Knowledge Revealed, by J. S. F.; 8vo, half calf, Lond., 1831.

85 to 87. DENON (V.)—Voyages dans la basse et la haute Egypte, two vols., 4to, text, and one vol. folio plates; Lond., 1807.

88. DE QUINCY—Confessions of an English Opium Eater; 8vo, cloth, London. (Contains his Article on Rosicrucians and Freemasons.)

89. DESPANGE (J.)—Shibboleth ou Reformation de quelques Passages de la Bible, etc.; 8vo, vellum, Geneva, 1671.

90. [D'ESPAGNET (J.)]—Enchyridion Physicae Restitutœ, or the Summary of Physics Recovered; 12mo, calf, Lond., 1651.

91. [D'ESPAGNET (J.)]—The Hermetic Arcanum of Penes nos unda Tag (Reprint), vol. I. of Coll. Herm.; 8vo, cloth, Lond., 1893.

92 to 103. DE VERTOT (L'Abbé)—Œuvres; 8vo, calf, twelve vols, Paris, 1819.

104. DICKINSON (Ed.)—Delphi Phoenicizantes, etc.; 8vo, calf, Oxon., 1655.

105. DICTIONNAIRE Hermetique—Contenant l'explication des termes, etc.; 8vo, calf, Paris, 1695.

E.

106. EGYPTIAN Antiquities, Catalogue of, in the Museum of Hartwell House; 4to, boards, illustrated, 1858.
107. EGYPT and the Great Suez Canal by St. Hilaire; 8vo, Lond., 1857.
108. EGYPT and Nubia, by J. St. John, illustrated; 8vo, Lond., 1845.
109. EGYPT (Burton, J.)—Excerpta Hieroglyphica; oblong folio, cloth (a valuable collection of plates on Egypt), Lond., 1828.
110. EGYPT—Congrés Provincial des Orientalistes Français; half calf, Paris, 1878. (A most valuable record of Egyptological Work.)
111. EGYPT—The Discoveries in Upper Egypt of H. Salt, by G. D'Athanasi, illustrated; 8vo, Lond., 1836.
112. EGYPT—De Symbolica Aegyptiorum sapientia symbola, etc., and the Symbolicus of Polyhistor, 1631; 8vo, calf, Col., Agrip., 1631.
113. EGYPT—Essay on Young and Champollion's system of Hierogyphics, by H. Salt, illustrated; 8vo, Lond., 1825.
114. EGYPT—On the Tombs of the Egyptians, with a Key to one of them, illustrated; 8vo, boards, Lond., 1822.
115. EGYPTIAN MAGIC, by S.S.D.D., vol. VIII. of Coll. Herm., illustrated; 8vo, cloth, Lond., 1896.
116. ERASMUS—Familiarum colloquiorum opus.; 8vo, cloth, Argent, 1628.

F.

10. FAMA FRATERNITATIS. 1681—(Rosicruciana).
117 and 118. FANTASMAGORIANA ou Recueil d'histoires d'apparitions des spectres, revenans, fantômes, etc., two vols.; half calf, Paris, 1812.
119. FAUST (Dr.)—Bücherschatz, with many magical diagrams; 8vo, cloth, Stutt., 1851.
120. FEITHIUS (E.)—Antiquit Homericarum, lib. IV.; 8vo, boards, Argent, 1743.
121. FISHER (R. C.)—A New Guide to Coptic; 8vo, calf.
275. FLAMEL (N.)—The Hieroglyphical Figures of 1624, ed. by W. W. Westcott.
122. FRANCK (A.)—La Kabbale on la Philosophie Religieuse des Hebreux; 8vo, half calf, Paris, 1843.

123. FRATRES LUCIS—Ritual in MSS., N.D.

124 and 125. FREEMASONS, Mag. and Masonic Mirror, The, vols. IV., and V.; 8vo, cloth, Lond., 1858.

126. FRIPP (E. I.)—The Composition of the Book of Genesis; 8vo, cloth, 1892.

G.

127. GAFFAREL (M. I.)—Curiousitez Inouyes sur la Sculpture Talismanique des Persans; 8vo, vellum, Rouen, 1631.

128. GAFFAREL (M. I.)—Des Talismans, De l'ungent des Armes; 8vo, calf, Paris, 1636.

129. GEBER (Rex Arabum)—His Treatises on Alchemy, in Latin, illustrated; 8vo, calf, Gedani, 1682.

130. GINSBURG (C. D.)—The Kabbalah : Its Doctrines, Development and Literature; 8vo, cloth, Lond., 1865.

131 to 134. GOULD (R. F.)—History of Freemasonry, illustrated, four vols, cloth, Lond., 1886.

H.

135. HAEN (Ant de)—De Magia liber; 8vo, boards, Venetiis, 1775.

136. HAMMER (J.)—Ancient Alphabets, from the Arabic of Ahmad bin Washih; 4to, 1806.

137 and 138. HANDWRITING—L'Autographie par J. Janin, 1st Series, 1864; 2nd Series, oblong folio, Paris, 1871-2.

139. HARRIS (A. C.)—Hieroglyphical Standards, representing places in Egypt; 4to, cloth, Lond., N.D.

140. HARTMANN (J.)—In the Pronaos of the Temple of Wisdom; 8vo, cloth, Lond., 1890.

141. HARVEY (G.)—Excercitationes de Generatione Animalium; 4to, calf, Amst., 1651.

10. HASELMEYER (Adam)—Antwort, an die Lobwurdige Bruderschafft, 1681 (Rosicruciana).

142. HAVILLAND (Saumarez de)—The Mystic Serpent; 8vo, cloth, 1891.

143 and 144. HEBREW—Latin and English Dictionary, by J. S. Frey; two vols., boards, Lond., 1815.

145. HEBRAICUM Lexicon ex ejus lexico heptaglotto, E. Castelli; 4to, vellum, Lipsiae, 1790.

146. HELMONT (F. M. B.)—Alphabet i verè Naturalis Hebraici brevissima, etc.; illustrated, 12mo, morocco, Sulz, 1657.

147. HERBERT (The Hon. G.)—Nimrod, a discourse on certain passages of History and Fable, vol. III.; 8vo, Lond., 1828.

148. HERMES—The Divine Pymander of, vol II. of Coll. Herm.; 8vo, cloth, Lond., 1894.

149. HERODOTUS, translated by W. Beloe; 8vo, cloth, Lond., 1830.

150. HEUCHER (M. J. H.)—Magic Plants; 8vo, vellum, 1886.

151. [HITCHCOCK (T.)]—Remarks upon Alchemy and the Alchemists; 8vo, cloth, N.Y., 1865.

152 to 155. HOFMANNIUS (J. J.)—Lexicon Universale, etc.; four vols, folio, Lug. Bat., 1698.

156. HORAPOLLO NILOUS, the Hieroglyphics of, by A. T. Cory; cloth, 8vo, 1811.

157. HOSKINS (G. A.)—Visit to the Great Oasis of the Libyan Desert, illustrated; 8vo, Lond., 1837.

J.

158. Jesu Regulæ Societatis; 8vo, vellum, Antwerp, 1635.

K.

122. KABALAH—Adolf Franck.

130. KABALAH—C. D. Ginsburg.

193. KABALAH—S. Liddell MacGregor Mathers.

202. KABALAH—Isaac Myer.

159. KAKERLAK oder geschichte eines Rosenkreutzers aus dem vorigen Jahrhunderte; 8vo, boards, Leipzig, 1784.

160. KELLY (W.)—Fifty Years' Masonic Reminiscences; 8vo, cloth : N.P., 1888.

161. KENDALL (G.)—An Appendix to the Unlearned Alchemist, etc.; 8vo, roan, Lond., N.D.

162. KILIANUS—Dictionary : Dutch, Latin, and French; 8vo, half vellum, Amst., 1642.

163. KIRCHER (A.)—Prodromus Coptus sive Ægyptiacus; 4to, vellum, Rome, 1636.

164. KIRWAN (R.)—Elements of Mineralogy; 8vo, calf, Lond., 1784.

165. KNEPH, THE—Vols. I. to VIII., 1888; 4to, cloth, London. (Official Journal of the A. and P. Rite of Masonry, and also contains occult information not to be found elsewhere.)

L.

166. LANDSEER (J.)—Sabean Researches, illustrated; 4to, calf, Lond., 1823.
167. LANE (E. W.)—An Account of the Manners and Customs of the Modern Egyptians; 8vo, Lond., 1890.
168. LEE (E.)—Animal Magnetism; 8vo, cloth, Lond., 1843.
169. LEE (E.)—Animal Magnetism and Magnetic Lucid Somnambulism; 8vo, cloth, Lond., 1866.
170. LELAND (C. G.)—The Hundred Riddles of the Fairy Bellaria, illustrated; 4to, Lond., 1892.
171. LÉVI (Eliphaz)—The Magical Ritual of the Sanctum Regnum, translated by W. Wynn Westcott; 8vo, London, 1896.
172. LÉVI (Eliphaz)—The Shemhamphorash and the Keys of the Tarot, in MSS., translated by W. Wynn Westcott from the original MSS. of the Author of 1861.
173. LILLY (Wm.)—Christian Astrology, in three books, etc.; 4to, sheep, Lond., 1659.
174. LIMBURG BROUWER (Van)—Akbar, an Eastern Romance; 8vo, Lond., 1879.
175. LOGIA IHESOU, or Sayings of our Lord, from an early Greek Papyrus; 8vo, boards, 1897.
176. LYTTON (B.)—The Coming Race; 8vo, cloth, Lond., 1872.

M.

177. MACARIUS (J.)—Abraxas seu Apistopistus, etc.; 4to (with charming illustrations of Gnostic gems), Antwerp (Plantin Press), 1657.
178. MACKAY (C.)—The Salamandrine, illustrated by J. Gilbert; royal 8vo, cloth, London, 1853.
179. MAHAN (A.)—Modern Mysteries Explained and Exposed; 8vo, cloth, Boston, 1855.
180. MAIER (J. A.)—Ueber Jesuiten, Freymaurer und deutsche Rosencreutzer; 8vo, half calf, Leipzig, 1781.
181. MAIER (M.)—Arcana Arcanissima, etc.; half calf, N.D.
182. MAIER (M.)—Cantilenœ Intellectuales de Phœnice redivivo, etc.; 8vo, calf, Paris, 1758.
183. MAIER (M.)—Scrutinium Chymicum, etc.; illustrated, 4to, vellum, Franco, 1687.

184. MAIER (M.)—Symbola aureœ Mensœ duodecim Nationum; 4to, vellum, Franco, 1617.

185. MAIMONIDES (Moses)—Porta Mosis sive Dissert aliquot; 4to, Oxon, 1655.

5. MAITLAND (Ed.)—The Pilgrim and the Shrine, by Herbert Ainslie, (pseud.), 1869.

186. MALCHUS—De Vita Pythagoræ, small 4to, vellum, Altorfii., 1610.

187. MANILIUS (M.)—Astronomicon ... cum Notis Bentleii; 4to, calf, Lond., 1739.

188 to 190. MASONIC MAGAZINE, The, vols. V., VIII., IX.; 8vo, cloth, Lond., 1877-82. (Contains inter alia valuable articles on alchemy.)

191. MASPERO (G.)—Guide au Musée de Boulaq; 8vo, cloth, illustrated, Boulaq., 1883.

192. MASSEY (Gerald)—The Ballad of Babe Christabel, etc.; 8vo, cloth, Lond., 1854.

193. MATHERS (S. L. M.)—The Kabbalah Unveiled; 8vo, cloth, Lond., 1887.

194. MELVILLE (H.)—Veritas, Revelation of Mysteries, etc.; illustrated, oblong folio, cloth, Lond., 1874.

195. MERCURY—A Theosophical Magazine, vol. III.; 8vo, cloth, San Fran., 1897.

196. MESMER (M.)—Mémoire sur la decouverte du Magnetisme Animal; 8vo, calf, Geneva, 1779.

197. MICHAELIS (S.)—The Admirable History of a Penitent Woman, etc.; 4to, calf, Lond., 1613. (Contains an account of the origins of "Luciferians," and deals with witchcraft.)

198. MORE (H.)—The Theological Works of; folio, half calf, Lond., 1708.

199. MORITZ (K. P.)—Die Symbolik Weisheit der Aegypter; 8vo, boards, Berlin, 1793.

200. MURR (C. G. van)— Uber den wahren Ursprung der Rosenkreuzer und des Freymaurerordens; 8vo, boards, Sulzbach, 1803.

201. MUSŒUM HERMETICUM reformatum et amplificatum continens Tractatus Chimicos XXI., etc., illustrated; 4to, cloth, Frankfort, 1749.

202. MYER (Isaac)—Qabbalah, The Philosophical Writings of Avicebron, etc., illustrated; 8vo, cloth, Pa., 1888.

N.

203 to 212.—NOTES AND QUERIES, Sixth Series, vol. X. (1884), XI., XII. (1885); Seventh Series, vol. I., II. (1886), III., IV. (1887), VII., VIII. (1889), IX. (1890); 4to, cloth, London.

O.

213. OCCULT MAGAZINE, The, vols. I. and II. (all pub.), 1885-6; 4to, cloth, Glasgow.

214 and 215. O'CONNOR, Chronicles of Eri, two vols.; 8vo, cloth, London, 1822.

216. OIMENEPTHAH I., King of Egypt, The Alabaster Sarcophagus of; 4to, cloth, London, 1864.

217. OLCOTT (H. S.)—Old Diary Leaves; 8vo, cloth, Lond., 1895.

218. [OLD (W. R.)]—Kabalistic Astrology, or your Fortune in your Name, by "Sephariel"; 8vo, cloth, Lond., N.D.

219. OLIVER (G.)—Institutes of Masonic Jurisprudence; 8vo, half calf, London, 1859.

220. ORACLES—Sibyllina Oracula ex vett codd auct renovata et notis illus a, J. O. Brettano; thick 8vo, calf, plates by T. de Bry, Paris, 1607.

221. ORACLES—The Chaldœan Oracles of Zoroaster, vol. VI. of Coll. Herm.; 8vo, cloth, Lond., 1895.

123. ORDER OF LIGHT—A MSS. Ritual of the Degrees of this Order privately copied; 8vo, cloth.

222. OWEN (M. A.)—Old Rabbit the Voodoo, and other Sorcerers, illustrated; 8vo, cloth, Lond., 1893.

P.

223. PALINGENIUS (M.)—Zodiacus Vitae, lib XII.; 12mo, vellum, Amst., 1628.

224. PALMER (A. Smythe)—Babylonian Influence on the Bible; 8vo, cloth, 1897.

225. PARACELSUS (Th.)—Compendium ex optimis quibus que ejus libris, etc.; 8vo, calf, Paris, 1567.

226. PHILALETHES (Eir)—Kern der Alchemie, aus dem Englischen ubersetzt; 8vo, calf, Leipzig, 1685.

227. PHILALETHES (Eug.)—Euphrates or the Waters of the East (reprint), Lond., 1655, vol. VII. of Collectanea Hermetica.

228. PHILALETHES (Eug.)—Lumen de Lumine, or a New Magical Light, etc.

THE SECOND WASH, or The Moore scour'd once more; 8vo, half calf, Lond., 1651.

229. PICUS (Joh. de Mirandula)—Cabalistarum selectiora, etc.; 8vo, calf, Venet., 1569.

230. PORPHYRY—De abstinentia ab esu aminalium, lib IV., Grace cum Latina. Notas adjecit J. de Rhoer; 4to calf, Trajecti, 1767.

231. PORPHYRY—De Antro Nympharum, Graece cum Latina. L. Holstenii versione; 4to, vellum, Trajecti, 1765.

232. PORTA (J.B.)—Magiæ Naturalis Lib XX.; 12mo, half calf, Lug. Bat., 1651.

233. PRASNOTTARA (The)—The Indian organ of the Theosophical Society, vols. I. and II., privately published, Madras, 4to, half calf, 1891-92.

8. PRICE (J.)—An Account of Some Experiments on Mercury, Silver and Gold in 1782; 8vo, Oxford, 1782.

234. PTOLEMY (Claudius)—Tetrabiblos, being four books of the influence of the stars, translated by J. M. Ashmand; half calf, Lond., 1822.

R.

235. REGNAUD (P.)—Le Rig Veda, et les origines de la mythologie indo—européene; 8vo, cloth, Paris, 1892.

226. REICHENBACH (C. Von)—Researches on the Dynamics of Magnetism, etc., by J. Ashburner; 8vo, cloth, Lond., 1851.

10. ROSICRUCIANA—A volume of the earliest German tracts, containing : —(1) Allgemeine und Generale Reformation, 1614; (2) Fama Fraternitatis; (3) Antwort, von Adam Haselmeyer; (4) Wolgemeyntes Auschreiben an die Hockwurdigste Fraternitat des Rosencreutzes, 1617; (5) Geistlicher Discurs und Betrachtung; (6) Vors Ander von der Liebe und ihrer Asrt, Natur und Eigenschafft; small 8vo, 1681, Regenspurg.

237. ROSICRUCIANA, Chymische Hochzeit Christiani Rosen-creutz, Aum 1459; 8vo, calf, Strasburg, 1616.

238. ROSICRUCIANA—Constitution der Gesellschaft zum "Rosigen Kreuz," privately printed; 8vo, bound, 1874.

239. ROSICRUCIANA—Der Heilige Balthasar ein Bruder Rosen-kreutzer, etc.; 8vo, boards, N.P., 1795.

240. ROSICRUCIANA—Geschichte des Bruder Gordians; 8vo, half calf, Kosmopolis, 1789.

241. ROSICRUCIAN, The, from 1868 to 1875, with Transactions of the Met. Coll. in Anglia, 1885-97; half calf, London.

S.

9. S.A.—The Science of Spiritual and Material Alchemy, 1893.

242 and 243. SABINE (Stuart de Chevalier)—Discours philosophique sur les trois principes, etc., two vols.; 8vo, calf, Paris, 1781.

244. SADLER (H.)—Notes on the Ceremony of Installation; 8vo, cloth, Lond., 1889.

245. SALMON (Wm.)—Polygraphics, etc; 8vo, Lond., 1701. (Contains valuable Articles on Alchemy.)

246. SCOTT (W.)—The Existence of Evil Spirits proved, etc.; 8vo, cloth, Lond., 1853.

247. SELDENUS (J.)—De Diis Syris syntagmata II.; 8vo, vellum, Amst., 1680.

248. SHARP (G.)—The Case of Saul and the Influence of Demons; 8vo, cloth, Lond., 1807.

249. SHECHINAH, The Revelations of the, or the Tree of Life in the Holy Royal Arch, by V.Q.S.V.; 8vo., P.P., 1887.

250. SHORT—Enquiry concerning the Hermetic Art, by a Lover of Philalethes, vol. III. of Coll. Herm.; 8vo, Lond., 1714 (reprint).

251. SMYTH (J. P.)—How we got our Bible; 8vo, 1896.

252. SOMNIUM SCIPIONIS, translated into English, by L. O.—The Golden Verses of Pythagoras, by A.E.A.; The Symbols of Pythagoras, by S. A., vol. V. of Coll., Herm.; 8vo, cloth, Lond., 1894.

253 to 255. SONNINI (C. S.)—Travels in Upper and Lower Egypt, illustrated, three vols.; calf, Lond., 1799.

256. [SOUTH (Thos.)]—Early Magnetism in its Higher Relations to Humanity, by THUOSMATHOS; 8vo, Lond., 1846.

257. [SOUTH (Thos.)]—A Suggestive Enquiry into the Hermetic Mystery, etc.; 8vo, London, 1850.

258. SPECTRES—Mirabiles Hist de Spectris, de Invocatione Sanctorum, etc.; 12mo, vellum, Lug. Bat., 1656.

259. ST. HILL (K.)—The Grammar of Palmistry; 8vo, boards, Lond., 1894.

260 and 161. STOBÆUS, Eclogœ Physicarum et Ethicarum Libri duo, two vols.; 8vo, calf, Gottingœ, 1792.

262. SWEDENBORG (E.)—Conjugal Love, etc.; 8vo, Lond., 1876.

T.

66. TABULA Cebetis, Lug. Bat., 1640; 4to, vellum.

263. TAYLOR (Thos.)—Iamblichus on the Mysteries, etc.; 8vo, Lond., 1895.

264. TAYLOR (Thos.)—Sallust on the Gods and the World, etc.; 8vo, calf, Lond., 1793.

265. TAYLOR (Thos.)—The Mystical Hymns of Orpheus (reprint); 8vo, cloth, Lond., 1896.

266. TEMPLE REBUILT (The), by V.Q.S.V.; wrappers, P.P., 1886.

267. THEOSOPHICAL Pamphlets—A vol. containing various pamphlets; The Vahan, American Section Reports, Notices, etc.; 8vo, cloth.

268. THEOSOPHICAL Society, Reports from 1891-94, etc.; 8vo, cloth, Lond.

269. THEOSOPHY—A volume of various pamphlets, including the Oriental Series, etc.; V.D., 4to, cloth.

270. TRITHEMIUS (J.)—Steganographia, etc.; 4to, calf, Norimb, 1721. (Contains valuable Magical Formulæ.)

V.

271. VAHAN (The)—Vols. III., IV., V., VI., in one vol.; 4to, cloth, Lond., 1893-97. (The official organ of the "Theosophical Society" in England.)

272. VALENTINE (B.)—His Triumphant Chariot of Antimony, illustrated; 8vo, calf, Lond., 1678.

W.

273. WELLING (G. von)—Opus Mago Cabbalisticum et Theosophicum, etc.; illustrated, 4to, cloth, Frankfort, 1784.

171. WESTCOTT (W. W.)—The Magical Ritual of the Sanctum Regnum, interpreted by the Tarot Trumps, illustrated; 8vo, cloth, Lond., 1896.

274. WESTCOTT (W. W.)—Numbers; their occult power and Mystic Virtue; 4to, cloth, Lond., 1890.

275. WESTCOTT (W. W.)—Reprint of the translation into English of "The Hieroglyphical Figures of Nicholas Flamel" of 1624; 4to, vellum, Bath.

276. WESTCOTT (W. W.)—The Rosicrucians, their History and Aims; 8vo, wrappers, N.D.

277. WESTCOTT (W. W.)—The Sepher Yetzirah, translated from the Hebrew, by W. W. W., 2nd Ed.; 8vo, cloth, Lond., 1893.

278. WESTCOTT (W. W.)—Suicide; its History, Literature, etc.; 8vo, cloth, Lond., 1885.

172. WESTCOTT (W. W.)—Translation of the Shemhamphorash and Tarot Keys, a MSS. work of Eliphas Lévi, of 1861.

279. WILKINSON (Sir G.)—The Egyptians in the time of the Pharaohs, coloured plates; 8vo, Lond., 1857.

280. WITSIUS (H.)—Aegyptiaca, etc.; 4to, vellum, Amst., 1696.

281. WRIGHT (T.)—Narratives of Sorcery and Magic, two vols. in one; 8vo, Lond., 1851.

Y.

282. YARKER (J.)—Continuation of the Comte de Gabalis (reprint); 4to, Bath, 1897.

283. YARKER (J.)—Lectures of a Senate, Chapter, etc., embracing all the Systems of High Grade Masonry; 8vo, cloth, Lond., 1882.

284. YARKER (J.)—Masonic Charges and Lectures, a series translated from the French; 8vo, cloth, Manchester, 1880. (Also excellent articles on the Mysteries, Mystic Symbolism, etc.)

Z.

285. ZOLLNER (C. F.)—Transcendental Physics, translated by C. C. Massey, illustrated; 8vo, cloth, Lond., 1882.

286. ZSCHOKKE (H.)—Tales from the German (2nd series); 8vo, cloth, Lond., 1846.

APPENDIX T

Impression of 6–5 Ceremony
Postulant Frater D.E.D.I. Oct. 16./14.

The Vision of Shekinah was not at all clear. Apparently the living figure should be enshrouded by a very large one, in this case the figure appeared to be imperfectly materialised. The alteration of the usual physical appearance of the Postulant was very marked – he was of a more refined substance, more transparent, and a clearer (more distinct) body illuminated, and permeated the physical one. He also had a much more beautiful appearance – one got a glimpse of what his Resurrection body might be. This alteration in appearance was obvious at once on his entrance, so must have been the result of his preparation. He had a surface of clear whiteness that could be written upon.

At first he appeared somewhat afraid. As he advanced slowly towards the Vault Door – before the Obligation – Great black Wings enshrouded him from behind, and seemed to make a Casket or Shrine for his Higher Self – who descended within them – the wings hovering above and behind him – (not touching him) during the Obligation. His Astral Feet appeared crossed as he stood at the Door during the Obligation, he also appeared divided in two. He gave himself a nasty jar by speaking, (repeating the Obligation at first). His arms stretched out formed the solid centre of the wings of the Figure which enshrouded him, one of great strength and delicacy, dark and semi-transparent, with irridescent blue, green, and orange tints, like a Pheasant's neck. He became larger towards the end of the Obligation, and also again was – afraid.

During the Prayer – at the beginning of the 2nd Point, "Knocketh at the Gateway of the Grave", he appeared to think of Water. (Was he ever nearly drowned?)

As he gazed into the Bowl of Water, he seemed to see his Higher Self enshrouding him from behind – but vaguely.

At the extinction of the Brown Candles – there seemed a

kind of Grill between them and the progress to the 4 Red Candles, difficult to get through. He felt the putting out of the Green Candles acutely, and sank down. He did not expect the extinction of the one Red Candle, it gave him a small shock. At the extinction of the seven violet Candles he rose up firmly again.

As he lay down in the Pastos – a great darkness fell over him – it began with the winding of the Bandage. There appeared to be great heavy pushing Powers trying to weigh him down.

The following occurred during the ringing of the 36 Bells, and the corresponding Sentences.

At the Fourth Bell Crossed Swords point downwards were held as a barrier before him.

At the Fifth Bell they were raised – and held straight across, level, before him, about the height of his thighs.

Between Six and Seven Bells his Arms went out in response, in the Form of a Cross and he passed through the Swords.

Eighth Bell. He became separated (left part of himself behind) and passed up.

At the Tenth Bell, he was only half conscious on the physical plane.

At the Twelfth Bell, he became firmer just before it.

At the Thirteenth Bell, he is faint.

At the Fourteenth Bell, he is very cold.

At the Sixteenth Bell, he again emerges into a further higher plane.

At the Seventeenth Bell, he is like a transparent Rainbow. The Colours of the Planets play upon him. They then merge into brilliant White Light and for the rest of the Bells he shone with it.

The sprinkling of the Salt appears to denote that Salt is the Purest form of Earth, for while ordinary Earth assists the decomposition of the Body, Salt preserves it.

The Rising from the Tomb, and the standing at the entrance to the Vault, and the Sprinkling appear to involve very great and serious effort on the part of both Postulant and Officers, in order that what has been obtained in the Tomb may be brought back to the physical man and incorporated with it, and retained.

APPENDIX U

Notes of Mr. Collison's Interview with Steiner re F.R.* & the Order.

F.R.   he says cares mostly about getting higher Grades. He is spiritualistic & Mediumistic.

Q.A.   is of no account, purely a Church-woman with strong leaning towards Rome.

Q.L.   is the only one who could be made anything of. She is a clairvoyant but is hopeless under her present influences. She is as it were on one side of a veil & calls for say Lloyd George who she supposes is on the other side, she gets an answer without making sure that it is Lloyd George, writes it down & even then may not write it down correctly.

A.B.S.   he knows nothing about & I presume does not wish to trouble about him.

C.R.C.   may be invoked in the vault. He does not think that C.R.C. himself comes, probably someone under his influence but on the other hand any evil spirit may come, it depends on who wishes.

Ceremonies   are not evil in themselves even under the present circumstances in our Order & are all right as long as one takes them as symbolism, tho' evil can come in according to who is invoking.

These ceremonies are in fact necessary to some people according to their stage of development.

F.R.   was permitted to be present during his (Steiner's) ceremonies (3 grades 1. 2. 3 the only ones he gives) but he gave him (F.R.) no grades.

He gave him no introductions to anyone. He thinks they (F.R. & Q.L.) may possibly have got some Masonic Grades somewhere in Germany, possibly Rosicrucian Masons. He knows nothing about it & apparently does not think that he or Q.L. received any recognised grades at all. He knows

* The initials stand for the following: F.R.: Dr R. W. Felkin; Q.A.: Miss Ethel Felkin; Q.L.: Mrs R. W. Felkin; A.B.S.: Ara Ben Shemesh; C.R.C.: Christian Rosenkreuz; I.F.C.: Miss Christina M. Stoddart. See Appendix X.

nothing of this claim to sole Continental authority put forth by F.R.

Details given to me by Mr. Sandrieux & given to him by Mr. Collison who saw Steiner in Holland & asked specially for information for us.

I.F.C.

APPENDIX V

Copy

In consequence of failure on the part of the Chiefs to take a plebiscite of the Order or furnish me with the official list of Members I am compelled by the lapse of time to call a meeting of those working members of the Order whose names & addresses are known to me. Should you know anyone not receiving a notice please show them this copy.

Pleacse attend a Meeting at

   7 Brunswick Place Harley St. N.W. 1

(by kind permission of Dr. Dickson)

on Saturday April 23rd at 3 p.m.

The matters to be decided are whether –

1. Members support those Chiefs who refuse to recognise F.R.'s authority.
2. Members support F.R. & wish to take the appropriate & consequent steps.
3. Members desire a deputation to investigate the authority vested in F.R. & in that case to formulate particulars.

Please attend if possible: if quite impossible a reply to Dr. Dickson marked personal, indicating the course favoured by yourself is desired.

(signed) Frat. Yrs. Q.A.*

---

* Q.A. is Miss Ethel Felkin.

APPENDIX W

V.H. Frater or Soror,

As you are aware, certain difficulties have arisen in the working of the Amoun Temple, and a considerable number of the Inner Members are anxious that some amicable arrangement should be made in order to facilitate our future working. For some time past, our G.H. Soror Q.A. has been endeavouring to obtain the co-operation of the present Ruling Chiefs to attain this end, but has not been entirely successful in her efforts – partly owing to a lack of agreement between these Chiefs themselves, and partly from their not having sent her the list of Members and their addresses, although the previous Inner Meeting decided that this should be given her.

As the present Chiefs will neither co-operate with others nor agree to carry out the work themselves, the only way out of the impasse appears to be to take a plebiscite of all the Inner Members on the active roll of the Temple. With this object in view, the G.H. Soror Q.A. called a meeting of all the Inner Members, including the Three Chiefs, whose names and addresses she could obtain. That Meeting was held at 7, Brunswick Place, on Saturday, 23rd April, 1921, at 3 p.m., twelve Members being present, and ten Members intimating their sympathy with the objects of the Meeting, though unable to be present.

In order, however, to carry out as fully as possible the wishes of the Temple as a whole, and to ensure its harmonious working in the future, it was decided to send round to all the Members, for their approval, the resolutions passed at the meeting.

A Committee of three Members (V.Q.S.V.: S.S.: and F.F.J.), with power to add to its numbers up to a total of seven, was appointed to carry out the wishes of the Meeting. Amongst other matters which the Meeting remitted to this Committee, the Members present unanimously decided :–

"That this Meeting, though fully assured of the bona fides of
F.R. himself, considers it advisable that the Committee
should, at a convenient season, discuss, and if necessary investigate, the Continental source of F.R.'s authority and
teaching – making use of the introductions granted by him
for that purpose."

If you are in favour of the Resolution, given upon the accompanying sheet, and unanimously adopted by the twelve Members who attended the Meeting, will you be so good as to
sign and return it at your early convenience? Should you
have any alternative and helpful suggestions to make, either
on the lines indicated, or in any other direction, the Committee will be grateful. Its members earnestly desire the
"SUMMUM BONUM" – the Greatest Good of the greatest
number; and they wish to avoid any such reproach as is
embodied in the words:– "Ye have taken away the key of
knowledge: ye entered not in yourselves, and them that
were entering in, ye hindered."

F.F.J.: S.S.: V.Q.S.V.*

Strictly Private.

Saint George's Day:
23rd April, 1921.

"We, the undersigned Inner Members of the Amoun Temple,
assembled on the invitation of G.H. Soror Q.A., who duly
issued the invitation to all the Ruling Chiefs and all Inner
Members whose names and addresses she was able to obtain,
hereby agree that the G.H. Frater F.R. is the ultimate authority in this Temple, and that we can therefore no longer
acknowledge the authority of those of the heretofore Chiefs
(appointed under the Constitution drawn up by F.R.), who
have refused both to accept F.R.'s rulings and to co-operate
with him and with his accredited Representative, Q.A.

We, therefore, have decided, with and under Q.A.'s authority
as F.R.'s Representative, to appoint a Committee to consider
and take the appropriate steps for the restoration and, if
necessary, reorganization of the Group according to the
intention of the Constitution drawn up by F.R."

* The initials stand for the following: V.Q.S.V.: Mrs Cecilia Macrae; S.S.:
J. W. Brodie-Innes; F.F.J.: Dr W. E. Carnegie Dickson; Q.A.: Miss Ethel
Felkin; F.R.: Dr R. W. Felkin. See Appendix X.

We, the undersigned members, unable to be present at the meeting held at 7, Brunswick Place on 23rd April, 1921, assent to the above Resolution passed unanimously at that meeting. (Please sign here :) .... (Date) ....

1. I desire to continue a Member under the Constitution drawn up by F.R., and in co-operation with those Members remaining loyal to him.
2. I desire to follow the lead of certain other Members or Ex-Members, independently and without the farther co-operation of F.R. and those working with him – such Members or Ex-Members then taking upon themselves all farther responsibility – so far as I am concerned – with regard to the authenticity or otherwise of the Order, its Teachings, and their source of origin.
3. I desire to go into abeyance for a period of one, two, or three years.
4. I desire to resign my Membership, and I herewith return all my Order Manuscripts, Papers, Implements, etc.
(Signed) .... (Date) ....
(Please delete the alternatives which you consider inappropriate.)

APPENDIX X

Order Names and Mottoes

Aitken, Andrew P.: Judico Lente

Aitken, Georgina: Sola Cruce Salus

Atherton, J. L.: Semper Fidelis

Ayton, Mrs W. A.: Quam Potero Adjutabo

Ayton, William Alexander: Virtute Orta Occidunt Rarius

Baker, Julian L.: Causa Scientiae

Bates, Miss Emily: Pro Veritate

Bennett, Allan: Iehi Aour

Berridge, C. M.: Respiro

Berridge, Edward W.: Resurgam

Birchall, Peter: Cephas

Blackden, Marcus Worsley: Ma Wahanu Thesi

Blackwell, Miss Anna: Essi Quam Videri

Blackwood, Algernon: Umbram Fugat Veritas

Borthwick, Miss Gabrielle: Sine Metu

Brettle, John W.: Luci

Briggs, Miss Mary: Per Mare Ad Astra

Brodie-Innes, J. W.: Sub Spe

Brodie-Innes, Mrs J. W.: Sub Hoc Signo Vinces

Bullock, Mrs Pamela Carden: Shemeber

Bullock, Percy W.: Levavi Oculos

Burry, Henry Pullen: Anima Pura Sit

Burry, Mrs Henry Pullen: Urge Semper Igitur

Carden, Alexander James: Fide

Carden, Mrs Anne: Amore

Cathcart, Mrs Agnes: Veritas Vincit

Cattanach, Andrew: Esto Sol Testis

Childers, Miss: Quis Seperabit

Clayton, Miss Fanny: Orare

Coleman, Frank: Audi Et Aude

Colville, Mrs Henry: Semper

Coryn, Sidney: Veritas Praevaleat

Cox, Benjamin: Crux Dat Salutem

Cracknell, Maud: Tempus Omnia Revelat

Crowley, Aleister: Perdurabo

Davies, Mrs Jane Anna: Excelsior

de Steiger, Juliette: Alta Peto

Dickson, George: Fortes Fortuna Juvat

Dickson, W. E. Carnegie: Fortes Fortuna Juvat (same as that of his father, George Dickson)

Drummond, Mrs Emily: In Deo Confido

Drummond, Miss Mary: Fideliter

Edwards, B. E. J.: Deus Lux Solis

Elliott, John Hugh: Nobis Est Victoria

Emery, Mrs Florence Farr: Sapientia Sapienti Dono Data

Felkin, Miss Ethel: Quaero Altissima

Felkin, Mrs Mary: Per Aspera Ad Astra

Felkin, Mrs Robert W.: Quaero Lucem (second wife)

Felkin, Robert W.: Finem Respice

Fitzgerald, J. C.: Deus Meus Deus

Fortune, Dion: Deo Non Fortuna

Fullham-Hughes, Mrs Reena: Silentio

Gardner, Frederick Leigh: De Profundis Ad Lucem, also Credo Experto

Gardner, J. K.: Valet Anchora Virtus

Gillison, Mrs Jean: Cogito Ergo Sum

Gonne, Miss Maud: Per Ignem Ad Lucem

Hamilton, Mrs Lina Bowatt: Fidelis

Hammond, William: Pro Rege Et Patria

Harrison, F. D.: Quanti Est Sapere

Haweis, Mary: Cede Deo

Heazell, F. N.: Evocatus Paratus

Hill, John: Ut Prosim

Horniman, Miss Annie E. F.: Fortiter Et Recte

Hughes, Miss C. E.: Lux Orta Est

Humphrys, W. E. H.: Gnōthi Seauton

Hunter, Edward A.: Hora Et Semper

Hunter, Mrs Harietta Dorothea: Deo Date

Hunter, William Sutherland: In Cornu Salutem Spero

Johnson, F. L.: Ora Et Labore

Jones, A. Cadbury: Faire Sans Dire

Jones, Charles S.: Achad

Jones, George Cecil: Volo Noscere

Kelly, Gerald: Eritis Similis Deo

Kennedy, Mrs Florence: Volo

Kirby, W. F.: Genetho Phos

Langridge, Miss Minnie Constance: Che Sara Sara

Machen, Arthur: Avallaunius

Mackenzie, Mrs Alexandrina: Cryptonyma

Mackenzie, Mrs M.: Magna Est Veritas

Macrae, Mrs Cecilia: Macte Virtute, also Vincit Qui Se Vincit

Maitinski, Mrs: **Abest Timor**

Mathers, Mrs Moina: **Vestigia Nulla Retrorsum**

Mathers, Samuel Liddell Mac-Gregor: **'S Rioghail Mo Dhream**, also **Deo Duce Comite Ferro**

Meakin, Neville: **Ex Oriente Lux**

Minson, George: **Equanimitur**

Moffat, Kate R.: **Servio Liberaliter**

Morris, H. C.: **Cavendo Tutus**

Murray, Mrs Grace: **In Excelsis**

Murray, Oswald: **In Utrumque Paratus**, also **Quaestor Lucis**

Nisbet, R. B.: **Ex Animo**

O'Connell, Miss Theresa Jane: **Ciall Agus Neart**

Paget, Mrs Henrietta: **Dum Spiro Spero**

Pattinson, Thomas Henry: **Vota Vita Mea**

Peck, William: **Veritas Et Lux**

Pollexfen, George: **Festina Lente**

Rand, Mrs Helen: **Vigilate**

Reason, Will: **Semper Sperans**

Regardie, Israel: **Ad Majorem Adonai Gloriam**

Rosher, Charles: **Aequo Animo**

Roy, Robert: **Nil Desperandum**

Scott, Mrs Maria Jane Burnley: **Sub Silentio**

Severs, Miss Ada: **Benedicamus Deo**

Simpson, Mrs Alice: **Perseverantia Et Cura Quies**

Simpson, Miss Elaine: **Donorum Dei Dispensatio Fidelis**

Smith, James Webber: **Non Sine Numine**

Sprengel, Anna: **Sapiens Dominabitur Astris**

Theobald, Robert Masters: **Ecce In Penetralibus**

Thiesen, Mr: **Lux E Tenebris**

Thomas, Robert Palmer: **Lucem Spero**

Todhunter, John: **Aktis Heliou**

Tranchell-Hayes, Mrs: **Ex Fide Fortis**

Waite, Arthur Edward: **Sacramentum Regis**

Waters, Miss Ada: **Recta Pete**

Westcott, William Wynn: **Quod Scis Nescis**, also **Non Omnis Moriar** and **Sapere Aude**

Williams, William: **Nurho Demanhar Leculnosh**

Wilson, Thomas: **Sub Rosa**

Windram, Thomas: **Semper Paratus**

Woodford, A. F. A.: **Sit Lux Et Lux Fuit**

Woodman, William Robert: **Magna Est Veritas Et Praevalebit**, also **Vincit Omnia Veritas**

Wright, Francis: **Mens Conscia Recte**

Yeats, Mrs Georgie Hyde-Lees: **Nemo**

Yeats, William Butler: **Demon Est Deus Inversus**

Index